T0311236

# FOLLOW
## *the* FEELING

**KAI D. WRIGHT**

# FOLLOW
# *the* FEELING

*brand building in a noisy world*

WILEY

Published by John Wiley & Sons, Inc., Hoboken, New Jersey.

Published simultaneously in Canada.

For general information on our other products and services or for technical support, please contact our Customer Care Department within the United States at (800) 762-2974, outside the United States at (317) 572-3993 or fax (317) 572-4002.

Wiley publishes in a variety of print and electronic formats and by print-on-demand. Some material included with standard print versions of this book may not be included in e-books or in print-on-demand. If this book refers to media such as a CD or DVD that is not included in the version you purchased, you may download this material at http://booksupport.wiley.com. For more information about Wiley products, visit www.wiley.com.

*Library of Congress Cataloging-in-Publication Data*

Names: Wright, Kai D., author.
Title: Follow the feeling : brand building in a noisy world / Kai D. Wright.
Description: First Edition. | Hoboken: Wiley, 2019. | Includes index. | Identifiers: LCCN 2019015127 (print) | LCCN 2019017753 (ebook) | ISBN 9781119600534 (Adobe PDF) | ISBN 9781119600480 (ePub) | ISBN 9781119600497 (hardback)
Subjects: LCSH: Branding (Marketing) | BISAC: BUSINESS & ECONOMICS / Marketing / General.
Classification: LCC HF5415.1255 (ebook) | LCC HF5415.1255 W745 2019 (print) | DDC 658.8/27—dc23
LC record available at https://lccn.loc.gov/2019015127

Cover Design: Wiley
Cover Icons: © thenounproject.com

Printed in the United States of America

V10011206_061419

*For Deborah Jean Wright*

**CONTENTS**

# PREFACE

I started my first business in fourth grade, around age nine. I made no money by collecting phone books to recycle. I later realized that this kind of business was called a nonprofit.

The second business I started was a for-profit, for sure. At 12 years old, drenched in humidity and hot breezes, I started a grass-cutting business out of my uncle and aunt's Florida garage. I learned how to define a problem: thick St. Augustine grass that grew like clockwork every week. I learned how to frame and package a solution: my time and grit. Constraints: family, homework, and extracurricular interests. And over the course of six years, I learned customer relationship management, customer acquisition, and loyalty techniques. But mostly, I learned there were many factors in a business's success or failure.

500 Startup founder Bill Gross looked at the dozens of successful bets that his firm made on startups—Airbnb, Instagram, Uber, YouTube, and LinkedIn. What he found was startling—out of the five factors of Timing, Team, Idea, Business Model, and Funding, timing was the most important.[1] Even bellwether businesses that rule the Fortune 500 are susceptible to becoming victims of timing . . . only 50% survive.[2]

An elder millennial by birth, but self-professed digital native by tribe, there was a major shift between "business" while growing up and "business" in the present day. Today, there's *social* business, *data-driven* business, *experiential* business, *content-driven* business, and *digitally-enabled* business. And with every new platform, technology, and service, the sea of metrics surrounding the business, consumer, and market can easily entangle a seasoned executive in a web of data. And that "timing" element doesn't stand still— it seems to be accelerating us into a standoff between data and meaningfulness.

I've long had a time management issue: I could never choose between learning and doing. It was a virtuous cycle that drove all my scholastic pursuits as a child, and later drove my career path as an adult. It's to blame for the magnetism that attracted me to become a scholar-practitioner. Between teaching at Columbia University and working as a strategic advisor to C-suite executives, startup founders, and talent time is precious. The yin and the yang of the theoretical and the practical produce a system of creativity being applied strategically, though, and that is my North Star.

The third business I started during college was steeped in business plan rhetoric and pitch competitions. Problem: college students have great local awareness but can often lack national attentiveness. Solution: a national news insert that would go into college newspapers, to deliver a broader lens beyond the campus. The company: *Accent Magazine*. I learned that this is called a social enterprise.

By the time I was on the Forbes 30 under 30, I had five jobs, and all were dream jobs: advising Fortune 100 companies on brand and marketing strategy for their $100 million campaigns; working for a celebrity to launch a $100 million media startup; and working on personal brand development for C-suite executives and entertainment influencers like Meghan Trainor. And in starting things over and over again, I've observed there are only five parts of any brand that matter most—whether it's a nonprofit, for-profit, social enterprise, or person.

As a social scientist who studied economics at the University of Chicago, and a self-proclaimed science-fair geek in high school, the power of pattern recognition is the sharpest tool in the shed of any strategist. Mapping patterns through trends enables the ability to steer focus, build lanes, and reduce friction for success.

Professionally, my work in communication has always centered on a singular fascination: How do companies navigate digital to connect with audiences? And every job, no matter which one, touched on the growing omnipresence of digital, platforms, and technology.

In studying and teaching communication, especially in an age when consumers are tethered to the Internet of Things, those "things" have made relationships feel cold. Devices. Servers. Screens. Chips. Dashboards. Mar-tech Stacks. Clicks. Endless Feeds. Is the dog chasing the tail, or vice versa?

Academically, I gravitate toward the field of behavioral economics. During multiple classes at the University of Chicago, the late Nobel laureate Gary Becker had to suffer my presence as an ambitious and eager student. Population. Demographics. People. Behavior. Incentives. Penalties. Working for a business school professor during college as a research assistant helped to sharpen my ability to pull insights from the data sets of company financial performance.

Fifteen hundred companies . . . that's the total number of companies whose performance data I analyzed to determine the five parts of a brand that matter most. From there, 100 anomaly companies emerged; companies profiled within this book as case studies.

This book takes the lessons from those fast-growing companies, and puts them into a back-of-the-napkin simple system—LAVEC— to offer busy marketers, strategists, employees, and entrepreneurs a quick guide to branding practices that lead to resonance in a digital age: (1) lexicon triggers, (2) audio cues, (3) visual stimuli, (4) experience, and (5) cultural connections. This book is about finding and expressing your brand's true North Star, and gives practical tips on how to hack and hijack culture to win the hearts and minds of tribes.

Having two military parents, my family's journey included several years in Germany. Infusing a sense of global citizenship in my DNA, I've trekked to over 20 countries. Branding has the power to and must transcend physical geographies, and a truly electrifying brand will light up the world stage. Regardless of what language you speak, the geography where you live, or what origins you have, these five areas of "brand" are universal igniters that enable your startup or 100-year-old company to join the fast-moving mavens who are mastering brand building.

## Notes

1.  Bill Gross, "The Single Biggest Reason Why Startups Succeed." TED, March 2015. https://www.ted.com/talks/bill_gross_the_single_biggest_ reason_why_startups_succeed.
2.  Capgemini, "When Digital Disruption Strikes: How Can Incumbents Respond?" LinkedIn SlideShare, February 20, 2015. https://www.slideshare .net/capgemini/digital-disruption-44929928.

# ACKNOWLEDGMENTS

A special thanks to all of those who opened the doors or gave me a front-row seat in brand and marketing:

My family and friends
Adam Schecter
Adele Myers
Adina Smith
Adrian Fenty
Afdhel Aziz
Aisha Staggers
Ajit Verghese
Akia Mitchell
Anastasia Williams
Andre Harrell
Andy Schuon
Angela Bundrant Turner
Aniela Kuzon
Ann Higgins
Arabella Pollack
Artie Kenney
Banch Abegaze
Ben Ezrick
Bennett Bennett
Bill Dunne
Bill Schroeder
Brian Feit
Brian Fetherstonhaugh
Brian Offut
Brooke Borell
Bryan Terrell Clark
Bukie Adebo
Bunita Sawhney

Carla Hendra
Charles King
Chris Graves
Christena Pyle
Christiaan Vorkink
Courtney Ettus
Dean Jason Wingard
Derek Scott
Donna Pedro
Eitan Miskevich
E'lana Jordan
Elizabeth Colomba
Felicia Mowll
Frederica Bonner
George Chisholm
Glen Patterson
Jacqueline Thompson
Jamie Henderson
JD Schramm
Jesse Scinto
Jiffy Iuen
Joel Johnson
John Frame
Jon Kamen
Jonathan Cohen
Julian Mitchell
Justin Williams
Kamasi Washington
Kaneisha Wright

Keith Clinkscales

Kenna Kay

Kim Ransom

Kristen Cavallo

Lara Oshea

Lindsey Osher

Loren Monroe-Trice

Lori Argyle

Love Welchel

Maomao Zhang

Maria Mandel

Mario Davis

Marlon Nichols

Mary Young

Max Wise

Meghan Trainor

Merri White

Michael Bailey

Michael Chapman

Michael Kassan

Michael Wasilewski

Paul English

Peter Fasano

Que Gaskins

Rebecca Heino

Reginald Greene

Rich Kronengold

Rishi Kadiwar

Robyn Turk

Rolo Vargas

Saptosa Foster

Sean "Diddy" Combs

Sean MacDonald

Semhar Amdemichael

Shante Bacon

Shirley Chisholm

Steve Pamon

Suzy Ryoo

Tanya Malcolm

Troy Carter

Trudi Baldwin

Walker Zavareei

Waverly Deutsch

Whitney-Gayle Benta

KAI D. WRIGHT is a strategy advisor to C-suite executives, founders, and talent. He advises on subjects including digital, technology, and marketing. He has been recognized as a leader by *Forbes*, *Adweek*, *CSQ*, *Cablefax*, and the Advertising Research Foundation. A frequent speaker at major conferences and Fortune 500 companies, Wright is a lecturer at Columbia University and global consulting partner at Ogilvy. His clients have included Bank of America, HP, McDonald's, Bacardi, Ford, Walgreens, Merck, and L'Oréal, in addition to startups and music talent. Wright graduated from Columbia University and the University of Chicago. An avid traveler, he lived in Germany during his childhood, and has visited over 20 countries. He lives in New York City.

# INTRODUCTION

For the past decade, I've roamed the halls of Columbia University—first as a graduate student studying communication and then as a lecturer. Before, I studied economics at the University of Chicago. After graduating, I worked as an advisor to Fortune 100 clients and startups. Through high-profile projects across advertising, PR, and media, I've navigated the landscape of hacking, hijacking, and steering hearts and minds. Influence . . . ish. In academic speak: applying principles of persuasion.

My journey as an intellectual misfit started abroad in my youth. My father and mother met in the military, and eventually, our family ended up in Germany. Coming back to the United States, strangely, I was a foreigner. Caught between languages and customs, every interaction with the world spawned a dozen questions. Identified as gifted, I was taught to untangle physical and mental puzzles through observation and question asking.

While a love of science may not be the coolest thing to talk about among friends more interested in playing sports, it nonetheless still teaches a lifelong lesson on how to apply research methods, interpret data, and extract meaning from disjointed variables. When your entrepreneurial spirit pushes you to do things others consider "too risky" for their liking, then you learn to live peacefully in a reality of change that others find daunting and uncomfortable. And when your military parents raise you in Germany and you've hit 20 countries by the time you're on the *Forbes* list of 30 under 30, then your worldview tilts to a new spectrum of gravitating toward what's next and new.

In many regards, all of this made me an intellectual misfit—a chaser of anomalies. A trend-eating, culture junkie disciplined in social sciences from an early age, accustomed to problem solving. Someone comfortable being uncomfortable. But, I've come to find a quiet power in being a "misfit"—although it took me some time to learn that. Over that time, an asset became manifest—a worldview informed by standing at intersections, namely a meeting of the roads of media, technology, and culture.

Through research, observation, and experience from a fast-moving career that has taken me from the boardroom to the classroom, from Harlem to Hollywood, and from advising celebrities to C-suite executives, I've seen one principle of influence ring true: *the most important "expression" of your brand—whether a person, company, or nonprofit—is simply how you make others feel.* This book is an ode to that principle, an argument for why we are ruled by feelings, and most important, how to leverage feelings as a competitive advantage through five core parts of your brand. We'll discuss over a hundred examples of how brands are both nailing the right message for their customers or failing to deliver on a central feeling, and what consequences it all has in a world that is rewiring our behavior with every new digital device, service, or platform. We'll dive into the broken rules of brand planning, and offer a new "back-of-the-napkin simple" system for mindfully designing a brand built for the digital age. This will include behavioral science principles from Nobel laureates and practical wisdom from today's most inspiring leaders. Your brand should've rebooted yesterday, so this will be a quick read. #LetsGetToWork!

## FORMING A WORLDVIEW

I made a career promise to myself—to be selfish. Yes, I volunteer. A lot. And yes, I've even started a charity for youth to have a pipeline into technology. I'm not talking about *Grinch* selfish . . . I mean *soul* selfish. Fulfillment selfish. True-to-my-roots selfish. From childhood onward, my curious mind turned into curious hands; and those hands built science fair projects on Mondays, wrote Latin on Tuesdays, buzzed answers during brain brawl on Wednesdays, worked as a photography assistant on Thursdays, waited for the family phone line to free up for AOL dial-up on Fridays, cut grass for my startup on Saturdays, and flipped through the Bible on Sundays.

Because even from an early age, my mother encouraging me to live outside of my comfort zone taught me the value of being able to navigate intersections. So, I set an ambitious goal: to manage my early career by having jobs for only 12- to 24-month periods. Like science experiments, answers continue to arise with continued experimentation; I was determined to learn as much as possible from each role before moving to the next. Getting paid to learn—the convergence of my two favorite interests.

My first job out of college at global advertising agency Ogilvy, which happened to be a rotational program, set my feet on the marketing path. Before long, one job period turned into the next, and within 10 years, I successfully maneuvered through five dream roles. Each job in a different place, with a different culture to adjust to, to rebel against, and to try to disrupt. Every opportunity was a new challenge, from contributing to the growth of $100 million advertising campaigns to helping launch a $100 million media startup. Some situations I found to be more beneficial for my career trajectory than others—but each role gave a piece necessary to fill-in the puzzle of brand building for both companies and people. I'll share those puzzle pieces with you in this book.

Whether teaching graduate students at Columbia University, speaking to leaders at Fortune 100 companies, or advising startup founders, people who were interested in my fast-moving career would bring me the most intriguing questions to untangle:

- What can my large company learn from startups, and how can my startup grow so fast that large companies can't catch up?

- How do we achieve brand relevance and resonance in a fleeting world of attention where there's an oversaturation of opinion, reviews, user-generated content, and direct peer-to-peer transactions?
- How do we prime our brand to survive this digital revolution of an always-on consumer tethered to the Web yet hidden behind firewalls?
- What are the new rules of brand building for today's culture?

## A CASE FOR CHANGE

As a strategist, I've built an armory of secret weapons—and now I want you to arm yourself with them, too. Back in 2015, Emilie Wapnick gave three tips for disruptors during an inspiring TED talk that will serve you well: learn to be adaptable, possess the ability to synthesize reams of data quickly, and recognize patterns.[1] It's her three signature traits of misfits destined to have a nomadic existence of quickly solving problem after problem, in place after place, rather than staying in one job. Mostly, it all comes down to the ability to make sense of data, trends, and patterns observed across fields. To see blind spots. Every team needs to consider how they're covering their blind spots; working with diverse leaders who know how to navigate intersections is one key solution.

For anyone considering starting a company, most seasoned executives will tell you that building loyalty and driving new consumer behavior is difficult in this world of digital abundance, regardless of the category in which you do business. And activating interest in the sea of disruptive competitors ready to assume a fast-follower strategy can take a culturally heroic feat to keep alive a 50- or 100-year-old brand. The technology chasm needs to be jumped faster than ever, from early adopter to mainstream pragmatists, in order for brands to thrive.

The practice of "branding" as defined by the emergence of the "planning department" in agencies during the 1960s brought with it a set of methodologies, including brand archetypes, "think, feel, do" shortcuts, and "look and feel" rules. The first agency planning department, contested to be at J. Walter Thompson (but formally developed into an agency function at Ogilvy), focused on understanding consumers, market conditions, and in-market communications.[2] Eventually, planning departments and adjacent marketing professionals were tasked with "brand stewardship."

Brand was interpreted as the external manifestation through creative assets—logo, font, shapes, colors, copy, and sometimes sounds such as jingles. As the years passed, more ephemeral elements of "brand" were added, such as experience, corporate culture, CSR, and purpose. And more "brand" elements will be added in the future—all with separate metrics that get thrown into a growing, entangled web of numbers.

Managing a brand today is like competing in a Tough Mudder. There are ebbs and flows of cultural ups and financial downs, calculated risks and unexpected obstacles, competition insight and foresight. And there's no company that goes up forever. At inflection points in a brand's life, there will need to be strategic decisions on how to progress through the mud and anticipate the next obstacle. The countless list of metrics tracked by brands—that's the mud. And digital is the next obstacle. I've long understood that the role of a strategist is to create viable pathways; so, this book will guide you down the pathways of branding that will get you past the next obstacle.

As communicators—and everyone is a communicator—we need to and must change the way we think about branding as the world moves into a new wave of computing, AI, and experience. We must adopt a new playbook built for now, rather than a playbook built for the 1960s dream of succeeding through reach and repetition. A playbook that recognizes that the speed of digital and innovation and disruption will force every iconic brand into a soft reboot and every startup into a tailspin if they don't nail their branding in an age where often the best story wins (rather than the best product or service).

*So, in a nutshell, here's the central argument made in this book:*

Reaching consumers tethered to the Internet of Things (IoT) has forced marketers, strategists, analysts, entrepreneurs, and decision-makers to analyze what seems like an endless firehouse of new metrics that accompanies the arrival of every digital platform and emerging technology. Pulling yourself out of that tangled web of numbers—and finding the value of your brand in all of it—isn't easy.

Brands can't sell to consumers the way they used to—through strong-armed push, push, push and repeat methods. *Head-on, apply directly to the forehead* . . . Nowadays, it is very much about lifestyle—how you make both consumers (nonbuyers) and customers (buyers) feel. And what today's consumer cares about is actually the same thing they've always cared about—empathy. It's not only empathy through direct dialogue on calls or in stores, but also as manifest in business practices, operations, and communication. The new brand-consumer relationship is: relate to me and creatively solve my problems, Brand X; that's how I invest in you by buying your product and/or service.

The frozen-in-time brands selling products during *The Andy Griffith Show* and *The Jeffersons* don't understand today's struggle; likely to continue to slowly disappear due to their fatigued business models. Consumers control brand visibility more than you do nowadays. How do you become one less reason for someone to throw shade on Twitter, and one more reason for that person's tribe to subscribe to your updates?

The answer to a lot of these questions comes at the junction of design and psychology. Think of it as a way to hack and hijack twenty-first-century hearts and minds mired in the digital quicksand of connectivity. Wading in the pond of behavioral science is this revolutionary and new idea (gasp!) that humans are just "feeling machines that think," and that the majority of times, rational thought is secondary. Again, rational thought is secondary . . .

At your brand's best, it's reduced to a feeling. Not a singular branded element like the logo, color palette, service tagline, or product shape. "Brand" is now how the consumer remembers you; and, we remember feelings all the way back to childhood. You might be surprised to know that researchers believe we remember feelings more when they're negative than when they're positive. And we are more apt to discuss only the negative ones. So how, as a brand, do you let consumers express themselves openly, listen, and help amplify positive feelings?

In a brutal world of continual change, we all look and are naturally attracted to things that give us a positive and consistent feeling. And a startup that ignites a central feeling—from SoulCycle to Airbnb to TaskRabbit to 23andMe—often benefits from the accelerant factor of emotions.

The iconic brands that have weathered decades of culture have done so because they have a positive feeling already wired into their DNA. Lucky them. For instance, Disney is more than its superheroes and theme parks—it is a source of *happiness* for its fans. Gatorade is more than colorful drinks and nutrition supplements—it is an *enabler of endurance*. Corona is more than just an import—it is a beach in a bottle, providing *escape*. You win out as a top brand by appealing through feelings to consumers, customers, and communities. Through marketing, licensing, partnerships, operations, and beyond, you must deliver on that appeal *consistently*.

In engineering that feeling—I hope you can follow the theme here—you need to specifically calibrate five brand territories: lexicon, audio cues, visual stimuli, experience, and culture. Just remember it as LAVEC. Or, CLAVE, for magic key. Today's iconic brands have mastery in more than one area. Brands built to be future-proof for a digital age should master all five areas. And you can.

Focusing on those five areas of "brand" specifically provides a shortcut to elevate the visibility of the branding elements that incite the most triggers for behavioral outcomes. We can thank recent Nobel laureates Daniel Kahneman and Richard Thaler for their life work of unpacking them. Now, we're going to apply their principles to brand building.

Following the feeling, not ironically, is the one brand metric that's truly cross-platform. It's your North Star. LAVEC, as a "back-of-the-napkin" branding system for entrepreneurs, marketers, creative professionals, and business leaders, outlines the five areas of focus that can increase the chances of surviving a time of digital transformation.

And in the most *Black Mirror* type of way, technology is becoming an enabler to measuring cognitive emotions and feelings in real-time through facial mapping, machine learning, biometrics, and eye tracking. Whether shopping in-aisle or browsing a site through a mobile device, measurement tools are becoming astoundingly more accurate and passive, allowing for an always-on data trail to optimize and recalibrate how a consumer, client, or customer experiences a brand.

## FEELINGS AREN'T THINGS TO GLOSS OVER

It's going to be a deep conversation over the next few chapters, but it won't be as painful as scrolling through 300 feet of content on a smartphone every day. We're going to go down the rabbit hole of emotions, feelings, secrets of why we behave the way we do, and shortcuts to branding in a digital age.

Tech is doing so much for society—improving our understanding of each other and ourselves, predicting future population needs, and decoding information we couldn't unlock in the past like DNA. As our existence in this world deepens with every new device that becomes plugged into the matrix, we must fight to simplify the output of meaningfulness. As I recall from my time as a student at Columbia University, when it comes to measurement, one goal is better than two, two is better than three, and so forth. An organization must fight the good fight to simplify how data comes together to deliver one indicator for brand meaningfulness.

Not so long ago, facial recognition, machine learning, and eye tracking were all sci-fi write-offs. It was considered weak fiction between the pages of George Orwell's *1984* and a far leap on the moviescreen in *2001: A Space Odyssey*. Not anymore. The age of surveillance and screen culture is here. The powerful analytics to come from tech are already paying dividends in improving customer experiences—and thus is already being cornered by Adobe, Amazon, Google, SAP, Oracle, Microsoft, and IBM. The question is no longer if the technology is going to help us conquer that final frontier of emotional understanding, but rather what that knowledge will enable us to do. How will it enable brands to grow? And which brand will win the race to that fantasy-land of decoding feelings first?

This book is an invitation into the brand, design, and psychology intersection where my work and teaching overlap. Condensing research on 1,500 fast-growing companies down to anomalies, I'll provide 60 case studies; this way, you also get to see how mentioned principles play out in real time around us. I'll also break things down into practical tips (and fire-starters) so you can brainstorm how to reboot your brand to infuse feeling back into your DNA and ways of working.

You will get pages from my life as well, from being an early adopter of technology and platforms to working with celebrities to traveling the world as a global citizen to teaching rhetoric principles from Aristotle at Columbia University. That way, I can show you how my worldview and perspectives meld together—and give you added reason to take this journey with me.

This intellectual misfit has something to say, and it could greatly impact your brand survival.

## Notes

1. Emilie Wapnick, "Why Some of Us Don't Have One True Calling." TED, April 1, 2015. https://www.ted.com/talks/emilie_wapnick_why_some_of_ us_don_t_have_one_true_calling.
2. Jack Martin Leith, "Planning Hall Of Fame." Plannersphere / Planning Hall Of Fame. Accessed January 30, 2019. http://plannersphere.pbworks .com/w/page/17146391/Planning%20Hall%20Of%20Fame.

# INSIDE OUT

*What's the Value of
Being an Outsider?*

When my family moved back to the United States from the Army base in Germany, I was shy of five years old. Because I was experiencing America for the first time, I was reserved and spent a lot of time observing others. I was a sponge; every new concept magnified through relentless question asking, learning, and doing.

When I was nine years old, teachers were mystified as to how I could finish my work so quickly. What was happening inside my mind in such a short period? And then the first indication that I was a misfit appeared: I passed a test for gifted students. Thereafter, a few hours weekly, in what now seems like a social experiment from science fiction, I was taught skills of pattern recognition, synthesis, and problem solving. For each session, we selected new puzzle boxes with surprising contents—sometimes cards, other times physical objects to untangle, and what felt like an endless number of tangrams.

I learned to be okay with being an intellectual misfit. Twenty years later, all those skills proved invaluable when I became a researcher and strategist. That experience of feeling like an outsider empowered me to live comfortably anywhere. Over time I learned how to define myself, and my own personal brand, and champion the point of view of the outsider.

One semester while lecturing at Columbia University, I started class by challenging students to think about subway systems. How would you use communication to design a new customer experience that encourages people to move away from the doors and toward the center of the cars? Many students thought about lexicon—asking people to move—while others were more inventive with experiential solutions—putting USB plugs in the middle of the cars to reward individuals who comply. After running that behavioral science simulation so many times, I started to take away a few observations: what a brand says (i.e., lexicon) and what it does (i.e., experience) are two gravitational forces around brands. And slowly, they informed two parts of the LAVEC system.

I also fill a role as a strategic advisor, working with marketers, celebrities, influencers, startup founders, and executives. Clients employ me to prepare and position their brands for the future by developing narrative (comms and public relations), storytelling (content), and experience (omnichannel) solutions. I work mostly within media, entertainment, and technology, but also have major clients ranging from financial services to consumer electronics to beauty, spirits, and food. You see, planners at agencies have a reputation for being what I like to call "brand promiscuous."

Whether teaching students or advising clients, my singular goal is always creativity applied strategically. These dual experiences helped me cultivate a scholar-practitioner mindset. There's likely a dual-mindset waiting to be unlocked in you, too, which will forever change your point of view and the way you approach work.

## A RED-HOT INDUSTRY

### *"Sell, or else."*

David Ogilvy was known for short, impactful phrases like this one. And when Ogilvy—the agency, not the man—hired me out of college, its purpose made its mark on me: to make brands matter. It was a magical time for the agency and its work: the launch of the iconic Dove Real Beauty campaign had the industry abuzz; Ellen DeGeneres and Beyoncé were new stars in American Express commercials; and a long-standing courtside courtship of the US Open had our IBM teams busier than ever applying data to sports. They were big brands . . . the biggest . . . and I was hungry to take a bite. I was soon steeped in the art of account planning, a function and set of tools developed over decades by an agency considered to be a pioneer in the field.

While those early lessons provided an ironclad framework for developing brand strategy, we were still essentially in the P.D.E.

(predigital era). Yes, social platforms such as Facebook, Twitter, and YouTube had just launched, but brands were not using them. It was 2007. Many didn't believe that digital media would gobble up traditional marketing dollars, but I did. Having been one of the initial 100,000 people on Facebook during college and having competed for five years during middle and high school in the Intel Science Fair—Intel's long-standing STEM investment—I had a hunch that this "digital" thing would win attention. And in 2018, digital spending finally reached an inflection of getting over 50% of budgets from the Top 100 advertisers.

While working at the world's largest advertising agency taught me how to combine observations and turn them into insights that could spark creative ideas for communication, it was in my next job in digital that I developed my mindset to "persuade, or else."

When you think about the goals of branding, public relations, business development, and licensing, they are all similar: to persuade people that a particular brand is superior to all others. And those people are more than just current customers: they are prospects, consumers, vendors, suppliers, partners, and everyone who has a hand in your brand's ecosystem.

Formerly, the options for persuasion were print, broadcast, and radio, and the field was relatively narrow. But this isn't our world today. As channels and platforms proliferate in every company's ecosystem, the most skilled Six Sigma marketer can lose almost total value in a digital world if they can't manage a social media team through an always-on reality. And with every new platform and technology, there's a wake of new metrics, forcing any decision-maker to assume the role of a data scientist.

When does an organization know it has enough data? Is there such a thing as enough data? Which data is more important than others? Is something unimportant just because you can't measure it?

Persuasion is a complex web, indeed.

## A FEW THINGS TO KEEP IN MIND

In the Introduction I mentioned that the role of a strategist is to simplify. And thus, in this book, we will redux all of the data down to meaningfulness in the single metric of feelings. And get comfortable living in that empathetic space. That feeling, though, does not emerge from staring at 100 metrics that are changing each week . . . instead, it arises from a conscious decision. A decision to focus on one thing rather than two, two things rather than three, and so forth.

When you can do that, you can start engineering that singular-minded feeling into brand expressions, experiences, and the ideal lifestyle that your potential customers are looking for. In addition, this singular focus will help in looking for places where the target feeling comes to life, to determine where the brand can thrive and interact with customers rather than just pursuing a "reach and repetition" approach.

Most undergraduate economics students or social science graduate students take courses on research methods, measurement, or analytics. I was no different. And the one takeaway from these studies, at whatever level you take them, is that *data can be skewed, faked, and misinterpreted.* When marketing teams, social media teams, PR teams, or any team gets their hand on data, and they're not data scientists or trained in data techniques, then as a strategist, I would be wary of their work. And when consumers, customers, or audiences only have to check a "man-made" box on a brand survey, then I'd be equally wary of how representative that response is when consumers are probed to reduce experiences down to only words or numbers (e.g., rating scores). Can words and numbers fully capture the spectrum of expressiveness of people? We'll dig into this more.

The science behind measuring feelings is leading to more accurate and real-time analysis of our emotions. Yes, there's some error. But as technology continues to iterate and as machine learning continues to reduce bias, just as in manufacturing, the errors will be driven to near zero. And when that happens, *feelings* will become one of the most universally relatable, subconsciously triggered, and age-agnostic methods of tracking brand health. What matters most in branding is the feeling that you convey to your customer.

Feelings can penetrate the skin and raise goosebumps, they can resonate and send shivers down your customers' spines, they can warm spirits and inspire actions. And they're also sensations that fewer than 1% of people can hide on their face, for instance.

In order to be an innovator for your tribe, your job is to keep showing up and exceeding expectations. According to Capgemini—a global consulting firm started in 1968 that boasts over 200,000 employees—pushing a brand to excel is rough going: from 2000 to 2015, over half of all brands on the Fortune 500 list either went bankrupt or altogether ceased to exist.[1] I know what you're thinking . . . all of those companies must have had a Kodak moment or a Blockbuster flop. However, the reality is that no one loses their brand overnight. Those companies lost their markets because of an internal culture of paying attention to cold numbers rather than to warm and fuzzy relationships with their customers. People were happier getting, seeing, and sharing their photos instantly, and people were happier getting content they wanted on demand. Brand building starts with audience empathy, and empathy lives in emotions and feelings, not dashboards full of data.

## Note

1.  Capgemini, "When Digital Disruption Strikes: How Can Incumbents Respond?" LinkedIn SlideShare, February 20, 2015. https://www.slideshare .net/capgemini/digital-disruption-44929928.

# 2

# GOING HAYWIRE

*What's the Relationship between Economics and Communication?*

I've always been attracted to "the next big thing." So, based on the University of Chicago's reputation for having produced the greatest number of Nobel laureates in economics, it was my first-choice school . . . and, besides that, Harvard wait-listed me. The university's open enrollment policy quickly lured me into the business school—first doing research for a professor and then taking classes.

Sarbanes-Oxley. Pink Sheets. Stock performance. Financial reporting. Somewhere there's a published paper by a brilliant Booth professor who was kind enough to give me a credit. In my sponge-like mode, I wanted to learn more about how all these Nobel laureates viewed the world and looked for classes to enroll.

There was one professor in the economics department whose classes I tried so hard, but failed triumphantly, to be in. His name was Steven Levitt, and he had just published his first book. You may have heard of it: *Freakonomics.*

There's a reason or two why Levitt's book sits on every smart executive's desk. First, the synergy Levitt had with *New York Times* journalist Stephen Dubner made for a great pairing of academic know-how with investigative journalism based on asking questions about everyday correlations. Dubner, arguably, helped translate the academic-speak of economics into language for the everyman, and in doing so attracted a cult-like following (including me) who wanted to absorb that ability to make the complex look simple and sound clear. That's what I will aim to do with this subject of brand building in a noisy world.

The second part? Levitt kept his questions simple and used them to probe the world, with surprising results. I'm sure there's nothing like being in his class in the mid-2000s, because the way he crafted his thoughts on economics make his lessons as timeless as any good brand.

There was another important economist at the University of Chicago at that time—the now late Gary Becker. Given that I wasn't taking a class with Steven Levitt anytime soon, Becker became my second choice. It was a decision that placed me at another important intersection. Becker broke down the world according to population dynamics, and it was my first exposure to the concept of "demographics." I became hooked; I took two classes with him. Becker's research on the levers of demographics and population change opened my eyes to the role of data in brand building.

*What's the relationship between economics and communication?*

Economics and communication are cousins, and in their DNA live *influence.*

When it comes to economics, we tend to think about the power of influence in terms of incentives and penalties. But in communication, we think of influence in terms of action. Whether it's economic policy or communication strategy, the measure of success is simply behavioral outcomes. At Columbia University, our program reinforces with graduate students that awareness is not an objective (thanks Frank). As marketers, strategists, communicators, and brand stewards, we are in the business of behavioral change; awareness is not an objective.

In the second season of Netflix's hit *Stranger Things*, the science teacher Scott Clarke tells his class about the railroad construction foreman Phineas Gage and the effects of an accident on his behavior. The story of Gage reveals that we can function without reason. Yes, we would be impulsive, but nonetheless, still functional. For Gage, who forgot to use sand when tamping down gunpowder with his iron rod, the result was a brain injury on the left side of his skull. After the rod passed completely through his head, from jaw to above his brow, he continued to function, but his personality changed. There's always been a belief, partly due to the medical anomaly of Gage, that the right sides of our brains are creative and the left sides are used for logical functions. Well, the truth is, the two hemispheres present a spectrum of logic and emotion. Like being extroverted or introverted, our brains toggle back and forth between the two, with the default set to emotions.

After winning the Nobel Prize in Economics for his lifetime research in behavioral science, Daniel Kahneman wrote in his acclaimed best-seller *Thinking, Fast and Slow* that, "Mental effort, I would argue, is relatively rare. Most of the time we coast."[1] It's in the coasting that our emotions assume control.

## "MOST OF THE TIME WE COAST"

Kahneman's belief expands upon the left-right positioning of the brand, evolving it into what he calls "dual-system theory." One system guides reason, and the other guides intuition. The more intuition-based system operates as our mental autopilot—influenced by triggers, traps, urges, physiology, our knowledge, and past experiences.

Kahneman's research, stemming from the 1970s, has led to a split within economics, creating a new branch known as behavioral economics. And what he had to say on behavior was quite important, because he concludes that our autopilot state accounts for 95% of the decisions we make. Again, 95% of decisions we make occur in autopilot mode. So in a noisy world where audience attention is a premium, is your brand betting too heavily on the "rational" drivers of your brand (e.g., features, benefits, claims) rather than the emotional drivers?

Let's reconsider what we've learned about economics—or what we thought was the right way to view it based on the foundations set by Adam Smith and David Ricardo. In that 1700s view of the world, we get five basic rules of behavior:

1. We are driven by **reason**.
2. We know what we **want**.
3. We can judge the **utility** (i.e., benefits) of our choice.
4. We can properly **value** our choices.
5. We behave selfishly, doing what is in **our own best interest**.

But, in reality, the lessons from Kahneman's *dual-system* theory sharpens our understanding of these areas (and aligns to a more empathy-based view of people):

1. We reserve reason for situations that include risk, discomfort, and first-time exposures to new situations.
2. We can easily be influenced by our proximity to others due to our need for belonging, and we have a natural tendency to conform.
3. We have to be "motivated" and "capable" in order to make a lasting decision, and to feel good about that decision.
4. We have a hard time evaluating chooses that are temporal (e.g., determining what mutual fund investment today will perform best over time for future ROI, or which health treatment today will yield the better long-term quality of life).
5. We are more altruistic than we think, with a prominent desire to protect and preserve the communities we belong to.

When the people we're trying to reach are head-down in devices, adapting those rules to get them to *listen* and *feel* requires sending an emotional signal and awakening the senses. Tapping into emotion sparks behavioral outcomes, and sometimes that requires no mention of "reasons to believe," such as features or benefits, at all. Instead, sparking behavior requires an understanding of what mental triggers to activate, walking the line of familiar and new. That's why the LAVEC system is powerful; it not only reminds us that autopilot is generally activated, but it builds upon dual-system theory to focus on the five parts of a brand that influence behavioral outcomes.

## THE VIRALITY COEFFICIENT

Ever been to a stadium and participated in "crowd wave"? If so, then you know that not everyone is coordinated at once to start the wave, yet somehow the wave can go full-circle. Our brands are like that: not everyone needs to be at the start, yet everyone can have the same pleasurable experience.

The "crowd wave" is how you should consider your media buys. In a noisy world, not everyone will be at the beginning of your brand's traction. But you still have to consider that the experience should be just as meaningful to each person who experiences it later.

Behavioral studies show that as few as 15% of people can create an inflection point for mass, group action.[2] In terms of media math, consider how you can strategically target 15% of people by building positive mental triggers around your brand, rather than attempting to reach 100% of a potential target audience through feature and benefit messaging to coordinate behaviors.

Kahneman posits, and I'd like you to remember this, that we are more conscious of our losses than of our gains. That concept, called loss aversion, highlights the tendency for negative emotions and experiences to be more salient than positive ones. Have you ever read Yelp reviews? Because we also are drawn to negativity—gossip, disasters, and tragedies—and have more language in our vocabulary to express negative sentiment, the majority of feedback reactions from customers tend to be negative.

What does that mean for a brand? It means more than avoiding a bad Net Promoter Score, it means more than implementing

Six Sigma to reduce errors, and it means more than iterating fast through lean tools. Ultimately, it means consciously activating a positive feeling often enough and consistently enough to build a brand moat. It means creating a feedback culture intended to identify negativity and resolve it as fast as possible.

A brand that can elicit good feelings can have a bandwagon effect. Consider President Obama's 2008 presidential campaign slogan of "Hope," which not only drew millions of new voters to politics but also led to the largest first-term margin win between a Democrat and Republican presidential candidate since the 1980s. He encapsulated one central feeling into language, visuals, a signature sound of a soulful symphony of classics, an inviting and open experience at rallies, and a campaign culture of values including "when they go low, we go high." It was a grassroots effort that stemmed from a minority of believers, which, like a crowd wave, grew into an experience that eventually reached the world stage as a formidable new brand in politics and social change.

## Notes

1.  Daniel Kahneman, *Thinking, Fast and Slow*. New York: Farrar, Straus and Giroux, 2011.
2.  University of Leeds, "Sheep in Human Clothing—Scientists Reveal Our Flock Mentality," February 14, 2008. www.leeds.ac.uk/news/article/397 /sheep_in_human_clothing-scientists_reveal_our_flock_mentality.

# 3

# RESONANCE VERSUS SHARE OF VOICE

*In What Direction
Is Technology
Propelling Us?*

Technology is changing us, and Facebook signaled the inflection point.

I'm an elder millennial; I didn't grow up with a cell phone. Yes, I had one during my senior year of high school in the early 2000s, but before then, the closest I got to digital technology was a couple of desktop computers. First was my friend's clunky Hewlett-Packard, with a loud, overheating hard-drive tower, followed by my neighbor's Compaq laptop, which he gave to me to use for schoolwork. Instead, I used it to access AOL through their free CDs available everywhere from direct mail to in-store.

But when Facebook appeared, the tectonic plates of community and content were starting to rub together. They had the second-mover advantage of watching Myspace grow to 100 million users, eventually nipping at its Achilles' heel of over-customization. While Myspace focused on individual expression, Facebook stood for the community. It was launched based on users' interests (i.e., colleges), allowed group pages (e.g., student clubs), and the only media it focused on was photos (at a time when digital camera sales were skyrocketing and the cameraphone was newish). As Bill Gross, the founder of 500 Startups, put it, timing is the most important factor for success, over team, idea, business model, or funding.[1] And as evidenced by Kodak and Blockbuster, timing is also the reason why many industry titans can equally fail. In a traditional economics model, it is expected that the market will force some startups to fail during these rapidly changing times.

I was a student at The University of Chicago when TheFacebook .com launched. Mark Zuckerberg's sister was in our college class. It didn't take long for news of the New England Ivy-League-only network to spread . . . Everyone knows the tale: Ivy-League college dropout builds a social network, gives access to the other

Ivies; then nonstudents like our parents and employers; and then the world.

As a student at the seventh school to get access to the nascent platform, I look back on being one of the initial 100,000 users, compared to the now three billion daily users. It's easy to get lost in the fact that Facebook has grown to touch more than half of the world's population; and in getting lost, miss the fact that all of their digital share and connectivity options have started to rewire us—along with Twitter, Siri, Alexa, iTunes, Tivo, smart home, smart car, smart luggage, instant delivery, and Roomba. We will never again be the same as a society. And new rules of economics are at play that lead us down a behavioral-based path.

Each day, the average person today scrolls through the equivalent of 300 feet of videos, tweets, images, books, articles, commerce sites, and comments. That's the equivalent height of the Statue of Liberty; imagine walking up it with your thumb. During this process, users are blocking ads, tuning out messaging, putting up digital firewalls, and adapting more effective ways to cut off access for brands—and governments are starting to lock down on data and privacy as well, through measures such as the European Union's General Data Protection Regulation (GDPR).

A decade after working at Ogilvy, where I was introduced to the mantra "make brands matter," *how* brands mattered had shifted significantly. To make brands matter in an increasingly noisy world, brands must first fight for visibility. But how you show up matters.

However, the goal isn't visibility through "share of voice" anymore. That's now called noise. And consumers have learned how to tune that out. Rather, visibility today means *resonance*. And the two are like day and night.

# A LESSON IN AUDIENCE PHYSICS

According to the way of thinking that Don Draper and his *Mad Men* ilk taught us, "share of voice" is the game of using repetition to reach more people than the competitors. *Head on, apply directly to the forehead.* The continued reliance of these methods has been nothing short of catastrophic as it collides with digital natives seeking the latest ad-blocking and ad-skipping technology.

I left the agency for a few years to work client-side in the media and music industries. The convergence within the music world was matched only by the acquisitions and mergers in media companies—one company after another merged to compete with digitally native companies, from Netflix to Spotify. Radio went from terrestrial to streaming through iHeartMedia, and hardware companies like Apple started making original content for their iTunes marketplace. In the midst of all this change, we realized that being successful as a company, and even as a music artist, no longer meant attracting large audiences through Top 40 or prime-time venues. Rather, success meant finding the right niche. And, arguably, that same principle of finding one's tribe is what got Donald Trump elected as president of the United States.

Not too long ago, the newspaper industry found itself publicly thrashing about in a cocoon, with local and international publications struggling to maintain a clear-cut stream of revenue. The explosive intersection of culture, politics, and opinion provided a growing audience, and once-declining media properties started to find new life with digital experiences that provided access to the right few within the crowd.

The music, television, and news industry survived as entertainment options because they were able to adapt to younger generations and to tech-driven consumers who wanted to live in that niche.

The music industry is at an all-time revenue high 20 years after fighting Napster and its culture of free music; television followed the lead of the music industry by offering streaming services to those who didn't want to be tethered to the cable TV on the wall, and the news industry is back in the black after converting content to bite-sized pieces easily consumed within consumers' digital scrolling habits.

Resonance with a defined tribe drives loyalty better than over-communicating with the masses. Don't focus on moving the whole crowd; focus on emotionally sparking a few.

*Resonance* is the physics-based term meaning "to oscillate at the same frequency as another being." So, resonating with an audience means maintaining the same level of energy.

When there are more channels than we know what to do with, how do we connect in a way that sparks consumers to turn up the brand volume? You resonate through emotion, turning those emotions into long-term positive feelings. And a dashboard full of data likely won't tell you which emotion or feeling to focus; your brand will have to set a destination.

## THE ECONOMY OF COMMUNITY

We will always yearn to belong. We scout for our community with every new platform, protect those who are aligned with us, and rally with those who share our love of the next new thing or the best old thing. So, to resonate with a tribe member, you need to resonate with an entire community.

Once upon a time, your community was your Girl Scout troop, your A/V club, or the other kids on your block. Social media has redefined the meaning of proximity—no longer is distance an issue if we're aligned by the same values and principles. Brands need to think in the same way in order to cater to their consumers' appetite. Yes, programmatic buying is making interest data actionable.

Additionally, brands need to understand the currency of any community: culture. Culture comes directly from communities: whether it's the Beyhive, your Tough Mudder crew, or the monthly sticker club, brands need to find ways to excite these audiences, help them connect with others in their tribe, and supports the tribe's purpose in the world. It's through our sense of belonging, paired with our unique experiences and our inherent flaw of irrational behavior, that we make decisions that could influence choosing one brand over another.

## ARE WE SPEAKING ON THE SAME WAVELENGTH?

Often, we look to verbal communication as the be-all and end-all of getting our messages across. We describe the features and benefits of our brands as if spelling it out still works, but our audience can now Google anything they want, and tune out anything they don't like. We often start marketing campaigns with a tagline or headline exercise (focused on words) and often start branding exercises with words on a page. Stop all that. Stop thinking in terms of words—it's a trap. The secret is to free your mind of words, and to recognize that lexicon (i.e., vocabulary) is so much richer than words alone. LAVEC shows how to use other elements such as audio and visuals to unite teams around purpose. Adopting LAVEC as a branding system means not only stronger behavioral outcomes for audiences, but also better briefings of teams using the richness of emotional expression.

One spring, Dr. Manuel Garcia-Garcia, a professor of neuroscience and behavioral sciences at New York University, and a behavioral science lead at IPSOS, explained to one of my classes the difficulty of resonating. Through research conducted by his team in his prior role at the Advertising Research Foundation, he noted that nearly 80% of television commercials are only *heard* rather than seen, due to viewers multitasking during the ads, due to the prevalence of mobile phones in our everyday life. Yet, in *Buyology*, Martin Lindstrom notes that over 80% of advertising features no sonic cues.[2] So, in a world where every branding element matters, yet marketers keep focusing on words and visuals, how does this cut through the noise?

Secret: sound matters. But sound doesn't necessarily mean verbal cues such as voice. In fact, communication has three core parts: only 7% of communication is **verbal** while 55% of communication is **nonverbal**—audio cues, visuals, and gestures—while the remaining 38% is the **para-linguistics** of delivery—tone, pauses, articulation.[3] So tell your copywriter to stop writing, and start feeling first. And tell your strategist to turn the one-page brief—full of words—into something more immersive with audio and visuals. The faster your team starts living in an empathy-based consumer reality full of senses, the faster your brand will start to grow at the pace of culture.

## AVOIDING DISSONANCE BEGINS IN THE BRIEFING

One last point about resonance: we just don't care about what we don't care about, and trying to get someone to care can be a waste of time. However, caring and action are unrelated. I'll give you a few examples.

First, traditional brand planning techniques teach that there's a linear path from thinking to feeling to doing. Throw that notion away. As shown in the work of behavioral economists over the past 30 years, that 1960s view is outdated. It's more likely that people first feel, *then* think. And the majority of times, consumers just "do" on autopilot, without thinking. For instance, in the grocery aisle, a brand has three seconds to capture attention and entice conversion; it's one of the hardest battlefields on which to influence a shopper. If you focus on the copy of the offer on the coupon, then you miss the bigger opportunity of the visuals (packaging shape and color) as distinctive elements. At home, children turn off lights not because they're thinking about the energy bill, but rather because of the emotional relationship to please the parent or avoid discipline. People can and do *feel* and *do* before they think. Bury your long features and benefits list in the brief . . . it's a red-herring distraction.

Second, traditional planners often assume we can "make" someone think about the big issues in their lives by giving them all the right information at the right time in the right format. Wrong.

The work of Ohio State professors Richard Petty and John Cacioppo in the 1980s built upon Daniel Kahneman's dual-system reasoning. Through their widely regarded *elaboration likelihood model* they demonstrate that people must have both (1) motivation and (2) ability to reason about a decision, if they are going to be successful at applying reason over emotion.[4] For instance, I can't make someone who is a nondoctor feel good about a medical decision if they aren't motivated to make a good decision, no more than a financial advisor can make a customer feel good about choosing a mutual fund if the customer isn't able to understand how the market works. When those two elements of motivation and capability are lacking, then people are susceptible to peripheral cues that serve as triggers (e.g., appealing endorsers, ratings and rankings, music). And the peripheral cues are present most of the time. It's these ever-present peripheral cues that influence our behavioral outcomes, such as the six described by Arizona State University professor Robert Cialdini in

*Influence*: reciprocity, scarcity, authority, social proof, liking, and commitment.[5]

As we live in digital autopilot, motivation is at a premium. For brands to resonate, "meaningfulness in the moment" matters. And according to researchers, meaningfulness shifts. Ipsos, an international marketing firm, studied the reaction of ads to World Cup viewers in losing and winning markets. They wanted to know if emotional appeals to audiences mattered based on the emotional climate within the country. They found that the brands that resonated most with their audiences were the ones that were in winning countries. The halo of negativity from the loss onto the brands signaled emotional context matters.

So then, why do we brief our creative teams in rational, word-based methods, and then expect them to produce creative work rooted in emotional appeals? Why do we start with taglines, headlines, and feature lists, and then build visuals, audio, and experience drivers? We need to help creative teams, and our organizations as a whole, bring to life a feeling, rather than filling pages, presentations, and sites with emotionless targeting numbers surrounding audience demographics, product features, or corporate missions.

That's what resonance is about—striking that right tone to get your target consumers humming at the same frequency with you. If you can deliver that, through a consistent feeling, your brand can break through in a noisy world.

## Notes

1. Bill Gross, "The Single Biggest Reason Why Startups Succeed." TED, March 2015. https://www.ted.com/talks/bill_gross_the_single_biggest_reason_why_startups_succeed?language=en.
2. Marin Lindstrom, *Buyology: Truth and Lies about Why We Buy*. New York: Doubleday, 2008.

3. Albert Mehrabian, *Nonverbal Communication*. Chicago: Aldine-Atherton, 1972.

4. Richard Petty and John Cacioppo, "The Elaboration Likelihood Model of Persuasion." *Advances in Experimental Social Psychology* 19 (1986), 123–205. doi:10.1016/S0065-2601(08)60214-2.

5. Robert Cialdini, *Influence: Science and Practice*. Boston: Allyn and Beacon, 2001.

# 4

# CREATIVITY APPLIED STRATEGICALLY

*What Parts of a "Brand" Matter Most to a Digitally Wired Audience?*

René Descartes, one of the most notable philosophers of the seventeenth century, is commonly known outside of academic circles for a series of principles best described as mind-body dualism. His central principle—"I think. Thought cannot be separated from me; therefore I exist"—is often truncated to "I think; therefore I am."[1] The ability to have thoughts is the essence of what makes humans supreme beings. But is *thought* the only thing that makes someone a being? Carl Jung and Sigmund Freud might vehemently disagree.

Descartes' ideas on the centricity of the power of thought (a.k.a. reason and rationality) became a bedrock of economic principles. And economists, including Adam Smith, therefore reasoned that homo sapiens must always act in rational ways. The puzzle of Phineas Gage prompted a Portuguese neuroscientist named Antonio Damasio to investigate the divide. Is thought more powerful than emotions, or vice versa?

## THE CRACKS IN THE AXIOMS

"Emotion, feeling, and biological regulation all play a role in human reason," Damasio contested in his 1994 book *Descartes' Error*. "We are not thinking machines. We are feeling machines that think."[2] His refutation of centuries-old theories included what he called the somatic marker hypothesis.

These somatic markers—indicators of feelings, of sorts—are tied to our emotions like bookmarks. Say a friend passes you a meme that almost elicits a vomit—that's disgust that is kicking in. Or if you're feeling the pressure of waiting for a first date to arrive and your heart is beating fast—that's a somatic marker telling you that you're anxious. Or if you're about to pitch to a prospective client, a new hiring manager, or an investor and your hands become sweaty.

These physiological and biometric responses that indicate emotional responses are driving what may happen next.

Damasio says that these emotions are essential to reasoning and decision-making. Emotions are bound together with the thinking process, leaving us unable to truly reason without them. So if we need emotions to reason, then do we need reason to feel emotions?

Carl Jung, the pioneer in psychiatry who spent his days mapping minds, once said there are levels to our thoughts. Your psychology professor may have given you an image of this concept: an iceberg. The high-up visible portion represents your conscious thoughts. Then, bobbing above and below the surface, is the portion that represents your feelings. Underneath the water, the largest portion is your subconscious: home to your freest expressions of self.

## EMOTIONAL HORSEPOWER DRIVES MANY A DECISION

Researchers have found that it's nearly impossible to make decisions without considering emotions. Of the 34,000 emotions identified by psychologists since the 1940s, a few core emotions are commonly experienced.[3] While many systems for codifying emotions have emerged, psychologist Robert Plutchik's 1980 Wheel of Emotions has earned the widest acceptance including mental health professionals, who use his work to diagnose bipolar disorder.[4] According to his system, our eight core emotions, around the world, include Anger, Fear, Pain, Joy, Disgust, Surprise, Interest, and Shame.

There are short-term emotional reactions, such as the shock of a bee sting, that may last for only minutes. And then there are longer-term emotional states known as feelings, such as waves and spells of joy or sadness, surprise and anticipation, that can last from hours to months to years. If we have not yet learned how to plumb the depths of our emotional complexity, the next generations of consumers probably will. And technology will help us better identify, distinguish, decipher, and express them.

Plutchik's Wheel of Emotions gives us a trustworthy view of these feelings and the emotions that thrust them forward. Plutchik envisioned a series of eight contrary emotions: joy versus sadness; anger versus fear; trust versus disgust; and surprise versus anticipation, all laid out across a circular model. Just like the blending of hues on a color wheel, the overlaps between these basic feelings reveal that a much more nuanced plethora of emotions is exhibited.

Each year, I spend two to four weeks outside my home base of the United States. I've traveled to 20 countries and have spent over a month at a time in Colombia, the UK, and France. Through teaching at Columbia University, I'm fortunate to have also had students from a dozen countries. In traveling across continents and immersing in cultures, I've learned that strong brands are as universal as digital borders. And that feelings represent a universal common ground.

Amy Cuddy, a Harvard Business School professor and body language specialist, notes that you're always communicating about your personal brand based on your presence. Her research brings to light the notion that you communicate from the moment you enter a room, down to your posture you take when seated. It's the ability to read body language and facial gestures that gives an edge to law enforcement and parents alike. It's the feeling someone gives you, which guides whether you trust them or not, before they even start talking.

Feelings are universal—they cross borders, bridges, and walls. They transcend age and income brackets. They're as global as soccer but without as much action. They pierce through the aged models of reason, they resonate, and they inspire you to act. And they're not something you can easily hide, due to our physiological responses (e.g., heart rate accelerating during fear).

Consider the expressions on your face. What does a hostage negotiator, officer of the law, and parent have in common? They all know how to read your face to tell if you're lying. And there's a secret science behind that ability . . . regardless of your race, gender, or geography . . . Because all homo sapiens have over 40 facial muscles that, when manipulated based on underlying emotions, form expressions such as a smile or the curled lip of contempt, then a face can become a biometric data point.[5] And AI and machine learning are unlocking the ability to decode these types of data points in real time.

## INFLUENCE RULES THE DAY, BUT WE CAN RULE INFLUENCE

Influence, the intangible, indirect power to cause an effect, follows the rules of social psychology. But just as social settings can be molded, the rules of influence can also be engineered.

Some of these emotions are hard-wired from childhood. Anytime a strange dog barked at you, you'd experience that rush of adrenaline that throws you into the acute stress response known as "fight or flight." Other emotions are experienced as you grow, such as anxiety over having to think about an uncertain future.

The way the twenty-first-century consumer is wired, a brand has only three to eight seconds to influence the decisions they make at points of sale (POS), online, or through mobile apps. Either there's a "click moment" for your brand or not. So, what type of "meaningful" connection can you possibly have in that time?

Often, as marketers, strategists, and leaders, we want only high-level interpretations of *meaningfulness*—brand recall, favorability, and preference. But that idea of meaningfulness can shift: media planners maximize against reach, PR professionals report in impressions, and brand managers worry about market penetration.

However, none of these metrics takes us as close to the consumer as *feelings* do, so you can better understand them. Optimizing brands to spark positive emotions reminds us that consumers are people—"feeling machines"—who are worthy of empathy. And in the pursuit of being a customer champion, we must not lose sight of empathy. Because as David Ogilvy said, "the consumer is your wife."

## SURVIVING BRAND QUICKSAND

At a time when brand loyalty favors the few companies that consistently exceed customer expectations, brands must set and sustain a vision that compels a community to buy and advocate. And with brands operating as 24/7 publishers living in accessible media backdrops, the ability to *not* fulfill customer expectations is higher than ever. Knowing negative experiences are felt more than positive experiences, we must be careful to avoid the quicksand of a negative culture.

Since "brand" is expansive, and the ability for "expression" is broad, where should one focus? There are five areas of any brand that matter most to elicit a consistent feeling:

1. **Lexicon triggers:** Language, vocabulary, associations, metaphors, schema
2. **Audio cues:** Tones, atmospherics, idents, voice, sonic logos

3. **Visual stimuli:** Symbols, shapes, colors, images, memes, emojis, gifs, video
4. **Experience drivers:** Feedback loops, omnichannel
5. **Cultural Connections:** Values, purpose, business practices, and policies

Brands that master one or more of the five areas tend to grow faster than competitors. And brands that excel at mastering multiple territories become the stuff of legends. Those companies defy market odds and achieve longevity, achieving an iconic status such as a being a *parachute of happiness* like Disney.

## A SYSTEM BUILT FOR BRAND "VALUE"

Think about your **lexicon**—what vocabulary and linguistic triggers do you use? What metaphors and schema have you utilized to help resonate with your customers? Would a consumer be able to identify your brand based on the language you use, or do you sound/read like every other brand in your category?

**Audio cues** are one of the most underleveraged branding tools. Does your brand have a signature sound (à la Intel or McDonald's)? Does your brand waste sonic inventory such as the first few seconds of an ad? Is your brand borrowing equity by licensing music so often that consumers wouldn't know what product is being sold if they didn't also see a screen? And does the audio around your brand spark behavior?

What **visual stimuli** does your brand use beyond logo and color palettes? What symbols are most associated with your category or industry? Does your brand book cover gifs, memes, emojis, infographics, stickers, video and newer ways consumers express themselves and identify within communities?

Today, brands are only as valuable as the last best **experience** delivered to a consumer. In a noisy world, a good experience in any category sets the bar for your category. So, what's your store atmosphere—messy and dimly lit? Are your sales associates friendly and helpful or pushy and aggressive? Are you delivering a consistent experience through mobile, phone, and in person? Whether your brand is a retailer, restaurant, or resort, what do you want people to feel when they step into your space or use your digital tools?

And finally, think about your internal **culture** before you double down on doing it for "the" culture. What is your purpose, what values do you stand for and take up, and what internal practices make your brand something people feel compelled to follow? And do those guiding principles carry through to your policies, practices, and protocols? Do you empower your employees to bring those values to life?

In this book, we'll bring those five brand territories to life in one system called LAVEC or CLAVE (i.e., key).

## EVERY HERO NEEDS A VILLAIN

Can't think of one positive feeling you'd like to own? Then pivot to taking on an enemy feeling. Here's a modern twist on a strategy that has placed a legacy brand well into the pantheon of cultural icons.

The brand? Snickers. Their marketing team created the message that hunger is the enemy, and used this sensation as the foundation for its 2010 Super Bowl ad featuring Betty White. You couldn't take your eye off the comedian getting tackled, then bespattered, and giving a snide remark. "Grab a Snickers. You're not you when you're hungry." That moment and that feeling led to the best ad recall of any Super Bowl ad that year, and later iterations slingshotted the brand straight into the number-one market position at a time of slow growth within their category. Their bravery to tackle hunger, literally, created a winning emotional hook.

The goal through following feelings is to champion the customer, and to elevate them in the world. Either name a positive feeling to reinforce for your consumers, or shelter them from enemy feelings by playing the hero. In the next section of this book, I discuss the nuances of each part of LAVEC, and how to engineer a feeling into each through tips and case studies on brands that nailed and failed each of these five areas, to help you quickly position your brand to win. And before long, you'll define your brand's North Star.

## Notes

1.  René Descartes, *A Discourse on Method*. Indianapolis: Hackett, 1998.
2.  Antonio R. Damasio, *Descartes' Error: Emotion, Reason, and the Human Brain*. New York: Penguin Books, 2005.
3.  Patty Mulder, "Emotion Wheel by Robert Plutchik." Toolshero. Accessed January 31, 2019. https://www.toolshero.com/psychology/personal-happiness/emotion-wheel-robert-plutchik/.
4.  "Robert Plutchik," Wikipedia, last modified January 10, 2019. https://en.wikipedia.org/wiki/Robert_Plutchik.
5.  Judy Foreman, "A Conversation With: Paul Ekman; The 43 Facial Muscles That Reveal Even the Most Fleeting Emotions." *New York Times*, August 5, 2003. https://www.nytimes.com/2003/08/05/health/conversation-with-paul-ekman-43-facial-muscles-that-reveal-even-most-fleeting.html.

# COMMUNI-CATION AS A SYSTEM

*How Does
Communication Work
in Society?*

Ever heard the phrase "lost in translation"? I'm not referring to the 2003 movie starring Bill Murray and Scarlett Johansson, but the phrase referring to a communication failure such as not being able to put something into words. In Italian, it's *ineffabile*, in Spanish, it's *inefable,* and in English, it's *ineffable.* It's in those moments when words can't express the depth and precision of feelings that we learn the limits of language, and bow to the power of emotions over vocabulary.

In the linguistic fight to win hearts and minds through the perfect brand name, tagline, positioning, value propositions, dialogue with customers, reasons to believe, proof points, and brand experiences, let's start with a discussion on the role of language in a communication system. Language, or, more formerly, lexicon, is the method of human communication consisting of the use of words in a structured and conventional way. As defined by the Oxford Dictionary, lexicon is "the vocabulary of a person, language, or branch of knowledge."[1] From its earliest beginnings, language has been an artifact of developed societies and a primary foundation of civilization.

## COMMUNICATION AS A "SYSTEM"

Communication is so powerful that it marks the advancement of society, and our very definition of a civilization. No civilization exists without some form of communication. It is as basic as the hierarchy of needs defined by Abraham Maslow, from physiological needs to self-actualization. Our need to express ourselves even supersedes what we call words and language; for instance, we have created instruments of expression that decode our environment (e.g., clocks, calendars, odometers, thermometers). Communication is owned by and respective to specific communities, and we will revisit the notion of appealing to communities frequently in this book. The Latin root of communication—*communicare*—means "to share."[2] And that sharing uses a combination of mixed media to inform a specific community through three core delivery channels: lexicon, audio, and visuals.

In this book, I use systems-thinking as an organizing framework. In her book *Thinking in Systems*, the late Donella Meadows, a MacArthur genius who specialized in creating the field of sustainability, breaks down the complexity of any kind of system into three core components: elements, interconnections, and purpose.[3] Nearly 30 million copies of her books have been sold, including one Pulitzer Prize–nominated work. The MIT researcher presents a valuable set of conditions that any system (e.g., corporate, economic, government, community, brand, and beyond) needs to instill for sustainability and resilience, ensuring that the behavior of the system fulfills its intended purpose and function.[4]

In branding, the elements of the system are lexicon, audio, and visuals. Meadows argues that in any system, the individual elements are the least important components. Most important are the interconnections—how those elements coordinate, interact, and enhance one another. In branding, the interconnections are expressions—an infinite set of combinations of three ever-expanding elements. An expression that could take the form of a Mona Lisa painting or a video game. Those interconnections evolve over time based on geography, community, and unforeseen pressures such as new market entrants or consumer behavioral shifts. Purpose, then, becomes the outcome of the system—its *function*. And sometimes the purpose (as intended by founders) and the outcome (as dictated by shareholders) may come to vary over time. The purpose is not in the lexicon (i.e., mission statements)—the purpose lives in the action. So in branding, my hope is that you're creating a brand that intends to have a positive outcome that leaves the consumer with a positive feeling.

Language, as an artifact, carries with it traditions, customs, and knowledge, from medicine to philosophy. It presents a *Matrix*-like reflection of human existence that evolves every second as meaning and context sway in and out of frame. In such an expansive system, one would think that lexicon is the most important element. Existing for over two million years in nonverbal form and 100,000 years in verbal form, language has long been a mark of a civilized society.[5,6] Language is believed to have been formed in tribal culture; born from the necessity to hunt, gather, and explore. Language meant coordination, and coordination meant survival. Whether direct, stern, colloquial, or flowery, the purpose of language is to spread information. Whether that information is fact, alternative fact, opinion, or fake news, it is transmitted through language. Based on the now widely accepted "communication model" (Figure 5.1), defined in the 1978 book *Looking Out/Looking In* penned by Ronald Adler and Neil Towne,[7] there are five core parts of any communication:

1. A sender (i.e., a messenger)
2. The receiver (i.e., the audience)
3. The coded message (i.e., combination of words, visuals, audio, etc.)
4. A medium (i.e., the channel the message is sent)
5. Noise (i.e., created by other unrelated stimuli, signals, or elements)

Translated into today's language, message transmission is successful based on whether it elicits a reaction—click, buy, like, donate, vote, and so on. If there is no feedback, then the message failed. Which is why at Columbia University, we are adamant in telling graduate students that awareness is *not* an objective . . . there is no feedback that anyone was persuaded to do anything when awareness is the end goal. In a marketing system, the audience's behavior closes the feedback loop.

In a digital world, creating a closed feedback loop in every communication is key. It is the difference between strategic communication and over-communication. Recall the "7-38-55" rule of

## FIGURE 5.1

# MESSAGE FEEDBACK LOOP

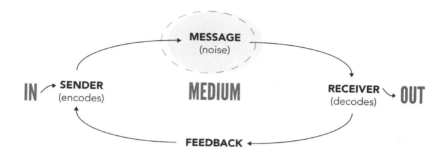

*Messages are pieces of information—words, sounds, visuals—that prompt feedback behavior.*

*Source*: Adapted from Ronald Adler and Neil Towne, *Looking Out, Looking In*, 2nd ed. (New York: Holt, Rinehart and Winston, 1978).

Albert Mehrabian, describing the relative impacts of verbal versus nonverbal messages.[8] Communication depends more on how we *feel* than on how we think about what the speaker is saying. So why do we attach so much importance to words in our communications? We elevate their importance because we've become a society that generates so much text-based data (e.g., tweets, articles, Web pages, books). In fact, more than 80% of data, as we know it, is text-based.

One of the core classes our students take is called *Principles of Persuasion*. We start off by focusing on the Greek philosopher Aristotle's rules of rhetoric and end with American economist and Nobel laureate Richard Thaler's behavioral nudges. Since half of my students are international, discussing global companies and navigating borderless issues is a mainstay during lectures. And, admittedly, multinational companies get an unfair share of class time due to the familiarity of those brands to all students. But, big or small, there's no protection for a company that can't keep pace with culture.

## WIRED TO THINK, FEEL, AND DO

Ignited by philosopher and educator Plato in 370 BC, "think, feel, do" has become a modern "go-to" strategy for brand planners, strategists, and marketers looking for a logic-based framework for converting audiences.[9] At 20, Plato became a student of Socrates, the founder of Western philosophy who gave us the Socratic method (i.e., asking question after question) commonly used in law and the groundwork for ethics and morality. In Plato's work *Phaedrus*, written when he was in his late 60s, he contends that our soul has a pilot—the mind—and that we should first think before acting impulsively. In his worldview, action needs to be balanced with rational thought.[10] It's a desired balance (at a time with more control over media and stimuli); today's consumer has evolved (at a time noisier than ever).

The forefather of modern philosophy has given us many gifts, including the modern university blueprint, based on his founding of The Academy, at which he taught students including Aristotle. The traditional branding construct of "think, feel, do" is showing signs of fatigue—likely because the pace of digital technology advancement doesn't allow most consumers the time to think before doing as we move toward an autopilot existence. As Daniel Kahneman notes in *Thinking, Fast and Slow*, "most of the time we coast."[11]

"Think, feel, do" leads to a heavy focus on taglines and slogans—over-compression in the meaning of a brand into assets that don't immerse, educate, or inspire employees about heritage, purpose, values, or roles.[12] After reading this book, you will gladly relinquish "think, feel, do" as a brand-building framework and upgrade your tactics to a system that represents an approach built for a culture of perpetual beta.

The relation between emotions, feelings, and expression is best described by San Francisco State University professor David Matsumoto and Bob Willingham, who believe "feelings are an important part of everyone's psychology because they are our private readouts of internal processes, informing us without words how we evaluate the world around us and events that happen to us, and what may be going on in our bodies. They are windows to our souls."[13] In his basic emotion system (Figure 5.2) he describes our eventual behavior as a series of dominos: events trigger associations that we have coded into

## FIGURE 5.2
# BASIC EMOTION SYSTEM

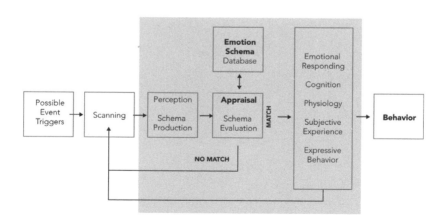

*Our emotion system masks a confluence of activity that results in an eventual behavior.*

*Source*: Adapted from David Matsumoto with photos by Bob Willingham, "The Origin of Universal Human Emotions." http://davidmatsumoto.com/content /NG%20Spain%20Article_2_.pdf.

our memory resulting in a behavior, and that the emotion that emerges may be the expression of "coordinated responses." All in milliseconds—in autopilot mode. We start to understand that the reasons why people react are due to a multilayered and often subconscious volley between cues that are mental, physiological, and environmental. It is through these windows to the soul that brands can start to unlock triggers to an audience's thinking, decision-making, and habits.

There are a few words we need to cozy up to, and they're as deep into psychology as we'll get.

Lexicon at its core is made up of three main interconnections to communication as a system (Figure 5.3): taxonomy, triggers, and framing. Collectively, they're going to give us the three main pressure points that you need to write a memorable tagline, create compelling brand positioning, develop poignant messages, or draft clever presentations.

**Taxonomy**: How we remember (e.g., coding, storing, cataloging)
**Triggers**: What prompts our memories (e.g., schema, associations)
**Framing**: How information is applied (e.g., perceptions, facts, and beliefs)

Let's start with taxonomy, which is essentially a system of categorizing to aid memory (i.e., information retrieval). At its core it is about organization. Imagine that every thought is tagged with keywords and hashtags. We are constantly compressing our knowledge into simple sparks. In 2009, researchers at UC San Diego calculated that the average American consumes 34 gigabytes of information daily, which amounts to 100,000 words.[14] Those billions of bits of information that you're processing every single second are similar to the binary computer language of 0s and 1s—good or bad, positive or negative, up or down. This process consumes 20% of our body's energy, and it's a process that

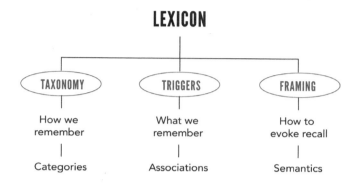

# FIGURE 5.3
## LEXICON ROOTS

*Three elements of a lexicon system include: taxonomy, triggers, and framing.*

our body is trying to minimize.[15] People want a break; a mental snooze button.

The secret behind taxonomy is that most people will at best remember three things at a time. This is why American phone numbers and Social Security numbers are split into three parts. It's one behavioral nudge that is intuitively built into complex systems. Whether we are cognizant of it or not, the majority of the time we naturally chunk information. Curiously, we prefer odd-numbered listicles (e.g., 3, 5, 7), echoing a fascination with the number three that stretches well beyond "three strikes and you're out" and "third time's a charm."

Imagine your mind is a server and each memory receives a meta tag for fast retrieval. In a game of balancing accuracy, speed, and efficiency, our mind creates as few tags as possible by compressing information into familiar chunks. Researchers have exhaustively cataloged the "science of memory," and in doing so, have concluded that memories intensify in saliency when chunks are tied to word/phrase triggers. In media, chunking translates into listicles. If pitching or writing a round-up, seven is the magical number. In social media, hashtags represent chunks, and platforms see drop-off when more than two or three are used simultaneously.[16] Those chunks of information are categories like an index table.

The British psychologist Sir Frederic Bartlett studied the ability to reconstruct memories using schema—puzzle pieces that unlock the taxonomy of information in our minds.[17] Through his work, psychologists have been inspired to study language as a "trigger" for emotions. A trigger is based on the association we have between words; those associations create language cues. For instance, if I were to say a series of words—stripes, black and white, horse—then you may deduce that I'm talking about a zebra. Surrounding a consumer with a breadcrumb trail of keywords creates associations. It's taking those keywords beyond paid search and using them throughout communication.

The third interconnection to communication is framing—how information is presented. Think of a news show: a host in the middle and guests flanking each side. Like in a debate, the host assumes a moderator role. Two different perspectives (i.e., "frames") are being applied: Democrat versus Republican, Wall Street versus Main Street, for and against, and so forth. Each frame can wholly be true, based on the facts being used. In that framing, both communities present arguments that represent the beliefs and socials norms shared by the members. They offer unique combination of facts, attitudes, and behaviors to bolster their arguments.

As Oren Klaff writes in *Pitch Anything*, "A frame is the instrument you use to package your power, authority, strength, information, and status."[18] He reduces frames to four types: (1) time, (2) power, (3) intrigue, (4) and prizing. In his theory, when frames clash, then only one frame wins, and that winning frame dominates the social interaction. If you have no frame (i.e., point of view), you become an automatic loser. Whether half-empty or half-full, the first step is simply having a "frame." As a business development expert, Klaff's point of view on framing concludes that the "stakes" are most important; the sooner the risks are known, the more receptive an audience will be to listen and act.

Framing is about choosing which set of facts and evidence to illuminate for an audience and, as culture evolves, ensure that the perspective is continually updated. If we fail to "frame" the information in a way that entices the audience, then we fail to resonate in a way that drives behavioral outcomes like purchase action. Try crafting a logic-based brand phrase about your brand. For instance, you can follow a similar construct as: We offer the **best** (i.e., a frame) **minty** (i.e., an association) **toothpaste** (i.e., a category).

## A FIGHT FOR EQUALITY

Since 2008, retail brand American Apparel has helped amplify the fight for "marriage equality" by donating over 100,000 shirts to support visibility for the Supreme Court victory that activists fought decades to secure.[19] But at first, not everyone was supportive of the "legalize gay" rhetoric. According to Pew Research Center, in 2004, only 31% of Americans believed in same-sex marriage. By 2017, over 62% of Americans supported same-sex marriage.[20] Why such a shift? In 2011, the year those in favor passed the number of those opposed of same-sex marriage, news lexicon started to shift.[21] More media outlets, online and broadcast, started consistently adopting the language "marriage equality," and along with that helping shift cultural frames. Aided by the shifting demographics that defined "family," the issue picked up steam all the way to the Supreme Court. In reframing the issue, it went from being about sexuality to being about humanity.

As the fight for marriage equality raged, women's rights were equally undergoing a shift during the 1980s. After the 1973 ruling of *Roe v. Wade*, antiabortion advocates reframed their argument in a positive light, tapping into the generally universal belief that those most vulnerable in society should be protected. They highlighted the fact that all human life matters, including the unborn. Today, "pro-life" appears online and in the news nearly four times more than the term *antiabortion*.[22] Framing is about winning the "semantics of perception" using the facts, metaphors, and narrative that build the mental image that moves your audience to action. We'll talk more about framing in the chapter on internal culture, related to a brand's point of view on issues and causes.

With those primers—reason, emotions, triggers, and framing—you have the necessary basic foundation to understand the relationship between psychology and decision-making that will compel consumers toward favorable brand thoughts and actions.

## Notes

1. "Lexicon," Oxford Dictionaries. Accessed January 30, 2019. https://en.oxforddictionaries.com/definition/lexicon.

2. "Communication," Oxford Dictionaries. Accessed January 30, 2019. https://en.oxforddictionaries.com/definition/communication.

3. Donella H. Meadows, *Thinking in Systems: A Primer*. White River Junction, VT: Chelsea Green, 2008.

4. Jørgen Stig Nørgård, John Peet, and Kristín Vala Ragnarsdóttir (Eds.), "The History of the Limits to Growth." Accessed January 31, 2019. http://donellameadows.org/archives/the-history-of-the-limits-to-growth/.

5. Sarah Knapton, "Language Started 1.5m Years Earlier Than Previously Thought as Scientists Say Homo Erectus Were First to Talk." *The Telegraph*, February 20, 2018. https://www.telegraph.co.uk/news/2018/02/20/language-started-15m-years-earlier-previously-thought-scientists/.

6. Paul L. Wattis and Phyllis Wattis, Foundation Endowment Symposium, Nina G. Jablonski, and Leslie Aiello, *The Origin and Diversification of Language*. San Francisco: California Academy of Sciences, 1998.

7. Ronald Adler and Neil Towne, *Looking Out, Looking In*, 2nd ed. New York: Holt, Rinehart, and Winston, 1978.

8. Ibid.

9. Plato, *Phaedrus*. Indianapolis: Hackett, 1995.

10. Ibid.

11. Daniel Kahneman, *Thinking, Fast and Slow*. New York: Farrar, Straus and Giroux, 2011.

12. Iris Bakker, Theo Van der Voordt, Jan Boon, and Peter Vink, "Pleasure, Arousal, Dominance: Mehrabian and Russell Revisited." *Current Psychology* 33 (2014): 405–421. 10.1007/s12144-014-9219-4.

13. David Matsumoto with photos by Bob Willingham, "The Origin of Universal Human Emotions." Accessed January 31, 2019. http://davidmatsumoto.com/content/NG%20Spain%20Article_2_.pdf

14. Doug Ramsey, "Computer Games and TV Account for Bulk of Information Consumed in 2008," *UCSD News*, December 9, 2009. https://ucsd news.ucsd.edu/archive/newsrel/general/12-09Information.asp.

15. Nikhil Swaminathan, "Why Does the Brain Need So Much Power?" *Scientific American*, April 29, 2008. https://www.scientificamerican.com /article/why-does-the-brain-need-s/.

16. Eric-Jan Wagenmakers, *The Oxford Handbook of Memory*, edited by Endel Tulving and Fergus Craik. Oxford University Press, 2000, *Acta Psychologica* 106 (3), 2001, pp. 329–331. ISSN 0001-6918, doi:10.1016/ S0001-6918(00)00065-2.

17. Claus-Christian Carbon and Sabine Albrecht, "Bartlett's Schema Theory: The Unreplicated 'Portrait d'homme' Series from 1932." *Quarterly Journal of Experimental Psychology* 65, no. 11 (November 2012): 2258–2270. doi:10.1080/17470218.2012.696121.

18. Oren Klaff, *Pitch Anything: An Innovative Method for Presenting, Persuading, and Winning the Deal*. New York: McGraw-Hill, 2011.

19. Michelle Castillo, "Brands Use Social Media to Back Same-sex Marriage." CNBC, June 26, 2015. https://www.cnbc.com/2015/06/26/ brands-use-social-media-to-back-same-sex-marriage.html.

20. Pew Research Center, "Changing Attitudes on Gay Marriage." Pew Research Center. June 26, 2017. www.pewforum.org/fact-sheet/changing-attitudes,on-gay-marriage/.

21. "Marriage Equality." Google Trends. Accessed January 31, 2019. https://trends.google.com/trends/explore?date=all_2008&geo =US&gprop=news&q=marriage%20equality.

22. "Anti-abortion vs. Pro-life." Google Trends. https://trends.google .com/trends/explore?date=all_2008&geo=US&gprop=news&q =anti%20abortion,pro%20life.

# 6

# LEXICON TRIGGERS

*Branding Objective:*
*Appeal to a "Tribe"*

## FLASH-FORWARD

Taxonomy

Associations

Schema

Framing

Audience appeals

Trigger words

Tribe

Normative language

Branded vocabulary

## BRAND SPOTLIGHTS

Aldi

CrossFit

Deliveroo

Dollar Shave Club

In-N-Out Burger

Refinery29

SoulCycle

StitchFix

theSkimm

Weight Watchers

Imagine searching on Google for a word. One minute later there will be the same relative "population" of words available online. That's because on average, a new word is added to the English language every eight hours. Now imagine searching on Google for an image. This can prove to be a moving target. Every eight hours, millions of new images are captured, uploaded, and indexed. The first lesson to realize about elements in a communication system is that they grow at different paces: words move slowly, images and audio much faster. So in the branding system we discuss in this book, we separate the three elements of lexicon, audio, and visuals into three different forms of expression. When combined, they present a more focused, less pixelated view of a "brand."

Words are powerful tools within the repertoire of lexicon. They can project a "binary frame" during a conversation or debate: positive versus negative, optimistic versus cynical, right versus wrong. They can incite emotions that prompt thought or action: urgency, scarcity, trust, respect, and beyond. And they can trigger emotional responses based on powerful associations rooted in negativity (e.g., war, crime, bomb, victim) or positivity (e.g., peace, tranquility, laughter). Our perfect irrationality, as argued by Dan Ariely,[1] contributes to language being a master key for exploiting the *triggers and traps* of cognition. Unlike audio and visuals, words evoke more binary interpretations, thanks to construct of *definitions.*

There are thousands of prominent dictionary companies in the world—from Merriam Webster, first released in 1828, to the Oxford English dictionary, first released in 1884.[2,3] In many regards, dictionaries are the measure of language through codification of acceptable framing. The emergence of new dictionaries signals new branches of communication and are a clear indicator of rising communities of thought. Language also shows the shared culture between countries. American English, for instance, is 60% Latin and Greek and 30% French. Language is comprised of words that are given meaning by the community that uses that language; and now more than ever, we have seen an explosion in communities redefining terms. Linguists who study the origins and evolutions of language are witnessing a golden age of communication: globalism creates more universal codes and tribalism creates more nuanced meaning. With new words being coined and coming into the common lexicon all the time, brands must pay particular attention to cues to drive new associations, triggers, and frames, updating their lexicon at the pace of culture.

Consider Urban Dictionary, started by college student Aaron Peckham in 1999 as a joke—really—to take a jab at more serious players like dictionary.com.[4] Already surpassing the one million definitions in Merriam-Webster,[5] the Urban Dictionary has well over seven million definitions. This feat became possible in an open source world, in which language is no longer determined by committee, but rather by community. Compared to the long-standing Oxford and Merriam-Webster dictionaries, which add 1,000 new words annually,[6] Urban Dictionary better represents the burgeoning growth of our language by adding over 2,000 new entries daily.[7]

Operating under a citizen-verified model, like Wikipedia, Peckman's pecking order of the hottest words in language attracts over 18 million visitors each year.[8] Webster's first volume in 1828 sold only 5,000 copies. Today, Noah Webster is now one of the most famous linguists in history, with his Merriam-Webster offshoot helping 40 million people annually navigate the turbulent waters of the English language.[9]

At 20 years of age, the average native English speaker recognizes about 40,000 words,[10] a mere fraction of the nearly 500,000 English words coded in Merriam-Webster, yet an incredible advancement over the initial 20–100 words shared by early speakers two million years ago.[11,12] Our inability to fully digest, memorize, and recall the totality of language leaves us with inevitable gaps in expression. Meanings are often being "lost in translation." And as a result, we find ourselves immersed in ineffable moments. Ever tried to launch a global campaign? If so, then you have experienced the limits of language firsthand: French has 100,000 words, German has 135,000 words, and Chinese has 350,000 characters/words. As a result, finding the right words to make the right impact often requires matching intent and sentiment, rather than precise translation alone.

The term "sentiment" has seen a surge in usage because of its popularity in social media bingo. The Latin root for "sentiment," *sentire*, encapsulates emotions, feelings, and metaphysical experiences—essentially, positive and negative reactions. Today, psychologists see one consistent winner in the thumb-wrestle between good and bad: we are more likely to express ourselves by using negative terms than positive terms. And, arguably, our primal defense mechanisms pose a barrier to brands that want to establish positive relationships with customers. At the MIT Media Lab, the "affective computing" project is busy assigning such sentiment to items within images: to predict behavior, to solve obstacles for individuals with disabilities, and to use emotional feedback to improve experiences.[13]

Research abounds on the saliency of negative language—we are more likely to click, more likely to repeat, and more likely to relay something negative . . . And in a system where feedback is required for a message to be transmitted, then negativity can become a strategy, as often seen in politics. For instance, the power of negative headlines results in a 60% lift in click-through-rates for articles than if the same headline were framed positively.[14] We know four times more negative words than positive words . . . an evolutionary defense mechanism for our "fight or flight" survival. So as brands engage with consumers online, and invite feedback, it's no wonder that the majority of online reviews are negative.

The single word that gets most associated with a brand, and becomes a mark of the quality, is the brand name. So, in a world in which search dominates, voice is on the horizon, less is more, and owning a hashtag matters, how do you even start to choose a brand name? For naming projects for companies, brands, products, services, or processes, it's common to go through hundreds of real and coined terms to find the word that hits the right chord. According to branding expert Sandra Bauman, who has studied hundreds of corporate identities, "Every name communicates something (and if that something is nothing, that's a problem)."[15]

In *50 Years of the Lego Brick*, German author Christian Humberg recounts the word play that led to the name of the one eternally modern company, LEGO.[16] Humberg notes: "When Ole Kirk Kristiansen established the company name LEGO in 1934, it was a fortunate play on words. The entrepreneur had been inspired by the Danish phrase 'leg godt'—'play well.' He took the beginning of each respective word and made what he considered to be a pleasant-sounding, imaginary word out of them. The company owner was unaware that as the first person present singular of the verb *legere*, 'lego' is also the Latin word for 'I assemble'—and therefore completely appropriate for the modularity of the company's later invention, the LEGO brick."

---

A brand name should be:
- Memorable (i.e., the average brand name is one or two syllables)
- Familiar (e.g., geographically, culturally rooted)
- Short (i.e., appropriate for hashtag culture)
- Distinguishable by spoken voice (more on the importance of voice in Chapter 7: Audio Cues)
- SEO friendly
- URL safe
- Autocomplete-proof
- Translation dexterous

---

During name evaluation, critical hurdles need to be cleared in finding one that can resonate now and into the future. Finding the perfect name can take hundreds of throwaways to result in a list of 10–15 viable candidates, in hopes that two or three can clear pressure tests for usage, including trademark and associations. Common naming trends to capture attention include (Figure 6.1):

- Modern, abstract words that can become ownable across search, trademarks, and hashtags (e.g., Amazon)
- Descriptive terms that can capture an unfair share of organic search traffic (e.g., SoulCycle, PopSocket)
- Phrases expressive of an emotion, feeling, or mental state (e.g., HappySocks)
- Traditional names that exude heritage and origins (e.g., Goldman Sachs)

Developing the name is a first step; testing the name for acceptability and resonance is the second step. When working with clients, there's a five-point pressure test that I apply to new names to check that associations are positive.

1. Basic word trademark search via USPTO
2. Google autocomplete results
3. Search engine top-page results for Web, images, and video
4. Hashtag search for negative conversation
5. In-category competitors

Now, more than ever, meanings of words are shifting as communities nuance terms, so trying to find a name relevant for today and "future-proof" can present a struggle. Follow the feeling to names and language that evoke emotions. Here's a common trap I see: in an effort to impress audiences through futuristic language—*innovation, disruption, and transformation*—we think we're capturing audience attention through buzzword bingo. However, cognitive confusion ensues. Our minds need simple building

FIGURE 6.1

# NAMING STRATEGY MATRIX

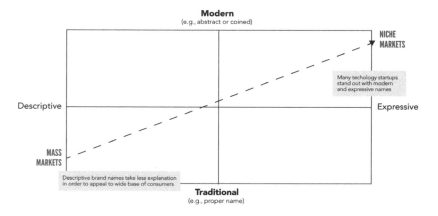

*Naming brands and/or products requires weighing key factors to achieve a niche or mass appeal—factors including modernity, tradition, descriptiveness, or expressiveness.*

blocks as stepping stones to larger, abstract constructs. Draw a bike. Chances are it has two wheels, a seat and a handlebar. Now draw innovation. And now draw disruption. And transformation. If you can draw it, then people can likely visualize it. If it doesn't pass a back-of-the-napkin sketch test, then the concept (or term) is too complicated to be a positive cognitive trigger as a single term or phrase.

**TRY THIS:**

Mission Image

Use your mission statement as a test to determine the concreteness of your company's language. Can you sketch the basic words that anchor the statement? If not, how can you shift the words to make them click with a clear mental image?

# DELIVEROO

*Creating a Sticky Name to Kick the Food Delivery Market into Full Swing*

Started in 2013, London-based food delivery service Deliveroo has become a $2 billion company through cashing in on a concept that speaks to the most basic sense of consumer convenience: food. When its cofounder William Shu worked as a banking analyst for Morgan Stanley and had been relocated from New York to London, he realized that the London food delivery market was not nearly as accessible as that of New York. The American banker-turned-businessman decided to take action. Shu employed his childhood friend Greg Orlowski, an American software developer, to help build a brand that resonates with an audience eager for ease and speed. After a few years of development and an original name of "Boozefood," Deliveroo was launched in 2013 with its first city being Brighton, England.

Shu and Orlowski ultimately decided on calling their concept "Deliveroo" prior to its launch. The name takes its inspiration from kangaroos, intending to blend a catchy-sounding name with the nature of the marsupial. "Kangaroos are known to be incredibly protective of their young. At Deliveroo we are equally protective of your dining experience," the website once stated. Shu's original concept with Deliveroo was to launch a food delivery service in London that was as convenient and far-reaching as the delivery options he knew in New York. To do this right, the company's aim had to be to deliver food that added ease and comfort to the customer's dining experience. In selecting the name "Deliveroo" for the company, Shu encompassed this notion into its name.[17,18,19,20]

## LIMITS OF WORDS

Bright-eyed out of college, I began working at global advertising agency Ogilvy. Started in the 1970s, their planning department is known within the marketing industry as the gold standard—one of the oldest, largest, and most influential. In a world where candidates are expected to hit the ground running, the department instead took the time to train people, and their processes for understanding consumers would slowly make their way throughout the industry as planners and strategists became clients, changed jobs, or gained media exposure.

From day one, they drilled home that the role of a "strategist" was to (1) create simplicity, (2) develop guardrails for saying no, and (3) illuminate achievable yet bold pathways forward. It's through that lens that a problem-solving mentality is engrained in anyone that touches strategy work. A clear job intent that should propel strategists to focus on creating singular positioning using the nuances of audience, market, product, or service . . . that ultimately steers teams to apply creativity strategically. And often, that strategic path starts to get illuminated based on finding the right trigger words to encapsulate a client opportunity, inspire a creative team, or rally action from an audience.

We live in a "PC" culture, in which significant care and consideration are now given to the words we use as citizens, or as C-suite executives, or as comedians, and so forth. A time when "labels" are being questioned more widely, often controversially, from gender to sexuality to heritage. And brands are no longer just reduced or remembered for their taglines, for example, "Just Do It," "I'm Lovin' It," or "A Diamond Is Forever." There's no doubt that words have purpose for brands—to make brands memorable, catchy, relevant, sticky, and clear in their value propositions . . . Yet, to put those expensive and flashy taglines back into perspective with our total communication system, recall that only 7% of a communication is verbal.[21] The majority of the effect of communication comes from visuals, sounds, tone, and delivery. This is not meant to suggest that copywriters aren't the most important people in an agency or that the writer is the least important person on a team; it's meant to give us a healthy understanding of the limitations of language. Because of those limits, we can't place all the pressure on words alone through creative briefs, case studies, presentations, speeches, positioning statements, or branding elements (e.g., name of company, brand, product, or service).

Language has two important limitations that every brand must consider—context and community. Context includes historical meaning, the current sociopolitical climate, and the moral landscape of society. And we must recognize that context changes as culture evolves. Community includes the ability to resonate through audience appeals. And marketers and strategists that have the most empathy for communities fare best in building strong brands. The limits of context and community can see-saw, requiring founders, brand builders, and communicators to continually reconsider how they are using framing to win hearts and minds. No brand should think it can stay frozen in time through a tagline or language that will always be meaningful in the future.

## CONTEXT

Context has two key layers: delivery and environment. Delivery is how something is being said. Delivery can be in written or spoken form (for instance, pacing and tone). It can also evoke feelings of calm, anxiety, or fear. Environment is the background for interpretation. Whether using PEST, SWOT, or TOWS analysis, no brand operates in a vacuum. Understanding the landscape—market, media, consumer, and beyond—is paramount to anticipating what "noise" might create friction between a brand and consumer. Context determines the motivation and ability of someone to make a favorable brand decision or form a favorable brand opinion. As a rule of thumb, always remember, all lexicon strategy starts and ends with the audience, and the more empathetic you are to your audiences, the more likely you are to craft language that spurs action.

The Elaboration Likelihood Model was developed by researchers Richard Petty and John Cacioppo while they were graduate students at Ohio State University in 1986.[22] The origins of their work on dual-processing can be traced to the early 1900s work of psychologist William James, who reasoned there were two paths to decision-making: "true" and "associative." Combined, these two pathways make what is dubbed as our "stream of consciousness." The "elaboration" is our desire to show either interest or disinterest—and which wins depends on two factors (Figure 6.2): (1) motivation to make a decision and (2) ability to make a decision.

### FIGURE 6.2
## ELABORATION LIKELIHOOD MODEL

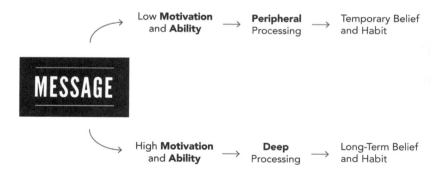

*Long- and short-term habit formation depends on the motivation and ability of the decision-maker.*

Source: Adapted from Richard Petty and John Cacioppo, "The Elaboration Likelihood Model of Persuasion," *Advances in Experimental Social Psychology* 19 (1986), 123–205.

Their dual processing system introduced central and peripheral pathways. Central processing leads to long-lasting behavior due to critical thought. It requires both (1) motivation and (2) ability. In centrally processed decisions, people may seek experts or access to information, to feel more assured in their decision-making. Peripheral processing happens the majority of the time. It is the 95% of decisions that Kahneman calls our autopilot (i.e., system 1). Susceptible to cognitive "triggers" (e.g., keywords, familiarity of colors/shapes, endorsements of respected people, audio), peripheral processing usually accompanies consumers being "tuned out" due to the frequency of purchase decisions, such as buying fast-moving commodities like toothpaste.

The communication implications for brands: save the long list of reasons to believe, the proof points, features, benefits, and the laundry list of words that are attempting to persuade. Instead, find the two to three keywords that trigger motivation, and then support the ability to make a decision with access to further information, experts, peers, testimonials, or reviews. It's a two-step process to spark behavior, and language only has a cameo.

## THE INVISIBLE HAND: COMMUNITY

Adam Smith, the one economist that the average Joe generally has heard of, warned us of the invisible hand—the forces at play that influence us. Those forces, in my professional opinion, are communities. But others may argue that those forces are "the market." Technology is bringing communities together in a way never imagined before, beyond geography or former avenues of knowledge, and brands that excel in culture understand their role to communities, and what a community is.

Communities can be physical or digital, public or hidden, religious or recreational, or localized or global. Definitions of *community* range from "groups of people in the same place"[23] to "groups of persons who come from the same ancestors."[24] Communities happen on several layers. People belong to multiple communities simultaneously (e.g., home, work, school, recreational, charitable), and must balance the values of each group. And, as Oren Klaff puts it, when faced with clashing frames, one community's views wins. One identity emerges above the others. The goal of a brand is to build, curate, or fuel a community so that it becomes so strong that it morphs into a "tribe." But at the same time, understand that audiences belong to multiple communities, and the values between those groups each have consequences for the brand.

While a consulting director at Ogilvy, helping clients unpack the future, a senior C-suite client asked us to think about his narrative for the future of their industry. For such a macro question, we broke the audience into several layers common in resiliency theory, because, of course, our goal is to build resilient brands.[25] Introduced in the 1970s by Dr. Urie Bronfenbrenner, an early childhood psychologist who's best known for helping create the Head Start program in the United States, the social-ecological model (Figure 6.3) uses a systems-thinking approach to untangle the relationship between individual and communities. Each year, the American Psychological Association, founded in 1892, awards their highest honor for lifetime achievement to a member; an award named after him.

His model has incredible applications for brand-building— because consumers exist in relation to and are influenced by many factors, including their community affiliations. The new brand social contract, then, is brand-consumer-community. By applying a sociology-based framework to brand building, we start to understand the depth of relationships, and thus triggers, for compelling action:

- Individual: Knowledge, attitude, behaviors
- Interpersonal: Family, spouse/partner, social network, friends

## FIGURE 6.3
# SOCIAL-ECOLOGICAL MODEL OF HUMAN DEVELOPMENT

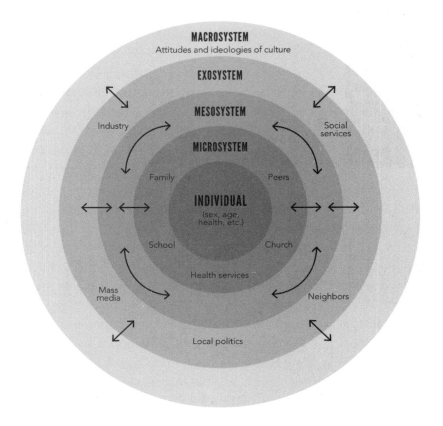

*Individuals experience simultaneous influences and pressure points, including micro interpersonal relationships and macro socioeconomics.*

*Source:* Adapted from Urie Bronfenbrenner, *The Ecology of Human Development: Experiments by Nature and Design* (Cambridge, MA: Harvard University Press, 1979).

- Organizational: "Work clique," clubs, associations, societies (e.g., fraternities and sororities)
- Society: Laws, regulations, social norms

Use the layers of the socioecological model to alter one key corporate value to appeal to a member of different communities (i.e., intrapersonal vs. society). What "sacred words" do you need to use? How does code-switching and code-signaling come into practice to make the message stickier for each target community? What does your tagline mean on each level; does it retain or lose its impact?

# DOLLAR SHAVE CLUB

*Connecting with Community by Cutting to the Chase*

When Michael Dubin and Mark Levine founded Dollar Shave Club in 2011, the duo had a simple mission: to provide customers with "a great shave delivered right to your door." Dollar Shave Club, or DSC, mirrors its consumer behavior through audience appeals. The brand is nestled within the notion of convenience, maintaining a friendly, relatable accord with its customers. This is accomplished through the brand's diction; in keeping a conversational tone throughout all of its correspondence, DSC appeals to its target audience in an approachable way that sparks motivation and ability to make a purchase decision. "American men are evolving in their bathroom routine," Dubin once said. "Five years ago, if you spent time in front of the mirror, people would have called you a metrosexual. We now live in the age where it's okay to hug guys and compliment and give advice."

The inclusion of the word "Club" in the name builds a sense of connection with the consumer. As a member of the club, consumers become a part of a thriving community that other brands failed to emphasize in their marketing. When talking to its members, DSC pokes fun at the common annoyances that people face when shaving. Each member receives the club's magazine, titled "The Bathroom Minutes," with their monthly shaving packages, establishing rituals for their community. "From our packaging to our digital presence to our media strategy, the DSC brand identity informs everything we do," the brand stated. The brand took a boring, monotonous routine and made it into an entertaining product and community, and in turn, was able to grow its consumer base at a rate much faster than most e-commerce companies. DSC was ultimately acquired by Unilever in 2016 for $1 billion, validating the success of the brand's tribe-like approach to personal care.[26,27,28,29,30]

## SHIFTING FROM TARGET AUDIENCE TO COMMUNITY

We spend a lot of time talking about "target audience." And many of my clients, rightly so, want to figure out how to be participants in "culture." Well, culture comes from communities. And communities grant permission for brands to leverage culture for consumerism. When you start to shift your thinking from cold, empty, data-induced language like "target audience" and shift to replacing it with "community" and "tribe," then you'll be closer to engineering a positive feeling into your brand.

Whether the "Beyhive" or "Black Twitter" our sense of existence and identity is deeply rooted in belonging to a community. Our instinctive state is to project that we are a part of a group—that we are not alone and are protected by the cloak of community. As early as 1943, Maslow cataloged our universal need to be a part of a group.[31] And as behavioral scientists have affirmed since the 1950s, a group develops its own psychology, which can override individual thought and reason. Deeper than peer pressure, the sense of belonging is predicated on survival. Thus, the role of communication, foremost, is to spark any alarm that could disrupt conditions. Over time, as communities develop more homogenous and singular-minded views, their communication can be reduced to shorthand, branded language.

**TRY THIS:**
—
A Tribe
Called . . .

Does your brand have a tribe? Is there a sense of "shared community" and consciousness between your customers?

FROM: Audience as a fragmented, scattered "target" demographic

TO: Audience as a unified community (i.e., "tribe") sharing one identity layer

# CROSSFIT

*Being a Tribe for the Weekend Warrior and Pro Athlete*

This past decade has seen the likes of Tough Mudder, Color Run, and a whole subculture revolving around fitness. The Santa Cruz–born fitness company started in 2000 and has grown to dominate conversations in the space, rivaling the spinning culture startups Peloton and SoulCycle. Over 140 gyms worldwide are CrossFit affiliates, with millions of community members plugged into their tribe through social media. Work-out Day routines (WODs) are peppered through many an Instagram timeline as novice and professional CrossFitters record their high-intensity workouts, including personal record box jumps, burpees, and kettlebell swings. The effect is contagious—much like running clubs or spin classes—and Cross-Fit has turned the art of weight training into its own tribal activity.

Two factors have led to the CrossFit brand's rise to dominance in the fitness world. One, a 10-year partnership and exclusive rights deal with Adidas-owned Reebok. Since 2010, that deal has helped to resurrect the fledgling shoe brand to a point where it's now synonymous with high-impact sports. (Reebok also has a long-running deal with mixed martial arts brand UFC.) Second, the CrossFit name—pithy and sharp off the tongue—founded a strong annual global competition that has included over 400,000 partici-pants who are athletes and weekend warriors. ESPN2 held media rights for the annual CrossFit Games and contests from 2013–2016, until CBS Sports took over broadcast and streaming coverage in 2017. As a niche brand, TV viewership has been comparable to audiences for drag and stock car racing. Like an iceberg, CrossFit has more than proven there's much below the surface, and its community continues to grow rapidly.[32,33,34,35]

The advent of the smartphone has been a blessing and a curse, and regulating its use in schools has become harder as researchers, have discovered that teenagers are capable of hearing ultrasonic sounds that adults cannot distinguish.[36] These high frequency sounds, akin to dog whistles, are what a linguist would call the audio equivalent of code signal. And in a digital age of hashtags, SEO, and data personalization, we are seeing more code signaling than ever. In *Thank You for Arguing*, a staple guide to rhetoric for all our graduate communication students, Heinrichs likens audience appeals to mirroring effects (e.g., talk like, look like, behave like . . .)[37] It's in this mirroring of audience that a brand's message is pressure tested for relevancy. And it's in those audience appeals that relevancy translates into a decoded signal to act. In politics, "dog whistle" appeals to specific audiences have taught us that code-switching based on the targeted crowd can trigger strong feelings and provoke actions, as well. Is your brand one-size-fits-all, or do you nuance language by audience to achieve appeal?

To help determine your brand's delivery style, imagine your company is having a dinner party. Who do you invite? How do those individuals talk? What's their linguistic style? What common words or phrases might you expect to hear? Now imagine you're having a meeting about financial performance. How are you code-switching around key topics to motivate favorable audience action in the moment?

# REFINERY29

*Creating a Business Model Anchored in Framing*

Though founded by a pair who had previously never worked within the fashion publishing realm, Refinery29 was the fastest-growing media publication for two years in a row, due to its success in appealing to women in a unique, personalized manner. Justin Stefano left his career in law to join his childhood friend, Philippe von Borries, who had left his career in politics, to form the content platform in 2005. After bringing on content strategist Piera Gelardi and magazine editor Christine Barberich, the then-small Refinery29 team expanded its mission as a fashion-focused city guide to New York City covering topics in home, music, and design to a publication that covered the angles that female readers were looking for. In its early days, the publication utilized a simple platform, which included "29 best lists"—hence the name Refinery29—to cover diverse topics across the fashion and beauty world, ensuring that women of all demographics are included.

Over the past decade, Refinery29 listened closely to its audience, and adapted to that audience in its editorial tone and the subjects that it covered. "It wasn't about feeding into this expectation that women have to be perfect or married or thin or beautiful, and it was really fun and satisfying for us to explore the fringe of what everyone else was talking about with beauty," said Barberich. Its innovative approach and evocative name proved successful to Refinery29; today the media platform reaches half a billion readers globally, with regional versions launched in countries including the United Kingdom and Germany.[38,39,40]

## A TALE OF TWO WORDS

More than signaling to specific communities, words, phrases, and terms also demonstrate the shifting morality of clashing cultures. It's an infinite thumb-wrestle battle to frame the pop culture landscape of acceptability. Almost 100 years after the passing of the Emergency Quota Act of 1921,[41] there's still widespread debate and dog whistling around undocumented immigrants. The tailspin debate exists within the framing choice of "illegal immigrants" versus "illegal aliens"—two frames familiar in debates today with an almost century-old origin.

While both terms were coined by writers at the *New York Times*— *illegal alien* in 1926 and *illegal immigrant* in 1937—the adoption of the term often splits along party line.[42] In 1939, a *Times of London* reporter used "illegal immigrant" to describe the migration of Jewish peoples to Palestine. Imbued with sentiments of foreign, other, and outsider, "illegal alien" has shifted over time to serve as a non-PC dog whistle that awakens an audience that feels threatened. The importance of these two words, and how they've tangoed over time by different communities, shows another example of social framing. Whether marriage equality, pro-life, or beyond, some brands experience success through words that ascend into "branded language" due to strong associations to ideas and ideals of one group.

## NICHE WINS

As marketers, we tend to think in terms of mass . . . that "efficiency" is executing as few deals as possible, to cover as many people as possible with as few messages as possible. Today's reality with communities is that niche wins, and given the pressure of personalization, we're approaching a soon-to-be AI-driven world of data-based messaging personalization that can deepen brand-consumer-community relationships.

The idea of Top 40 radio was introduced in 1950s by Todd Storz,[43] a radio programmer in Nebraska who astutely observed a rise in radio and music listeners during the 1940s, when *Billboard* magazine starting publishing "charts."[44] The primary strategy within the music industry, then, was to break into that cohort of top-selling music. And while payola, or "pay to play," began to determine what was broadcast on the radio, the charts were controlled by a few powerful labels, managers, and artists. Fast-forward to today, when DIY and an indie culture has led to a reform of traditional music models, allowing talent to be discovered and supported through niche communities of fans and brand sponsors. It's not about the charts any more than it's about being in primetime; it's about resonating with a connected community of any size.

By the time Nielsen expanded from radio and retail measurement into television ratings in the 1950s, there were only a handful of channels including ABC, CBS, and NBC. Most broadcasts were local only. By the time HBO launched in 1972, there were over four million subscribers with cable.[45] At its height, there were over 500 cable channels available on services, including Comcast and Time Warner (now Spectrum). Until streaming and on-demand were available, channel line-up mattered. Now, being accessible across devices matters. On YouTube, there are a million "channels" for subscribers. From music artists to filmmakers, the ability to go directly to an audience is making niche marketing strategies more and more successful as the algorithm of digital platforms surface what's relevant. Gone are the days when messaging and engagement need to utilize "mass" channels to reach an audience: niche and relevant wins over mass and repetitious.

**TRY THIS:**

Community Approach

Shift your language: from "target audiences" to "communities." Think of the audience as amorphous clusters of culture, rather than defined demographic cohorts. What community attributes might rally action based on group dynamics (e.g., bandwagon effect)? What about the community is important, which may not matter on the individual level (e.g., status, badging)? What does the community care about as a group?

## BRANDING LANGUAGE

Strong tribes create a gravitational pull on culture. For instance, hip-hop, as a tribe, took over 20 years to reach a mainstream

# THESKIMM

*Hitting All the Right Trigger Words*

NBC alumni Danielle Weisberg and Carly Zakin launched theSkimm, a daily newsletter built for busy Millennial women like themselves, in 2012. Named after the quick, digestible nature of news curation it offers, it's set the tone for many subscriber-based offerings that have come after it, from major publishers like Vox Media's outlets to upstarts like the subscriber-only *The Information*. Five million subscribers, 45 employees, and a valuation of over $50 million later, theSkimm has paved the road that many newsletters today now follow—a strong editorial voice, a distinct look, and an appreciation for their readers. Each letter follows a winning formula: a pithy quote based on recent news, a major news headline (with at least six different outlets to pull additional info from), four to six other newsworthy pieces, curated reads and picks, and an ever-growing list of Skimm readers celebrating birthdays. For the young woman who wants to stay in the know, the newsletters provide them with enough ammo to take on the world. The brand has since expanded to an app for mobile devices, as well as live events, and a more intimate Skimmbassador community that helps young women tackle their bucket list goals.[46]

gravitational pull, and now permeates global culture as the best-selling music genre, in addition to its influence over trends in fashion, sports, art, and even language. Okurrr. Tribes are communities—they operate with a consciousness of the other members. They are a not-so-hidden force in the brand-consumer relationship. They are more powerful marketing constructs for an audience because of the group dynamics of conformity, which enables a brand to start to develop branded language to appeal to them.

Tribes redefine the brand-consumer relationship because their social norm is herd mentality (i.e., individual members of a group follow the dominant behavior of the group, often without regard to their own decision-making abilities). It's the "fear of missing out" or FOMO syndrome born in the wake of tech- and Web-connected Millennials and Generation Z. And whether friends or strangers with someone else in a community, behavioral mirroring happens. Remember that crowd wave, in which a few people can set a whole stadium of people in motion? Well, tribes work like that. Researchers at University of Leeds believe a herd needs only a small nudge to move overwhelmingly in a single direction.[47,48]

As a community, herds experience leadership dynamics. Herd (or tribe) leaders are usually people at the top of information cascades: executives, religious figures, parents, principals, politicians, celebrities (a.k.a. influencers). People conform to the actions and attitudes of others, assuming that those individuals have access to "better" information. Consider the medical field: before any marketing messages go to consumers, medical researchers and pharma companies talk to universities, hospitals, NGOs, the Food & Drug Administration (FDA), manufacturers, and governments. The decade-long process of taking a drug to market, then, produces cascades of information—and in that process, power shifts to the knowledge holders. And around those individuals, institutions, or brands, tribes form.

# SOULCYCLE

*Developing a Tribe Psychology*

When you walk into one of SoulCycle's nearly 100 locations, you'll experience a buzz throughout the studio, the feeling of a beehive that is echoed by the lemon-yellow spoked wheels. Motivational tenets are plastered on the walls and along the corridors—but one saying sticks out: "Find Your Soul." Members call themselves "warriors" and "rock stars" and ride in packs, tribes, crews, or communities. Julie Rice and Elizabeth Cutler joined forces with cofounder Ruth Zukerman in 2006 to launch the fitness startup, in an effort to breathe new life into the fitness space. In giving its riders something to aspire to, the company has risen above the typical grind mentality of traditional gyms. Cycling, very fittingly, served as a metaphor for life's journey, and SoulCycle's spin classes quickly led a revolution that spawned rivals such as Peloton and Flywheel (owned by Zukerman).

Aside from the bright, communal atmosphere, the staff that coaches each group of riders have easily become the backbone of the business. Rice, a former talent agent and now WeWork's chief brand officer, had scouted each of her first coaches personally. Often, members would enter as actors, cheerleaders, and dancers, and end up "rock stars," more famous within studio walls than the celebrities who'd regularly come to classes. Rice said to The Hollywood Reporter: "Making sure people feel taken care of, that they're having the opportunity to shine—it's what I loved about being a talent manager and what I spent a lot of time doing at SoulCycle." Equinox took interest in the company in 2011, first taking a majority stake in the brand and receiving the remaining ownership shares from Rice and Cutler in 2016. By 2018, SoulCycle had been valued at over $900 million and recently opened a talent arm with Hollywood powerhouse WME to further expand its reach and help millions more find their souls.[49,50,51,52]

## A PLANNING PROCESS MINDSET SHIFT

Demographics reduce an audience to averages and indexes. By contrast, a "tribe" conjures up the warm feelings of belonging through shared experiences. Demographics-led marketing leads to data privacy concerns. Tribes-led marketing leads to listening, collaboration, and empowerment.

If you want a new lexicon for your brand, then understanding the natural language people use to describe you is key. Rather than analyzing how many four- or five-star ratings you have, probe and provoke conversations that can later reveal insights. Do you know what product gets the most praise? Least? Why are you keeping the one that garners the least likes in your inventory? Democratize access to information—and influence tips and tribes restructure. By unlocking shifts in language through artificial intelligence of text mining, you can realign your brand lexicon to keep resonating at the pace of culture.

---

How do you identify key audience appeals?
- **Social media analysis of audience conversations:** Identification of frequently used terms, common associations (e.g., word clusters), and emerging language (i.e., slang)
- **Ethnographic studies:** Allows firsthand understanding of how consumers describe situations, products, and services
- **Text mining:** Using artificial intelligence to analyze large volumes of information produced by the community for other community members (e.g., white papers)

---

# STICHFIX

*Winning the Hearts of Busy Professionals One Seam at a Time*

One of the youngest billionaire brands, StitchFix was launched in the Cambridge, Massachusetts, apartment of its founder, Katrina Lake, while she was working on her graduate studies at Harvard in 2011. By 2018, the company had attracted nearly three million active customers, earning it a net revenue north of $1 billion. Lake founded the clothing box service with a mission "to blend the human element of personal styling with high-quality clothing and proprietary algorithms." In other words, customers provide a detailed profile of their size and style preferences to receive a box of clothing curated by a remote personal stylist. Describing its boxes as "snowflakes," because no two are alike, each box is an invitation to experience surprise and delight. The approach to apparel retail adds ease and convenience to the process, saving time throughout and streamlining selection.

StitchFix makes its simple, easy motive clear to consumers through its use of language in speaking to its consumers. Prospective customers find a welcoming tone online: "We're here to help you save time, look great and evolve your personal style over time." The company directly speaks to its shoppers, in a personal and to-the-point manner, addressing the common concerns today's consumers feel with the current retail landscape, and telling them how StitchFix will solve these concerns. StitchFix is unique from both subscription box services and traditional retail methods. Its brand is built within the personalization aspect of its service, which it reflects through the clear-cut and conversational tone it takes when addressing its shoppers.[53,54,55,56,57,58]

# THE DOUBLE-EDGED SWORD OF BEING A "HOUSEHOLD NAME"

My mother sold Tupperware when I was a child. She was one of the two million salespeople finding empowerment in an entrepreneurial spirit rivaled only by Mary Kay salespeople. Launched in 1948, at its height Tupperware had annual sales exceeding of $2 billion.[59] The branding for Tupperware was so strong that in my home, every type of storage container was called Tupperware. And this was happening all across the country in other households, too—so much so, that the brand had become genericized.

Owning a term in society is fluid. Consider music, once associated with Napster, then iTunes, and now Spotify. Google, on the other hand, has marched consistently toward becoming a verb and synonym for "search" through marketing, ease, and ubiquity across devices; the cognitive strength of their name sparks envy among marketers. The ascension of a brand to becoming the generic default may look good on paper when reporting market share, or feel good from a cultural impact standpoint, but can present legal challenges.

Global, industry-leading brands are not shielded from genericism. As recently as 2017, Google had to defend its trademark against claims that it had become too commonplace of a term to warrant a trademark. While marketing groups can celebrate that they created a synonymous relationship between "googling" and "searching," their legal teams have spent millions defending their right for brand protection for their name. This provides a cautionary tale for marketing and legal teams, and the need to collaborate to protect brand value, as consumers naturally hijack brand names to describe generic behavior in an attempt to keep mentally coasting. The runaway success of brands that become genericized brings this question to the forefront: Does a brand landing in the pop culture zeitgeist build or destroy brand value? In other words, should Uber be concerned that people are "ubering" places? As determined in the ruling, a brand is protected only if the name denotes a product attribute (e.g., "who" they are or "where" a product comes from), but not "what" a company does. So, if you're name becomes a verb, you're safe, for now.[60,61]

The temptation to make companies "household names" is driving countless agencies and brands to produce demand-driven work that builds behavior but not brand differentiation. In *Positioning: Battle of the Mind*, authors Al Ries and Jack Trout note that "the basic approach of positioning is not to create something new and different, but to manipulate what's already up there in the mind, to retie the connections that already exist."[62] Their work brings to life the timeless advice of Mark Twain: "There is no such thing as a new idea. It is impossible. We simply take a lot of old ideas and put them into a sort of mental kaleidoscope." Examples of brands that have become genericized over time include:

- Band-Aid—bandage
- Google—search
- Kleenex—tissue
- Xerox—copy
- Jacuzzi—hot tub
- Popsicle—ice cream push
- Frisbee—flying saucer
- Tupperware—storage containers
- Velcro—adhesive

The goal of a strategist is to strike a balance between familiarity and novelty—paving a path to consideration with the fewest stepping stones possible. A strategist seeks to find the right trigger words to inspire action by tapping into emotions of a community and to understand the tribal dynamics around culture that will incite favorable brand behavior. Only in a rare case, over time, might a brand want to lose trademark . . . Bayer actually held a trademark on "heroin" until 1917, when the word became too commonly used.[63] Brands that lost their trademark include items you may use on a regular basis: Griswold-Nissen lost "Trampoline" and Otis lost "Escalators." So as a new brand, if your sights are on being household, don't forego protecting and policing your brand name and branded language. Otherwise, your brand value could ironically erode with your success.

## ANCHORS AND NORMATIVE MESSAGING

To make decisions, we are constantly scanning internally for shortcuts like familiar cues. Those cues—lexicon, audio, and visuals—become anchors to memories. And it's through that mental process of coasting in which anchors become important cognitive markers for which behavioral path to take.

Through research from Dan Ariely and Richard Thaler, we've learned that anchors are deep-rooted and inform how we navigate a noisy world of choice overload and choice indecision. Their body of research since the 1970s mostly focuses on anchors as numbers, which matters when you're handling salary negotiations, selling value-based goods (e.g., real estate, arts), or getting someone to donate to charity.

Anchors are a framing technique. Aside from numbers, anchors can be used in other methods—words, audio, and visuals. Brands have anchors—key messages that take root as claims, slogans, taglines, and branded language. One of the most famous claims and slogans in branding is an anchor: Geico's "15 minutes can save you 15%." This slogan has been used for over 20 years since it was first coined by The Martin Agency, and is one of the longest-running agency-created campaign slogans ever, alongside McCann's "Priceless" MasterCard positioning in 1997, with over 90% ad recall.[64]

*Conquering Context through Experience Simplicity*

Aldi's roots belong in Germany, but it has long been a global force. In the United States, Aldi operates 2,000 locations in 16 states. Globally, Aldi's has over 10,000 locations. The family-owned chain—named after Albrecht Diskont—opened its first store in 1961, touting a cost-effective approach in which 90% of the products it sells carries the same store label, borrowing an experience strategy from fashion retailers. Often retailers tend to work with the same manufacturers and suppliers of name-brand products, but because Aldi has stuffed its shelves with its own branded items, most money that would be used for mass marketing campaigns instead goes to enhancing the customer experience. Which, for any family looking for a bargain, means shoppers can enjoy up to 50% in savings compared to its main competitors: Kroger's, Walmart, and Amazon. A little-known fact: California-based Trader Joe's is owned by Aldi. Purchased in 1979, Trader Joe's has grown to over 500 stores across the United States in a brewing fresh-format supermarket battle with Amazon-owned Whole Foods.[65,66,67]

One of the most famous taglines, dubbed by *Advertising Age* as the top slogan of the twentieth century, is DeBeer's "A diamond is forever."[68] It delivers a feeling of commitment while symbolizing permanence . . . even despite a 40-year rise in divorce rates in the United States. During that time, while the slogan has endured, the company's market share has gone from 90% to under 40%.[69] But the tradition of buying a diamond ring is now normative behavior, etched into Western society with the help of a powerful branded message.[70]

Where else do these anchors live? Well, hotels. If you've reused towels and sheets in your hotel room, then it's likely that you've been coaxed by normative language that creates an anchor so powerful that it can alter your behavior from what you might commonly do at home. If you've stayed in a hotel room since 2010, then you've likely seen signs about recycling towels and sheets. And while that behavior seems standard today, once upon a time, it wasn't. LEED (Leadership in Energy and Environmental Design) certification is the gold standard in construction, and while few hotels fully achieve it, many strive to be as green as possible to save money, thus offering lower rates. For hotels, washing sheets/towels is one of the largest expenses and biggest contributors to energy use. In terms of energy, hotels consume upwards of 15% of local water supplies; reducing washing can save a hotel between 20 and 30% on energy costs and labor.[71]

After writing his global bestseller *Influence*, Arizona State University professor Robert Cialdini joined University of Minnesota professor Vladas Griskevicius and University of Chicago professor Noah J. Goldstein on a journey to change behavior. In the 1990s, they conducted a series of experiments to determine how to trigger behavior. Through several messaging tests, they found that posting signs with wording that indicates that other guests are complying leads to a nearly 30% increase in compliance among all hotel guests.[72] The "normative messaging" approach of evoking communal behavior continues to be powerful today in driving behavioral change and is used for services ranging from Match.com (i.e., ads that state over 25,000 people join a day) to Geico (i.e., ads that reinforce you being able to save 15% in 15 minutes). Reframing through use of statistics such as compliance, or giving the impression of high compliance (e.g., IRS with paying taxes), can lead to a larger individual participation rate from fear of being outside the norm. It's that clash between individual and community, and the fear of missing out, that prompts behavior when messages are normalized through evoking what others are doing.

| | |
|---|---|
| **TRY THIS:**<br>———<br>Normative<br>Language | What normative language could you offer consumers, clients, customers, partners, or vendors, to encourage decision-making? |

# CUTTING ANCHORS LOOSE

Anchors can be created to aid brand recall, associations, and triggers; and they can be dropped as a reframing technique also. Fast food brands have experienced a slim down trend in naming: Dominos dropping pizza, Dunkin dropping donuts, Subway becoming less of a mouthful (original name was Pete's Super Submarines), and McDonald's rolling out simpler experiences through "McD" Cafes. The fast food industries strategy of "single-word dominance" helps emphasize keyword triggers because less is more. Stemming back to naming strategy, switching from descriptive to evocative is often a luxury for brands once market penetration and familiarity are high. But consider, also, wouldn't your brand be better off calling itself what consumers call it? To appeal to audiences, mirror their language back, and if it means dropping a few letters, words, or numbers, then allow lexicon to shift with culture.

Furthermore, understand that the tides of culture have long pushed other long-enduring companies to change with culture:

- Consumer Value Stores became CVS.
- American Telephone and Telegraph became AT&T.
- Minnesota Mining and Manufacturing became 3M.
- The Government Employees Insurance Company became GEICO,
- Hennes and Mauritz is known to consumers as H&M.
- Weight Watchers became WW.

# WW (WEIGHT WATCHERS)

*Slimming Down to Grow the Bottom Line*

Founded during a time of empowerment, Weight Watchers was launched in Queens in 1963 by homemaker Jean Nidetch to build a community of people aiming to lose weight in a setting that functions as a support group. Today's consumer is not the same as the ones who joined Weight Watchers in Nidetch's time. In the age of publications such as Goop and health movements like yoga and meditation, the health conversation focuses more on terms like "wellness" than it does terms like "weight loss." Consumers want to see promotion of healthy, positive lifestyle choices. They don't want to be told to lose weight. To keep up with these health and fitness trends, Weight Watchers slimmed down to just "WW."

With its new name, WW shows consumers that its focus is on overall health and wellness, rather than simply the yin/yang experience of weight loss. Its new tagline, "Wellness that works," reflects this further. The new WW promotes wellness and healthy living, while the former Weight Watchers preached weight loss. "It's not just about weight anymore," Mindy Grossman, president and CEO of WW International said. "Today's generation is more preventative; they want to live healthily. They want to educate themselves." The company elected to utilize an abbreviation of its heritage name rather than select an entirely new name. In choosing this option, WW accomplishes its goal of speaking to the new generation while staying true to its heritage and remaining the same company it had been during the past 50 years.[73,74]

Brands that ascend into the pop culture zeitgeist using lexicon are good at one more thing—developing "branded language." Since language is shared, then language is a bonding agent. In *Primal Branding*, Patrick Hanlon introduces seven methods to build brands, one focusing on "sacred words" that signal to the community that you are a member.[75] For instance, employees at a restaurant may use a different shorthand language among themselves than the language they use with diners. Imagine this as the language you need to use when you knock on their door to get them to invite you in, to make a memorable impression, and to be a brand with a story worth sharing.

Consider the preflight experience: the same on every plane and thus easily tuned out by frequent flyers. But what if that experience didn't have to be so bland? Southwest Airlines flies 4,000 flights daily with a fleet of nearly 800 planes.[76] A company with consistent annual growth, the airline has delivered a profit to shareholders for a record-setting 46 consecutive years.[77] According to Elise May, the Southwest executive in charge of cabin safety, "as long as all of the safety and regulatory requirements are met, our Flight Attendants are encouraged to make onboard Safety briefings engaging through the use of humor, song, or other individual twists."[78] Their spirited stewards have been viewed over 100 million times in online videos. Ironically, Southwest uses language as an anchor with consumers to create a positive brand feeling immediately during every journey.

**TRY THIS:**

**Branded Language**

What two to three words are most common in your industry? How would your company express that word/phrase as a branded term? Can you invent a new lexicon guide (e.g., In-N-Out Burger)?

# IN-N-OUT BURGER

*Developing Branded Language for an N-sider Experience*

It's close to Southern Californian custom—the act of pulling up to the white and red drive-through lane, sifting through the not-so-secret menu, and pausing to consider the Animal Style burger. In-N-Out Burger has had that effect on many native Californians and tourists since its first store opened in 1948. Harry and Esther Snyder immediately made waves with their burger chain. In the early years, McDonald's hadn't quite served billions worldwide, but it was a growing national force that In-N-Out would have to compete for market share with, as well as regional rivals Jack in the Box and Carl's Jr. In the United States, where it seemed as if everyone was creating their own fast-food startup, In-N-Out relied on customer service and a bevy of memorable burger names to help it stand out in a market that was deepfried, but with little differentiation among burger joints. Customers would soon become familiar with the chain's unique lexicon: mainstay meals such as the Double-Double, or unique options such as the bun-free Protein Style or mega-sized 3x3 and 4x4s. The chain built a branded language system all its own that resonates internally among its 300-plus West Coast locations. While it may never reach the global status as the Golden Arches, In-N-Out has retained a loyal following that appreciates its positive messages.[79,80]

## CONCLUSION

In an age of abundance, when brands are trimming down, appealing to their tribes through branded language and normative messaging, marketers are finding that less is more. Whether names truncate to fit hashtags or capitalize on catchphrases du jour, lexicon is alive and evolving; and brands must remain open to shifting their lexicon at the pace of culture.

The rules of the road for building a brand foundation with lexicon requires finding the right trigger words through mixed methods, which, in the future, will be greatly aided by artificial intelligence capable of scraping texts, conversations, and voice, to develop next level vocabulary sets for brands that are personalized to the individual. As tech improves its ability to accurately find the right word in the expansiveness of language, success will come through branded vocabulary that helps unlock a shared feeling among community members. And as AI improves, the ability for brands to deploy sets of lexicon triggers dynamically to audiences in digital communication will turbocharge tribes through language that sparks familiarity, favorability, and action.

##  FIRE STARTERS

### BUILDING A "TRIBE"

**LEXICON TRIGGERS**

- ☐ What three adjectives would you want people to use most often when mentioning your brand?

- ☐ In meetings, what are the three to five most commonly used terms on a daily or weekly basis?

- ☐ Who are your five most important relationships or strategic partnerships, and what phrases do they use the most?

- ☐ If you were hosting a dinner party for five ideal customers and/or clients, who would you invite, and what would the invite say to get their attention?

- ☐ Is there any framing you could use to "normalize" product or service usage?

# Notes

1. Dan Ariely, *Predictably Irrational: The Hidden Forces That Shape Our Decisions*. New York: Harper, 2008.
2. "About Us." Merriam-Webster. Accessed January 31, 2019. https://www.merriam-webster.com/about-us/americas-first-dictionary.
3. "History of OED." Oxford Dictionaries. Accessed January 31, 2019. https://public.oed.com/history/.
4. Terry Heatony, "10 Questions with Urban Dictionary's Aaron Peckham." Terry Heaton's Pomo Blog, April 14, 2010. http://thepomoblog.com/index.php/10-questions-with-urban-dictionarys-aaron-peckham/.
5. "How Many Words Are There in English?" Merriam-Webster. Accessed January 31, 2019. https://www.merriam-webster.com/help/faq-how-many-english-words.
6. "We Put a Bunch of New Words in the Dictionary." Merriam-Webster. Accessed January 31, 2019. https://www.merriam-webster.com/words-at-play/new-words-in-the-dictionary-september-2018.
7. Jenna Wortham, "A Lexicon of Instant Argot." *New York Times*, January 3, 2014. https://www.nytimes.com/2014/01/04/technology/a-lexicon-of-the-internet-updated-by-its-users.html.
8. Kimberly Lawson, "How Urban Dictionary Became a Cesspool for Racists and Misogynists." Broadly, May 31, 2017. https://broadly.vice.com/en_us/article/qv4dwp/how-urban-dictionary-became-a-cesspool-for-racists-and-misogynists.
9. "About Us." Merriam-Webster. Accessed January 30, 2019. https://www.merriam-webster.com/about-us.
10. Jessica Boddy, "An Average 20-year-old American Knows 42,000 Words, Depending on How You Count Them." *Science Magazine*, December 8, 2017. www.sciencemag.org/news/2016/08/average-20-year-old-american-knows-42000-words-depending-how-you-count-them.
11. Andrey Vyshedskiy, "Language Evolution to Revolution: From a Slowly Developing Finite Communication System with Many Words to Infinite Modern Language." Biorxiv, July 20, 2017. doi:https://doi.org/10.1101/166520.
12. Ibid.
13. "Advancing Well-being by Using New Ways to Communicate, Understand, and Respond to Emotion." MIT Media Lab. Accessed January 31, 2019. https://www.media.mit.edu/groups/affective-computing/overview/.

14. Shawn Paul Wood, "Bad News: Negative Headlines Get Much More Attention." *Adweek*, February 21, 2014. https://www.adweek.com/digital/bad-news-negative-headlines-get-much-more-attention/.

15. Steve Rivkin, "Brand Naming Research Q&A." *Branding Strategy Insider*, June 9, 2009. https://www.brandingstrategyinsider.com/2009/06/naming-research-q-a.html#.XFlwCdlza00.

16. Christian Humberg, "50 Years of the Lego Brick." Germany: Heel Verlag, 2008.

17. Shona Ghosh, "How Deliveroo Went from Being the Idea of a Hungry Banker to a $2 Billion Food Delivery Giant Coveted by Uber." *Business Insider*, September 29, 2018. Accessed February 4, 2019. https://www.businessinsider.com/deliveroo-history-and-timeline-2018-9#may-2018-deliveroo-announces-that-it-will-plough-5-million-65-million-into-finding-celebrity-chefs-to-partner-with-to-create-new-experimental-concepts-35.

18. "Introduction to Deliveroo." Accessed January 31, 2019. http://ec.europa.eu/information_society/newsroom/image/document/2016-6/deliveroo_13855.pdf.

19. "The Story of Deliveroo." Deliveroo. Accessed January 31, 2019. https://deliveroo.co.uk/about-us.

20. "Application Deadline Extended For Fall 2019." Brand New, September 12, 2016. https://www.underconsideration.com/brandnew/archives/new_logo_and_identity_for_deliveroo_by_designstudio.php.

21. Ronald Adler and Neil Towne, *Looking Out, Looking In*, 2nd ed. New York: Holt, Rinehart, and Winston, 1978.

22. Richard Petty and John Cacioppo, "The Elaboration Likelihood Model of Persuasion." *Advances in Experimental Social Psychology* 19 (1986), 123–205. doi:10.1016/S0065-2601(08)60214-2.

23. "Community." Oxford Dictionaries. Accessed January 31, 2019. https://en.oxforddictionaries.com/definition/community.

24. "Tribe." Merriam-Webster. Accessed January 31, 2019. https://www.merriam-webster.com/thesaurus/tribe.

25. Marc Zimmerman, "Resiliency Theory: A Strengths-Based Approach to Research and Practice for Adolescent Health." *Health Education and Behavior: The official publication of the Society for Public Health Education* 40 (2013), 381–383. doi:10.1177/1090198113493782.

26. Michael Dubin, "How Dollar Shave Club's Founder Built a $1 Billion Company That Changed the Industry." *Entrepreneur*, March 28, 2017. https://www.entrepreneur.com/article/290539.

27. Maddy Osman, "Dollar Shave Club's Marketing Strategy." M., August 31, 2016. https://www.mabbly.com/dollar-shave-club-marketing-strategy/.

28. Ben Zifkin, "How Psychographics Made Dollar Shave Club a Winner." *MediaPost*, September 12, 2017. https://www.mediapost.com/publications/article/307133/how-psychographics-made-dollar-shave-club-a-winner.html.

29. Ramona Sukhraj, "How Dollar Shave Club Grew From Viral Video to $1 Billion Acquisition." *IMPACT*, July 21, 2016. https://www.impactbnd.com/blog/how-dollar-shave-club-grew-from-just-a-viral-video-to-a-615m-valuation-brand.

30. Anna Henderson, "Brand Story Hero—Dollar Shave Club." All Good Tales. Accessed January 31, 2019. https://allgoodtales.com/brand-story-hero-dollar-shave-club/.

31. A. H. Maslow, "A Theory of Human Motivation." *Psychological Review* 50, no. 4 (1943), 370–396. doi:10.1037/h0054346.

32. "What Is CrossFit?" CrossFit. Accessed January 31, 2019. https://www.crossfit.com/what-is-crossfit.

33. Michelle Markelz, "Has CrossFit Made Reebok Relevant Again?" American Marketing Association. Accessed January 31, 2019. https://www.ama.org/publications/MarketingNews/Pages/has-crossfit-made-reebok-relevant-again.aspx.

34. Kevin Skiver, "CBS Sports to Telecast CrossFit Games through 2018." CBS Sports, July 19, 2017. https://www.cbssports.com/crossfit/news/cbs-sports-to-telecast-crossfit-games-through-2018/.

35. Sara Gottfried, "Dr. Sara Grades Different Forms of Exercise for Women: CrossFit Gets a . . ." Dr. Sara Gottfried Blog. Accessed January 31, 2019. https://www.saragottfriedmd.com/dr-sara-grades-crossfit/.

36. "Ultrasonic Ringtones." Accessed January 31, 2019. https://www.ultrasonic-ringtones.com/.

37. Jay Heinrichs, *Thank You for Arguing: What Aristotle, Lincoln, and Homer Simpson Can Teach Us about the Art of Persuasion*. New York: Three Rivers Press, 2017.

38. Alyson Shontell, "How Two First-Time Founders Went from $28,000 Salaries to Owning a $100 Million Media Brand." *Business Insider*, April 22, 2013. https://www.businessinsider.com/How-Two-First-Time-Founders-Went-From-28000-Salaries-To-Owning-A-100-Million-Media-Brand/articleshow/21160072.

39. "Get to Know Us." Refinery29. Accessed January 31, 2019. https://corporate.r29.com/about/#about-intro.

40. Bartie Scott, "How Refinery29's Founders Built a $500 Million Business on 1 Simple Idea." *Inc.*, September, 26, 2016. https://www.inc.com/bartie-scott/2016-inc5000-refinery29.html.

41. "Emergency Quota Act," Wikipedia. Last updated on January 17, 2019. Accessed January 31, 2019. https://en.wikipedia.org/wiki/Emergency_Quota_Act.

42. John Hudson, "Looking for the First Use of the Term 'Illegal Immigrant,'" *The Atlantic*, September 28, 2012. https://www.theatlantic.com/national/archive/2012/09/looking-first-use-term-illegal-immigrant/323086/.

43. Richard Harrington, "From Hit Parade to Top 40." *Washington Post*, June 28, 1992. https://www.washingtonpost.com/archive/lifestyle/style/1992/06/28/from-hit-parade-to-top-40/4550deaf-6e31-4e99-bcbe-0c7378bf1cd3/.

44. "Billboard Charts." Wikipedia. Last updated on January 29, 2019. Accessed on January 31, 2019. https://en.wikipedia.org/wiki/Billboard_charts.

45. "The Rise of Cable Television." Television in American Society Reference Library. Encyclopedia.com. Accessed January 30, 2019. https://www.encyclopedia.com/arts/news-wires-white-papers-and-books/rise-cable-television.

46. Marguerite Ward, "This Financial Risk Allowed TheSkimm Founders to Launch Their Multi-million Dollar Company." CNBC, May 5, 2017. https://www.cnbc.com/2017/05/03/the-risk-theskimm-founders-took-to-launch-their-55-million-company.html.

47. "Sheep in Human Clothing—Scientists Reveal Our Flock Mentality." *Leeds*, February 14, 2008. http://www.leeds.ac.uk/news/article/397/sheep_in_human_clothing-scientists_reveal_our_flock_mentality.

48. Rick Nauert, "'Herd' Mentality Explained." Psychcentral, August 8, 2018. https://psychcentral.com/news/2008/02/15/herd-mentality-explained/1922.html.

49. Elizabeth Fournier, "SoulCycle Shelves Plans for U.S. IPO After Three Years in Limbo." *Bloomberg*, May 26, 2018. https://www.bloomberg.com/news/articles/2018-05-25/soulcycle-shelves-plans-for-u-s-ipo-after-three-years-in-limbo.

50. "Welcome." SoulCycle. Accessed January 31, 2019. https://www.soul-cycle.com/about/#welcome.

51. Kathryn Romeyn, "How an Ex-Talent Manager Co-Founded SoulCycle and Sold for $90M." *Hollywood Reporter*, July 3, 2017. https://www.hollywoodreporter.com/news/how-an-talent-manager-founded-soulcycle-sold-90m-1015009.

52. Filings. SEC. Accessed January 31, 2019. https://www.sec.gov/Archives/edgar/data/1644874/000119312515270469/d844646ds1.htm.

53. StitchFix. Report. San Francisco, California, 2018. Accessed January 31, 2019. https://investors.stitchfix.com/static-files/6e0572f2-5f59-4891-90e1-fe96f34b985e

54. "StitchFix Is the Personal Style Service for Men and Women That Evolves with Your Tastes, Needs and Lifestyle." StichFix. https://www.stitchfix.com/about.

55. "StitchFix Company Fact Sheet." StichFix. Accessed January 31, 2019. https://investors.stitchfix.com/system/files-encrypted/nasdaq_kms/assets/2018/10/01/19-50-45/StitchFix_FactSheet 9.28.18.pdf.

56. Tracey Lien, "StitchFix Founder Katrina Lake Built One of the Few Successful E-commerce Subscription Services." *Los Angeles Times*, January 9, 2017. https://www.latimes.com/business/la-fi-himi-katrina-lake-stitch-fix-20170609-htmlstory.html.

57. Ryan Mac, "Stitch Fix: The $250 Million Startup Playing Fashionista Moneyball." *Forbes*, June 1, 2016. https://www.forbes.com/sites/ryanmac/2016/06/01/fashionista-moneyball-stitch-fix-katrina-lake/#723d89fb59a2.

58. Nathan Chan, "220: Building Community as the Foundation for a Successful Content Business, with Carly Zakin and Danielle Weisberg of theSkimm." Foundr, October 11, 2018. https://foundr.com/building-community-carly-zakin-danielle-weisberg-the-skimm/

59. Marsha Bryant, "How Tupperware Became a $2 Billion Brand." *Fast Company*, September 10, 2019. https://www.fastcompany.com/90233279/how-tupperware-became-a-2-billion-brand

60. "Court: 'GOOGLE' Not A Generic Trademark. Lessons Trademark Owners Should Learn About Genericide." Gerben Law Firm PLLC, July 5, 2017. https://www.gerbenlaw.com/blog/court-google-not-a-generic-trademark-lessons-trademark-owners-should-learn-about-genericide/.

61. "Don't Let Your Trademark Become Generic." Caesar Rivise Intellectual Property Law. October 25, 2017. www.caesar.law/news-resources/dont-let-trademark-become-generic/.

62. Al Ries, *Positioning: The Battle for Your Mind*. New York: McGraw-Hill, 1986.

63. "15 Product Trademarks That Have Become Victims of Genericization." *Consumer Reports*, July 19, 2014. https://www.consumerreports .org/consumerist/15-product-trademarks-that-have-become-victims-of-genericization/.

64. "US' Most Creative Partnerships: Geico & The Martin Agency." The Martin Agency, June 23, 2016. https://martinagency.com/news/us-most-creative-partnerships-geico-the-martin-agency.

65. "ALDI History." Aldi. Accessed January 31, 2019. https://corporate.aldi .us/en/aldi-history/.

66. "Aldi." Wikipedia. Last updated on February 3, 2019. Accessed February 3, 2019. https://en.wikipedia.org/wiki/Aldi.

67. Ashish Pahwa, "Aldi Business Model: Why Is Aldi So Cheap?" *Feedough*, January 19, 2018. https://www.feedough.com/aldi-business-model-aldi-cheap/.

68. "Ad Age Advertising Century: Top 10 Slogans." *AdAge*, March 29, 1999. https://adage.com/article/special-report-the-advertising-century/ ad-age-advertising-century-top-10-slogans/140156/.

69. "In U.S., Proportion Married at Lowest Levels." Population Reference Bureau, September 28, 2010. https://www.prb.org/usmarriagedecline/.

70. Leonie Mercedes, "The Stories behind the Most Famous Slogans (Info-graphic)." Clickz Marketing Technology Transformation. August 3, 2015. https://www.clickz.com/the-stories-behind-the-most-famous-slogans-infographic/20570/.

71. Robert Mandelbaum, "Consumption and Pricing Influence Hotel Utility Costs." CBRE. Accessed January 31, 2019. http://www.cbrehotels.com/ EN/Research/Pages/Consumption-and-Pricing-Influence-Hotel-Utility-Costs.aspx.

72. Noah J. Goldstein, Robert B. Cialdini, and Vladas Griskevicius, "A Room with a Viewpoint: Using Social Norms to Motivate Environmental Conservation in Hotels." *Journal of Consumer Research* 35, no. 3 (October 2008), 472–482. doi:10.1086/586910.

73. Rina Raphael, "Here's Why Weight Watchers Changed Its Name." *Fast Company*, September 24, 2018. https://www.fastcompany .com/90241019/ww-heres-why-weight-watchers-changed-its-name.

74. Cherly Wischhover, "As Dieting Becomes More Taboo, Weight Watchers Is Changing Its Name." *Vox*, September 24, 2018. https://www.vox .com/the-goods/2018/9/24/17897114/weight-watchers-ww-wellness-rebranding.

75. Patrick Hanlon, *Primal Branding: Create Zealots for Your Brand, Your Company, and Your Future.* New York: Free Press, 2006.

76. "Southwest Corporate Fact Sheet." Southwest Media. Accessed January 31, 2019. https://www.swamedia.com/pages/corporate-fact-sheet.

77. Maylan Stydart, "Southwest Airlines Jumps after Profit Beat." *The Street*, January 24, 2019. https://www.thestreet.com/investing/southwest-airlines-stock-jumps-on-profit-beat-14844160.

78. Joel Christie, "'In the Event of an Emergency, the Cabin Crew Will Be the Ones Carrying the Liquor Kit': Extravagant Male Flight Attendant's Hilarious Safety Speech Takes Web by Storm." *Mail Online*, June 20, 2014. https://www.dailymail.co.uk/news/article-2663710/Extravagant-male-Southwest-airlines-hosts-hilarious-safety-speech-takes-web-storm.html.

79. "History," In-N-Out. Accessed January 31, 2019. www.in-n-out.com/history.aspx.

80. Myrna Oliver, "Esther Snyder, 86: Co-Founded the In-N-Out . . ." *Los Angeles Times*, August 6, 2006. http://articles.latimes.com/2006/aug/06/local/me-snyder6.

# AUDIO CUES

## *Branding Objective:*
## *Develop Instant Recognition*

| FLASH-FORWARD | BRAND SPOTLIGHTS |
|---|---|
| Atmospherics | Adidas 🏋 |
| Product sound design | Barry's Bootcamp 🏃 |
| Heuristic engineering | Corona 🏝 |
| Sonic signatures | Harley Davidson 🏍 |
| Mood | Intel 🔲 |
| Mnemonics | Y7 Studio 🎿 |
| Audio branding | |
| Diffused sonic cues | |
| Behavioral triggers | |

Netflix's sonic signature, which opens every piece of its content, might be as popular among millennials and Gen Z as Intel's iconic chimes are to Gen X and boomers. With consistent, industry-beating annual growth over the past 20 years, Netflix has offered investors a blockbuster success in streaming to every screen. But what happens when consumers can't see a screen? Imagine that Sandra Bullock in her role in Netflix's record-shattering *Bird Box* thriller represents your consumers: forced to navigate the world blindfolded and reliant upon audio only. With all of your shiny commercials, microsites, packaging, billboards, out-of-home signage, and experiential touchpoints, can audiences identify your brand if they can't see you?

Many brands fail the *Bird Box* test. Consider advertisements, generally the highest visibility touchpoint for brands: over 90% of ads feature a sound.[1,2] Yet, according to Martin Lindstrom in *Buyology*, over 80% of brands fail to be recognizable through audio.[3] The presence of sound and the ability to be recognizable by sounds are two completely different things. By far, then, audio continues to represent one of the most underutilized channels for branding, all while streaming and voice assistance gains significant momentum.

## EVERY BRAND LONGS TO BE HEARD

Between 2002 and 2011, Verizon Wireless used an audio cue to great affect as a service differentiator with its "Can you hear me now?" slogan. Defending their slipping 25% market share, Verizon's rhetorical slogan marked today's billion-dollar question, which every aspiring brand should be posing to its customers and other important constituents.[4] And though it can be posed in many different strategic and creative ways, it's the use of audio that unlocks cognitive triggers among consumers to produce feedback responses; the kind that translates into increased market share and top-of-mind awareness.

Knowing their message is being heard gives new meaning and life to brands fighting for visibility, relevancy, and resonance. This is not only true metaphorically, but also literally, given the rise of audio, voice, streaming music, gaming, and experiential marketing. In 2018, the power of audio led to double-digit sales growth in both vinyl albums and cassettes.[5] Amazon sold over 100 million voice-controlled Echoes.[6] Spotify crept closer to 100 million user accounts as streaming music reached 15% penetration in the United States.[7,8] And, podcasts crossed a technology chasm into mainstream at over 40% adoption in the United States.[9] Although it's crystal clear that audio cues can add a huge upside to marketing impact, it's astonishing to see, from my own involvement in developing agency campaigns and working in talent management, that audio is still frequently left to the last production step rather than a strategic central character.

When I say audio or sound, I don't just mean music. Audio includes vibrations and rhythm, elements that are constantly changing, growing, and expanding as a library of human artifacts. As such, sound (speaking up, making noise) is a big part of our "raison d'être," our very reason for existence of how we communicate within communities and leave our mark on history. Sound is so important that it is the first sense we develop in the womb. We have a relationship with the world through audio before we can see, touch, or smell. It is an acute and exacting sense, and encodes memories down to the day, location, and ambiance. We are all on a search for purpose, and that quest includes a soundtrack that informs, drives, heightens, and inspires. For brands—startup and Fortune 500 alike—your soundtrack might then play out in environments (e.g., stores, events), through products and service (e.g., call centers, waiting areas), engagement campaigns (e.g., marketing), or internal culture (e.g., anthems, chants).

Two of my former bosses have a long and storied history in music, and my work with them reinforced the importance of the universal language of audio. As a passion platform alongside fashion, art, sports, and film, audio is a big business. For instance, the music industry alone hit a six-year high in 2018, fueled by a radical business transformation from CDs to digital, full albums to EPs and singles, and label-backed performances to indie breakouts.[10] Touring is stronger than ever, marked by nearly 100 new festivals that have emerged in the past decade, and Web-connected devices are empowering each consumer to have a unique soundtrack to their lives.[11]

Among the many events we would attend, one year we trekked to Fast Company's Innovation Festival where my boss Troy Carter took center stage with NPR's Kai Ryssdal. During their interview, Troy noted that "music sells everything but music."[12] And to a degree, that is very true. The branding industry is a $20 billion juggernaut—tied to the hip of music as companies license tracks for commercials, stream playlists in-store, sponsor festivals, or license audio clips for usability cues in technology and platforms. Unlike other passion platforms, music is a drug. Well, almost. Researchers at McGill University, for example, have shown that music triggers a dopamine release akin to reward sensations like having sex, using drugs, or eating food.[13] Some people contest that music has a 20% higher dopamine hit than both sex and drugs.[14] And music is only one aspect of audio.

In *Sonic Boom: How Sound Transforms the Way We Think, Feel, and Buy*, Man Made Sound's CEO and founder Joel Beckerman notes: "Whether you're scoring films, ads, or products . . . [y]ou should be focusing on the experience . . ."[15] Sound is an experience driver, and as an emotional trigger, different sounds produce different feelings. To start to unlock meaning behind sounds, there's one framework to understand: pleasure-arousal-dominance (PAD). The 1970s PAD theory was proposed by now–Boston College professor James A. Russell and his doctoral advisor, Albert Mehrabian, a former UCLA psychology professor. In *An Approach to Environmental Psychology*, released in 1974, at a time when behavioral science was gaining popularity, they focused the psychology community on a simpler understanding of how we process experiences.[16] Their three-part system gave clues as to how we navigate the physical world, making sense of emotions and feelings in relation to correlated factors:

**Pleasure:** Positive versus negative feelings (e.g., spectrum from pain to ecstasy)
**Arousal:** Level of stimulation (e.g., from sleepy to excited)
**Dominance:** Order of priority of emotions (e.g., anger overrides fear)

**TRY THIS:**

**Mood Mapping**

If you were having a party, what music would you invite people to hear and dance to? Is that the same music you would play in your office? At a brand event or venue (e.g., store)? This is about strategic engineering, placement, and use of audio to spur action.

## AUDIO'S ROLE: HARDLY NEW, BUT CERTAINLY EVOLVING

Audio branding goes by several names including "sound branding, acoustic branding, sound identity, acoustic identity, and corporate sound."[17] Sonic brand assets are also often referred to as earcons, sogos, idents, sonic signatures, and atmospherics. In computer science, an eracon is a sound denoting a user-computer interaction (e.g., the noise made when clicking on a folder to notify the user an action was done).[18] In branding, an earcon is a nonverbal audio message, carefully coded to spread information, evoke an emotion, or induce a physiological response.

Sonic logos (also called "sogos" or "idents") are becoming more common. The few brands that have them—Netflix, Intel, and NBC—benefit from astoundingly high brand recall despite the noisy world we live in. And there's a science to creating them. Researchers have started to explore the optimal number of chimes, and thus far believe six tones are a sweet spot for sogos.[19] All kinds of sounds, both simulated and natural, are finding their way into commercials and other marketing instruments. The sounds are carefully engineered, down to just the right decibel of fizz for Alka Seltzer versus Coca-Cola. This heuristic engineering is subtly prompting physiological responses (e.g., thirst), nostalgic memories, and, most important, action to buy.

"Atmospherics" was coined by influential Kellogg professor Philip Kotler in the 1970s.[20] He described atmospherics as "the conscious designing of space to create certain effects in buyers."[21] Kotler reasoned that "in some cases, the place, more specifically the atmosphere of the place, is more influential than the product itself in the purchase decision. In some cases, the atmosphere is the primary product."[22] While his initial model included only volume and pitch for audio, researchers have now confirmed the effect of tempo in music, also. His thinking has significant modern-day bearing on the role of audio as more brands consider their stores as immersive experiences—from IKEA to Lululemon. From DJs in Adidas to curated playlists in grocery stores, the positive benefits of music abound, from higher employee morale and productivity to increased spending among consumers due to longer dwell times. Fashion retail brands are evolving in-store music beyond atmospherics into live entertainment, and turning sound into an experience.

# ADIDAS

*Creating an Atmosphere That Mirrors Culture*

Adidas was created by Adolf "Adi" Dassler, a World War I veteran. In 1924, his brother Rudolph joined him in his venture and they successfully launched Dassler Brothers Shoe Factory. After nearly 20 years in business and a second world war, communication between the brothers grew hostile and they parted ways. Rudolph or "Rudi," as he was called, went on to form a company he branded Puma and Adi created his own, Adidas, in 1949. The two athletic shoe brands remain competitors to this day.

It is the music industry—specifically hip-hop—that not only brought the Adidas brand into the mainstream but designated it as a symbol within fashion for communities of artists and creatives. The first hip-hop artists to make Adidas "their" brand were the members of Run-DMC. In the 1980s, the trio were famous for wearing the original Adidas sneakers and black tracksuits, which they accessorized with black Fedoras, thick gold chains, and four-finger rings. In 1986, they released the song "My Adidas," an ode to their favorite brand of clothing and shoe wear. Following the release of this song, Adidas became more than a brand and a staple of what was a growing hip-hop culture.

By having DJs "spin sets" in their flagship locations around the world, often to mark a new store opening, Adidas leverages music as a cognitive trigger for shoppers and music fans. In addition to the physical aspect of sound in the stores or commercials, Adidas has partnered with a number of well-known music artists like Rihanna and Kanye West, both of whom have had their own clothing line under the retailer, with West's "Yeezy's" being a global success.[23,24,25,26]

## SOUND AS A MOOD SHIFTER

Audio is a springboard for brands to accomplish three key objectives (Figure 7.1): (1) create mood, (2) spread messages, and (3) spur behavior.

First, sounds create mood through atmosphere—shopping in-store, attending an event, navigating a digital experience, or dining. Wish you could have a more pleasant experience while flying rather than hearing clanking, coughs, cries, and people crunching on chips? In 2018, Finnair composed a song for each of their in-flight meals, helping customers immerse further into their brand by tuning out annoying plane mechanics to allow the mind to be guided through pleasant, calming soundscapes.[27] We are all attuned to having sound control our mood; finally, brands are tuning in, too.

### FIGURE 7.1
# TRIAD OF AUDIO TRIGGERS

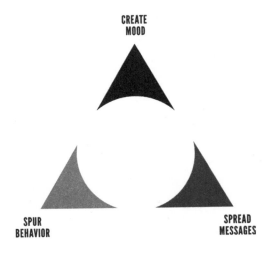

*Audio can trigger behavioral responses—create mood, spread messages, and spur behavior.*

Sound is more than what makes you want to shop more in-store or dance at a sporting event; it's also, ironically, the thing to create more calm, focus, and productivity. According to Deloitte, by 2017, nearly 25% of employers offered a wellness program, and the benefit was sought by two-thirds of employees.[28] Companies that now include meditation as a wellness offering include Salesforce, Nike, Google.[29] The surge in calls for wellness has resulted in an evaluation of the environment that spurs productivity, and in 2017, raking in over 30 million downloads to become Apple's App of the year for 2017,[30] the Calm app helped lead to the "mainstreaming" of emotions, feelings, mood and sound. Sound is a powerful yin and yang in brand building, helping companies resonate at the same frequency as audiences.

Second, sound functions to spread messages by disseminating information through verbal cues such as voice. Imagine passing through an airport—there's a barrage of audio that presents messages such as prerecorded instructions like reminders about moving escalators, revolving doors, flights departing, and moving baggage carousels. For brands, turning up the volume on sound can help deliver an improved customer experience through ambient messages that inform or inspire.

Third, sound spurs behavior through nonverbal functional cues such as alerts and notifications. For instance, without thinking, functioning on autopilot, a doorbell means answer the door, a laundry buzzer means check the clothes, a ringtone means answer the phone, and a fire alarm means leave the building. Sound is a powerful trigger for common behavior. Roughly 60 miles from Los Angeles, the city of Lancaster was experiencing an increasing crime rate, and eventually turned to music as the peacemaker. By playing soothing soundscapes of bird songs through 70 city-owned speakers, downtown dwellers dissipated and the minor crime rate had a 15% decline while major crimes experienced a 6% decline.[31,32] As we look for shortcuts for survival, sounds become key in navigating the world. For brands, this means managing a sound bank and evolving the traditional brand book to create an orchestra around the consumer.

# CORONA

*Leveraging Nonverbal Cues to Induce Feelings*

Although we tend to associate Corona Beer with tropical islands, it was founded by German immigrants to Mexico in 1925. One of Mexico's most popular brands of *cerveza* (Spanish for beer), Corona began an aggressive campaign in 1937 to edge out all of its local competition and assert itself as *the* beer preferred by discerning drinkers. It worked, and by 1976 the brand became popular in the United States as well. So popular, in fact, that a black market for the beer thrived—which wasn't supplied adequately to meet the consumer demand. Corona has always been offered in glass bottles, however, in 2009, the light version was offered in cans and the company has taken strides to "expand their full line of beers." Corona's commercials use the typical sounds of a tropical setting: seagulls, waves crashing against sand, and steel drums. The orchestra of diffused sonic cues creates an atmosphere of relaxation so that when people buy and consume their product, they associate it with the escapism vibes that accompany a vacation getaway, relaxation in the warmth of the sun, and lounging on the beach while being served your favorite beer (with a twist of lime, of course).

Building from its simple sonic cues into a full symphony, in recent years, Corona has taken music even further for branding. Corona Electric Beach, a national tour of DJs who spin records that evoke summertime vibes 365 days a year, delivers an experience where "beats meet the beach" in select cities throughout America like Miami, Atlanta, Los Angeles, Dallas, and Las Vegas. Corona Electric Beach also makes appearances at festivals like Insomniac Orlando, HARD Summer Music Festival, and Spring

Awakening. Corona has expanded its reach to the global stage through its new festival series called Corona SunSets, again focusing on creating an atmosphere of relaxation focused on sunsets across the world.[33,34,35]

## IS AUDIO THE MOST SALIENT PART OF "MEMORY"?

Music triggers memories and feelings, and dozens of researchers have proven the interconnections between sound, emotion, and memory, reducing the connection down to the simple notion that processing sound and storing memories both use the same part of the brain.[36] In *The Sonic Boom*, Man Made Music's CEO and founder Joel Beckerman likens the emotional effect of sound to a "startle."[37] Using research from academics such as Petr Janata, a professor at University of California–Davis who has published over 50 papers, Beckerman offers a layman's explanation of the role of music on emotions and memory: it takes milliseconds for the brain to recognize sounds, using the same part of the brain that codes memories, causing immediate total body alertness. It's in that stimuli-experience exchange that the "boom moment" occurs, where sound triggers a physiological response (e.g., increased blood flow to the brain).[38] And in that boom moment, audience behavior is spurred.

**TRY THIS:**

Bird Box Test

Can someone identify or differentiate your spot (eyes-closed) within three to five seconds? Is audio one of your top five brand assets? What singular audio branding thing do you do today that you could turn up the volume on across channels, touchpoints, screens, or experiences to drive differentiation from competitors?

# OUR FIREWALL WORKS LIKE THIS: "TUNING OUT"

Each year, I teach a behavioral science course called Battle of the Mind. For one assignment, students are instructed to use a diary to log all the brands they're exposed to during a 24-hour period. Students always, without fail, record fewer than 100 brands. In actuality, researchers have concluded that the average American experiences over 10,000 brand exposures daily.[39] From hitting the snooze button, opening the medicine cabinet, and making breakfast in the kitchen, most individuals are exposed to hundreds of brands before they even put their shoes on to walk out the door. Over the lifetime of a millennial, Gen Xer, or boomer, they'll be exposed to over two million commercials, for instance, all filled with sounds that eventually all blur together into a cacophony of background noise.

As Martin Lindstrom, a psychologist who has conducted research in 77 countries with over 2,000 participants, noted in his 2007 work *Buyology*, an estimated 83% of branding and marketing dollars goes toward visuals.[40] He estimated that 40% of consumers felt audio was crucial to a brand communication, yet only 12% of brands actually spent money on audio branding. Fast-forward to today's reality, and the landscape has remained fairly unchanged with brand's investing in audio as a growth opportunity rather than a necessity. The data and studies remain missing, with brands underreporting their investments in audio. The best indicators are spending on popular music in commercials, where traditionally television has been the most expensive media investments. With shifts to experiential and direct-to-consumer engagement, a more comprehensive study on sonic branding is needed to start tracking brand impact.

Started in 1936, the Advertising Research Foundation represents 400 members from the largest advertising agencies, media companies, and brands.[41] Not only do they catalog the most promising research techniques and results achieved by brands related to marketing, but they also conduct original research to close insight gaps. One study conducted by Dr. Manuel Garcia-Garcia, a neuroscientist and assistant professor at New York University, investigated the attentiveness of consumers in watching millions of commercials. One key stat was startling, yet expected: nearly 80% of people multitask across multiple screens while watching television. Potentially then, marketers are wasting billions of dollars by concentrating brand assets in visual appeals with no (recognizably ownable) audio cues. Most audio is in elements such as a throwaway audio cue of a brand mention during the last three seconds or the use of a licensed track that might be claimed by another brand next year.[42]

To cope with consumers' tuning out of commercials, waning attentiveness has led to the compression of traditional 1-minute and 30-second commercial formats down to 15-second and even 6-second durations. Launched in 2009, the audio app Shazam surpassed 100 million users in 2014.[43] Taking the sound-ID craze to primetime in 2017 on Fox, households across America try to beat Shazam. The question is—does your brand pass the Shazam test of being identifiable during the initial three to eight seconds of content in which consumers are likely to mentally or physically hit "skip?" Most brands, unfortunately, would fail the Shazam test, too.

# HOW BRANDS LEARN FROM TELEVISION THEME SONGS

In an effort to win the initial three- to eight-second battle for consumer attention, sonic cues that include mnemonics (i.e., memory aids such as jingles and melodies) are important. With 90% of people listening to radio or another form of audio in the car,[44] driving attentiveness through voice and sound is key to an audio branding strategy. In the United States, the average American is within 100 miles of a McDonald's, so winning the battle of attention in the car is crucial. Intended to be a two-year campaign, McDonald's "I'm Lovin' It" jingle was created by the German advertising agency Heye & Partners in 2003.[45] Over 15 years later, the jingle has been translated into 11 different language and featured in over 100 countries.[46] The iconic slogan features a little-known hook by Justin Timberlake, who sings "ba da ba ba ba," to the tune of over $1 billion advertising spend annually.[47] As a result, audio has helped sell billions of burgers for McDonald's by placing sonic cues just in time for the consumer to reach the next exit.

Intel's "chimes" (aka "bongs") are a four-tone sonic signature known instinctively by millions of users who have never actually held a chip in their hand, and never will. This level of product placement in the brain's frontal lobe comes at a cost of a $10 billion annual marketing budget, to ensure that the tune closes co-branded commercials.[48] HBO's iconic "white noise," launched in the 1970s, has become a programming must-have to immerse viewers in the expectation of a premium experience. An ident strategy from the movie industry that now manifests itself in programming through theme song music and network ident cues. For all these brands, audio represents an invitation, a reminder of quality, and the beginning of an experience.

# INTEL

*Creating a Sonic Logo That Transcends Holding the Product*

Founded in 1968 by Gordon Moore and Robert Noyce, this Fortune 500 company is one of the original Silicon Valley tech companies. The company is a combination of two tech terms: *integrated* and *electronics*. Intel was an early producer of micro memory chips, which was the foundation of the company's business until 1981, when personal computers became more accessible to the public. Steve Fund, former CMO of Intel, says the company's longevity as a recognizable brand is because, "We've inserted Intel into pop culture, showing up when and where Millennials were receptive to our message. We're leveraging their passion points: music, sports, entertainment and gaming."

In 1994, Whitney Houston's "I Will Always Love You" won Grammy Record of the Year, and later that year Intel debuted their now famous sonic logo (i.e., the "Intel Inside Bong"). Composed by Walter Werzowa, the three-second note is composed of 20 sounds, including a tambourine, an anvil, an electric spark, and a hammer on pipe. The "Bong" has now become one of the highest valued intangible brand assets. In 2016, Yogiraj Graham, director of production for Intel Global Production Labs, told *Forbes*, "We're always looking for ways to showcase the amazing experiences that Intel enables, and the Intel bong sound helps keep our messaging consistent." In 2017, Intel experienced one of its best quarters, earning nearly $20 billion. The company credits this success to the branding consistency of using the recognizable "bong," bringing all their branding work in-house, and partnering with music and pop culture icons who appeal to millennials.[49,50,51,52,53]

So, is the success of sonic cues for global brands leading to a rise in usage? Weirdly, no. While jingles first appeared in 1923 (i.e., Wheaties), researchers in the 1980s started dissecting their influence.[54] Longtime researcher Wanda Wallace began studying the efficacy of jingles in the late 1980s when she was a graduate student at Duke University, finding that they do aid recall.[55] Villanova University marketing professor Charles R. Taylor highlights that "consumers like and have fond memories of many jingles. Over a period of time, they can conjure up good memories that are then associated with the brand."[56] In 2008, a research team at Saint Joseph's University analyzed music in television commercials airing during prime-time on broadcast networks (i.e., NBC, ABC, FOX, CBS), discovering that only 5% of commercials used jingles. The majority of commercials, over 80%, used generic music.[57] So then, what's the value of a jingle if they're in decline?

In 2017, the law partner duo behind the successful injury firm Cellino & Barnes decided to split. Known for their "Don't Wait, Call 8" jingle, the firm had over $1 million profit monthly with over $2 billion in revenue generated in the firm's history.[58] The firm paid $5,000 to the composer of the jingle, and another $1.7 million to secure the 1-800-888-8888 phone number.[59] Arguably, the firm's jingles will become the most valuable intangible brand asset, alongside their phone digits.

The decline of the jingle was signaled by a consortium of advertisers. American Association of Advertising Agencies tracked jingle usage in television commercials for a decade, finding a decline from 153 jingles in 1998 to only 8 in 2011—a drastic decline of over 80%.[60] While brands from McDonald's to Alka Seltzer benefit from mnemonics such as jingles (Figure 7.2), thousands of other brands have yet to unlock the power of having a tune stuck in a consumer's head.

# FIGURE 7.2

## HIT JINGLES

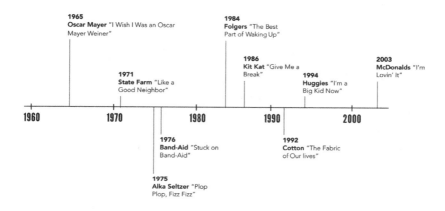

## TRANSLATING SOUNDS

Transmutation of properties between audio visuals and feelings is being explored by technologists, researchers, artists, and audio-philes, all looking for ways to enhance the creative process, aid how individuals navigate the world, and create more immersive engagements. In 2016, during an interview with Ellen DeGeneres, Kanye West introduced millions of viewers to synesthesia, a sixth sense (and superpower) only experienced by 5% of the world's population.[61] The Greek word "synesthesia" means bringing together senses, and for those with the neurological condition, that combination happens automatically and involuntarily.[62] For synthetes like Kanye West, their superpower is being able to see color when they hear sound. Years earlier, in 2012, a joint research team from University of California–Berkeley and University of Guadalajara found that there's truth to synesthesia, and that it may hold the answer to understanding the relation between two key senses of sight and sound.[63]

While researchers were looking for links between senses, in his 2012 TED Talk, fellow synthete and colorblind artist Neil Harbisson

# FIGURE 7.3

# CROSS-MODAL PATTERNS OF ACOUSTIC CUES FOR DISCRETE EMOTIONS

## SUMMARY OF CROSS-MODAL PATTERNS OF ACOUSTIC CUES FOR DISCRETE EMOTIONS

| Emotion | Acoustic cues (vocal expression/music performance) |
|---------|---------------------------------------------------|
| Anger | Fast speech rate/tempo, high voice intensity/sound level, much voice intensity/sound level variability, much high-frequency energy, high F0/pitch level, much F0/pitch variability, rising F0/pitch contour, fast voice onsets/tone attacks, and microstructural irregularity |
| Fear | Fast speech rate/tempo, low voice intensity/sound level (except in panic fear), much voice intensity/sound level variability, little high-frequency energy, high F0/pitch level, little F0/pitch variability, rising F0/pitch contour, and a lot of microstructural irregularity |
| Happiness | Fast speech rate/tempo, medium-high voice intensity/sound level, much voice intensity/sound level variability, little high-frequency energy, high F0/pitch level, much F0/pitch variability, rising F0/pitch contour, fast voice onsets/tone attacks, and very little microstructural regularity |
| Sadness | Slow speech rate/tempo, low voice intensity/sound level, little voice intensity/sound level variability, little high-frequency energy, low F0/pitch level, little F0/pitch variability, falling F0/pitch contour, slow voice onsets/tone attacks, and microstructural irregularity |
| Tenderness | Slow speech rate/tempo, low voice intensity/sound level, little voice intensity/sound level variability, little high-frequency energy, low F0/pitch level, little F0/pitch variability, falling F0/pitch contour, slow voice onsets/tone attacks, and microstructural irregularity |
| Note | F0 = fundamental frequency |

Source: Adapted from Patrik Juslin and Petri Lukka, "Communication of Emotions in Vocal Expression and Music Performance: Different Channels, Same Code?" *Psychological Bulletin* 129 (2003), 770–814.

unveiled technology to help translate sound into color, building on long-held theories that the two sensory pathways are connected. His "eyeborg" translates color into matching audio frequencies, and through those frequencies he's able to perceive a world in color. The research he conducts through his Cyborg Foundation enables technology to create a new field that converges color, sound, and emotions, making a connection between three once unknown variables.[64] In 2003, researchers Patrik Juslin and Petri Laukka analyzed over 100 studies from 1930 to 2000 to determine observations related to voice and music, ultimately creating a sonic key for triggering five basic emotions: anger, happiness, fear, sadness, and tenderness. At Uppsala University in Sweden, researchers were busy digging through over 100 studies to determine the link between music and emotions, including voice delivery, tone, modulation, and tempo (Figure 7.3).[65] As chefs say, people first eat with their eyes and then taste with their nose. The halo effect of sensorial-based experiences is just beginning to be explored. Brands that can unlock the relationship between connected senses will drive deeper emotional connections and memories with consumers.

| TRY THIS: | In the haste of moving through a hyper-digital world, audio becomes a way for brands to |
|---|---|
| Brand Playlist | demonstrate their personality. Imagine your brand were walking down the street. Which street? What five songs are playing on its playlist? |

## RESULTS AT THE SPEED OF SOUND

When audio hits the right chord with consumers, we see increases in brand recall, favorability, and brand consideration. One company leading the pack is Man Made Sound, who prides themselves on sound-scoring experiences. In 2011, while Verizon was saying, "Can you hear me now?," Man Made Music was helping AT&T win the audio wars by developing new sonic cues for the telecom giant. Within three years, the new four-tone note they composed for AT&T had become the second most valuable brand asset, following their circular visual logo. According to their research, by 2015, the new AT&T sonic logo became so familiar that it was the second most recognized audio cue among Americans, following the chimes used in NBC's sonic logo introduced in 1954.[66] Speaking to *Adweek*, Lauren Nagel, a senior Pandora executive, noted that many brands are behind in sonic branding despite the fact that "We are now in a currency of language and sound, as opposed to screens."[67] And if you listen to lyrics, it's apparent how inseparable music and brands have become in a tango to move product.

---

In mid-2017, Bloomberg analysts reviewed the top 20 songs on Billboard Hot 100 from 2014 to 2017 to determine which brands were mentioned most.[68] The top brands mentioned in music lyrics:

1. Rolls-Royce
2. Ferrari
3. Hennessy
4. Porsche
5. Chevrolet
6. Lamborghini
7. Bentley
8. Cadillac
9. Jordans
10. Mercedes Benz
11. Rolex
12. Xanax

---

## SOUND AND PRODUCT DESIGN

Product managers not only need to worry about the brand eco-system, product attributes, and service channels, but also need to fret about the sounds created by the products. So, add heuristic engineering to their qualifications.

Furthering research around two types of product sound—consequential and intentional—Rosana Sanz Segura and Eduardo Man-chado Pérez at the University of Zaragoza–Spain hints at secrets for heuristic engineering. The research team posits that "product sound design can be applied to modify or deliberately create a sound not only to increase consumers' comprehension of the functionality of the product but also to enhance the customer experience on an emotional level."[69]

First introduced by Dutch researchers Elif Özcan and René van Egmond in 2008, "consequential sound" is a function of the acoustics of a product operating in its normal state.[70] For instance, the whirring noise generated by a computer fan that's preventing overheating. Brand marketers often acknowledge and recycle these natural product sounds to aid brand recall or drive product category usage. As brands attempt to become synonymous with audio triggers, these consequential sounds are amplified for behavioral reminders—the crunch of a Kit Kat bar or Rice Krispies, the fizz of Alka Seltzer or Coca-Cola, or the pop of a Snapple lid. On the other hand, "intentional noises" are active sound design features (e.g., beeps) to give functional feedback or create ambiance. These types of noises are engineered to occur when electronics and appliances power on or off—typical sounds for operating systems, gaming consoles, and television programming openers. These heuristically engineered sounds are stimuli fire-crackers, notifying the user that an experience is about to happen or completing.

# HARLEY DAVIDSON

*Protecting the Culture of Their Community*

Harley Davidson Motorcycle is synonymous with leather jacket-wearing, tough guy, American culture made popular by James Dean. Known as a rugged and quality product, the century-old brand continues to dominate the auto industry with a loyal base into the millions, including one of the largest global fan clubs of over a million members. Launched in 1907, the company founded by William S. Harley and the Davidson Brothers, Arthur and Walter, created a product that would define rebel culture and craftsmanship. In 1994, realizing the power of the Harley "sound" within pop culture—the V-twin engine—the then 90-year-old company sought a trademark sound patent. Initially, other motorcycle manufacturers challenged Harley Davidson's trademark application. Each entity lost their case and appeal, and the courts granted Harley Davidson their trademark for the iconic sound.[71,72]

Ever waited in line: to ride a coaster at Six Flags, to enter a stadium for a game, or to attend a concert? Well, there's a psychology to managing big crowds through audio. In research from 2000, reviewing literature from 20 studies, researchers Steve Oakes and Adrian C. North from the University of Liverpool and Curtin University, respectively, furthers their "musicscape" theories on how to increase spend and pleasure in wait times using music. Their research offers four variables to consider in creating an ideal service environment: genre, tempo, volume, and liking.[73] In 2008, the duo applied their musicscapes theory to service environments (i.e., places accessible by consumers).[74] Their literature review brings together potential secrets for experiential marketing: slow tempo music enhances an experience for big crowds while fast tempo music is better for "waiting" experiences, such as standing in line. Knowing what chords to strike can enhance your brand experience; sometimes the right chord is vocal.

## VOICE

Ask Disney how important James Earl Jones's voice is to the *Lion King* franchise, ask Visa about Morgan Freeman's voice in advertising, or ask Amazon about Alexa's voice. In Amazon's 2018 Super Bowl commercials, which celebrated the highest brand recall for commercials airing during the game, their spot featured Alexa, the virtual assistant, losing its voice and being replaced by prominent celebrities with globally distinguishable voices. The voice of Alexa, is now in 25% of all US households, likely making it one of their most valuable intangible brand assets not only for the brand but also alongside Intel's chimes.[75]

We are becoming a voice-driven society. Digital, streaming, and virtual assistance are all increasing the need for a brand to have a "voice" strategy. Sound triggers not only emotions and memories but also physiological responses (e.g., palms sweating when scared by ominous sounds or relaxation caused by soothing voices). Voice delivers qualities of personality and value. With so many experiential brands relying on coaches and instructors, voice is a key ingredient to success for the likes of CrossFit, Peloton, SoulCycle, Equinox, and Barry's Bootcamp.

# BARRY'S BOOTCAMP

*Understanding the Power of Voice*

It is rare you find someone who is willing to work out without music in the background. Music helps to set a pace and keep engagement high, and, for those who do not like to exercise, it distracts from the time. Boot Camp style workouts have grown in popularity in the past 15 years. They are intense, based on the workouts commonly used to get the military in shape. They are highly disciplined, and most boot camps occur over a period of time, mostly three weeks, and include daily sessions that range from 90 minutes to three hours. They are also highly effective and participants see results in as little as two to four weeks. One of the most popular is Barry's Bootcamp.

The founder of Barry's Bootcamp, Barry Jay, was a celebrity personal trainer who created the concept in the late 1990s. With a small loan from

HSBC bank and a five-year business plan, the company has grown to being the most popular workout program in America and is significantly popular abroad. While some of their fitness gurus advocate that their customers stay in "beast mode," Barry's Bootcamp's music keeps its consumer base in "beat mode." Accompanying the voice of instructors that have ascended to near celebrity status themselves, each class features a soundtrack with the hottest tunes on the charts, in the streets, and spinning in clubs. There are a number of different genres that push enthusiasts, and regardless of the style of music you're hearing, the company guarantees the same: you can burn up to 1,000 calories (one-third of a pound) in a single class.[76,77,78,79]

As of January 2019, Amazon's Alexa was available as a voice assistant in nearly 30,000 smart-home devices made by 4,500 manufacturers.[80] Voice is creating an ecosystem that stretches far beyond hardware alone, enabling branded content distribution and a new medium for consumer-brand interaction.

Susan Bennett is a name you wouldn't recognize, but a voice you hear weekly if you own an Apple device. The real-life voice of Siri, Susan, was recorded in 2005 in an initial 100 hours of recording sessions, first appearing publicly on devices in 2011.[81] With several localized voices for regional relevancy, Susan is the most known voice of Siri, although there are several others, including male counterparts.[82] The right voice does more than sell or motivate; it trains new behavior.

---

In 2016, 2,600 U.S.-based adults were surveyed to evaluate the brand-recall strength of leading U.S. companies as determined by Interbrand ranking, Dow Jones, and the S&P 500.[83] The top 10 recognizable trademarked sonic signatures from brands included:

1. Nationwide
2. Farmers Insurance

3. Intel
4. Green Giant
5. Hot Pockets
6. McDonald's
7. Chevy
8. Folgers
9. State Farm
10. T-Mobile

---

# THIS COULD GIVE YOU A HEADACHE

In 2006, Miralus Healthcare launched "HeadOn," a product targeted to migraine sufferers. The ad promised instant relief, and posed a challenge to category leaders Tylenol and Advil, who were outspending the new brand by 10-to-1.[84] Delivering four brand mentions every 15 seconds, it's one of the only ads that's both the problem and solution. But, was it effective in generating ad recall or purchase action? Despite being called the "most annoying ad on television" by NBC news anchor Brian Williams, HeadOn's 200% sales lift had marketers asking, "Does repetition really work that easily?"[85]

Remember Life Alert (the brand that saves a life every 11 minutes made famous in the 1980s premiere of "I've fallen and I can't get up")? Its repetitious slogan was not only successful, but also so memorable that the companies received trademark protection in 1992.[86] The business of saving lives is deeply in tune with sonic branding. Paying attention to audio can become a matter of survival, from the sounds of ambulances, fire trucks, and hospital alarms to sirens of more than 100 decibels and patient-monitoring machines with whisper-soft beeping sounds. Researchers at the University of Adelaide in Australia discovered that regardless of how loud a siren is, people generally misperceive the distance as being about twice as far as it actually is.[87] In the United States, this miscalculation helps contribute to the over 200 crashes between emergency vehicles and cars, trucks, pedestrians, or property.[88] So for emergency vehicles, repetition means survival.

But repetition for a brand is losing support. Dramatically diminished are the "share of voice" days of repetition and reach. Today, winning in an already noisy world doesn't mean making more noise over-and-over; rather, prompting action today requires resonance and relevancy.

## REPETITION IS MARKETING MYTHOLOGY

In teaching, pedagogy varies. Children learn by repetition—hence elementary school lessons are based on activities such as writing word lists again and again to learn spelling. Rote learning proves useful until high school, when our brains start to require us to apply the information in order for it be "learned." In college, teaching techniques shift to analysis. And by graduate school, instruction tends to focus on creation (i.e., a dissertation). Somehow, marketers have introduced the idea that repetition works for adults, when in reality this is a misapplied and elementary principle.

Media math has become a race to reach and repetition. Gaining more impressions, gross rating points, and conversions-per-click has become the optimization lingo du jour. However, chasing those metrics has resulted in scandals ranging from fake followers to fake video counts, which make these goals meaningless. For presentations, we often follow the adage to "Tell them what you're going to tell them, tell them, and then tell them what you told them;" ancient advice that originates in the teaching style of Aristotle. In 2017, research from Nielsen on advertising impact affirmed that our memory lapses after just 24 hours—details fade, saliency decays, and recall loosens.[89] So, whatever you tell them better activate a feeling that triggers or creates a memory.

In *Audio Branding*, Columbia College Chicago professor Laurence Minsky and audio branding expert Colleen Fahey team up to deliver a modern guide to building an "audio system" flexible enough to capture and connect across touchpoints.[90] They give a stark reminder to the reader: brands develop an audio imprint whether we manage it or not, and that imprint can be unpleasant and dissuading. Minsky and Fahey evoke imagery of a hospital—a consistently miserable audio experience for patients, visitors, and staff—and then ask people to imagine their own company or brand's experience as an audio journey. Is your brand journey miserable like a hospital or pleasant? Is that audio journey actively being managed, or the consequent of oversight? And does it elicit a positive feeling from those immersed in it?

According to Adrian North, a professor at Curtin University in Australia who has studied the intersection of music and psychology for 25 years, "If you use music to make people more aroused they'll act more quickly, they'll eat more quickly. Other research shows that they'll drink more quickly or walk around a shop more quickly whereas slow music will have the opposite effect."[91] We know sound spurs behavior, yet marketers continue to underleverage audio in branding and experiences.

Savvy marketers are implementing bold and ambitious sonic branding efforts for organizations that span from consumer packaged goods to B2B and every type of company in between. Joining the Effies, Cannes Lions, and One Club in recognizing lead work, Clio Music launched in 2014 to promote the power of sound in branding. The organization's mission is to demonstrate that sonic branding is more than just background music in commercials—it's as important as the visuals that go into branding or the tactile experiences of packaging. In 2018, top honors went to music artist Logic for his work to raise awareness for the National Suicide Prevention Lifeline, and Finnair was recognized for enhancing the dining experience on its aircrafts with custom music soundscapes.[92]

**TRY THIS:**

Brand Sound Bank

Struggling to find the identity of your brand? Ask employees to generate a shared music playlist of 10 tracks that best present the company's spirit. As a cross-cultural effort, each core team, department, or business unit might contribute one track for the company or brand's soundtrack. Now test it. Play the music to audiences in presentations, tradeshows, conferences, lobbies, stores, and beyond, to determine if audiences react favorably to the brand's soundtrack.

By this point, you have either come to the realization that your brand is rocking audio or you have acknowledged that your brand would fail a *Bird Box* test, Shazam test, and any other audio test given to consumers. If the latter, what then, should brands include in their sonic branding strategy? In *Sonic Branding,* Daniel Jackson lays out the elements of sound—voice, ambiance, and music—that can be included in branding (Figure 7.4).[93]

An audio strategy and brand sound library should minimally include:

- Sonic logo (e.g., original compositions)
- Mnemonics (e.g., memory aids)
- Signature sounds (e.g., brand-related tones)
- Experience atmospherics (e.g., playlist strategy for stores, events, etc.)

FIGURE 7.4

# ELEMENTS OF SOUND

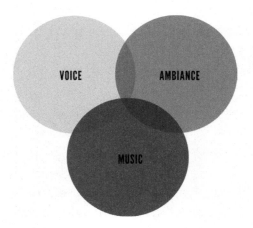

*Source*: Adapted from Daniel Jackson, *Sonic Branding: An Essential Guide to the Art and Science of Sonic Branding* (London: Palgrave Macmillan, 2003).

- Usability cues (i.e., start-up sounds, notifications, alerts)
- Media distribution (e.g., radio, streaming audio)
- Atmospherics (e.g., music selection for commercials, video)

More advanced audio strategies might include:

- Jingles
- Dialogue management (e.g., call center scripts)
- Voice/virtual assistance (e.g., telephone, voiceovers, IVR systems)
- Product heuristics (e.g., low-noise emissions of engines, "quiet mode" appliances)
- Sound bank (e.g., original compositions)
- Brand anthems (e.g., member/employee chants and songs)
- Playlists (e.g., samples of music cues to create mood)
- Branded audio (e.g., podcasts, whitepapers, news)
- Music partnerships

Can the sound work in various formats of short and long-form: video intro (i.e., initial three seconds), soundtrack for brand video, in-store, etc.

# Y7 STUDIO

*Unlocking the Power in Voice, Ambiance, and Music*

Sarah Larson Levy is the newest maverick in the booming group fitness movement. Founder of the Y7 Studio, a five-year-old franchise of yoga studios in New York and Los Angeles. One would think she began the business because she is a fan of yoga when in truth, Levy says it is just the opposite. In an interview with *Inc.*, Levy, 31, said, "This all came about because I actually hate yoga." It was her displeasure with a yoga class she took in Michigan where there was "endless chanting or confusing terminology or bright lighting and mirrors that made her self-conscious about her body." Frustrated that she paid money to be ridiculed, Levy decided to rent out a small space where she could offer yoga classes that were fun and empowering, that found beauty in every body type and offered an experience that people wanted to stick with for the long haul.

Y7 Studio is a boutique fitness club and ranks on *Inc.*'s 2018 5000 list of Fast-Growing Companies at number 80. What makes Levy's studios so appealing is that she challenges conventional ideas of what constitutes yoga. The flagship studio is located in Brooklyn. Levy and company recall the hip-hop roots in this locale through the music that is for the classes, an unconventional choice for yoga. According to Forbes, if you take a class, "forget ambient music, Y7 Studio is famous for featuring hip-hop artists including Beyoncé, Jay-Z, and Fetty Wap."[94,95,96]

## CONCLUSION

Marketers try to check off the "sonic branding" box by using a tune from an existing pop or rock song, hoping it will trigger a sense of familiarity. But does that borrowed equity actually work? Brands often leave sync rights until the last step in production, using whatever budget remains, borrowing equity from tracks likely shuffled between brands. The new rules of consumer behavior in a noisy world matter when brands only have a few seconds to capture and connect with audiences; audio creates a hook. In a reality where every second counts, waiting until the end of content or commercials to play recognizable audio or leverage voice is a total waste of money. Use audio, immediately, as an extension of the visuals around a brand, investing in it a driver of action.

Whether an entrepreneur, brand planner, or CMO, remember that audio is one of the most underleveraged branding triggers. As a result, a sonic signature becomes a competitive advantage. When treated as a system (i.e., voice, ambiance, and music), music can become the instant recognition factor that shapes mood, informs, and triggers product use. In the future, with the help of artificial intelligence, expect a more precise composition of tunes that motivate action and sophisticated delivery of the right tune to the right touch point, an always-on algorithm learning from audience reactions. The evolution of the brand book to include audio will result in a brand getting closer to its North Star of owning a feeling.

## 🔥 FIRE STARTERS

### DEVELOPING INSTANT RECOGNITION

☐ *If your brand was a person, who would it be?*

☐ *If your brand were a music genre, what would it be?*

☐ *If your brand was encapsulated in a playlist, what tracks would be on it?*

# Notes

1. Rickard Aronsson, Christian Hansson, and Daniel Wierup, "International Marketing and Brand Management." Master's thesis, Lund University, 2009, 4–72. Accessed January 31, 2019. http: //lup. lub.lu.se/luur/download? func=downloadFile&recordOld=1437373&fileOld=2435552.
2. David Allan, "A Content Analysis of Music Placement in Prime-Time Television Advertising." *Journal of Advertising Research* 48 (2008). doi:10.2501/S0021849908080434.
3. "The 10 Most Addictive Sounds in the World." *Fast Company*, February 22, 2010. https://www.fastcompany.com/1555211/10-most-addictive-sounds-world.
4. "Market Share of Telecom Private Lines in the U.S. from 2002 to 2011, by Service Provider." Statista. Accessed January 31, 2019. https://www.statista.com/statistics/214193/us-market-share-of-telecom-private-lines-since-2002-by-company/.
5. Jon Porter, "Vinyl and Cassette Sales Saw Double-Digit Growth Last Year." *The Verge*, January 6, 2019. https://www.theverge.com/2019/1/6/18170624/vinyl-cassette-popularity-revival-2018-sales-growth-cd-decline.

6. Rich Duprey, "Amazon Is Losing Its Grip on the Smart Speaker Market." *The Motley Fool*, January 6, 2019. https://www.fool.com/amp/investing/ 2019/01/06/amazon-losing-its-grip-on-smart-speaker-market.aspx.

7. Ross Winn, "2018 Podcast Stats & Facts (New Research From Dec 2018)." *Podcast Insights*, January 9, 2019. https://www.podcastinsights.com/ podcast-statistics/.

8. "Number of Paying Spotify Subscribers Worldwide from July 2010 to November 2018 (in Millions)." Statista. Accessed January 31, 2019. https://www.statista.com/statistics/244995/number-of-paying-spotify- subscribers/.

9. "Music Streaming." Statista. Accessed January 31, 2019. https://www .statista.com/outlook/209/100/music-streaming/worldwide.

10. Nick Routley, "Visualizing 40 Years of Music Industry Sales." *Visual Capitalist*, October 6, 2018. https://www.visualcapitalist.com/music-industry-sales/

11. "FESTatistics: Festivals By The Numbers." FestForums. Accessed February 1, 2019. http://www.festforums.com/new-blog-1/2017/5/31/fe statistics-festivals-by-the-numbers.

12. Kai Ryssdal and Tommy Andres, "Atom Factory's Troy Carter: 'Music Sells Everything but Music.'" MarketPlace, November 19, 2015. https://www .marketplace.org/2015/11/19/world/corner-office-marketplace-corner- office/atom-factorys-troy-carter-music-sells.

13. "Musical Chills: Why They Give Us Thrills." McGill Library, January 7, 2013. https://www.mcgill.ca/newsroom/channels/news/musical-chills-why-they- give-us-thrills-170538.

14. Panelist comment during Sostereo panel, "Making Brands Memorable Through Music," Advertising Week New York, October 3, 2018.

15. Joel Beckerman and Tyler Gray, *The Sonic Boom: How Sound Transforms the Way We Think, Feel, and Buy*. Boston: Houghton Mifflin Harcourt, 2015.

16. Albert Mehrabian and James A. Russell, *An Approach to Environmental Psychology*. Cambridge: MIT Press, 1974.

17. Meera M. Blattner, Denise A. Sumikawa, and Robert M. Green- berg, "Earcons and Icons: Their Structure and Common Design Princi- ples." *Human–Computer Interaction* 4, no. 1 (1989), 11–44. doi:10.1207/ s15327051hci0401_1.

18. Ibid.

19. Vijaykumar Krishnan, James J. Kellaris, and Timothy W. Aurand, "Sonic Logos: Can Sound Influence Willingness to Pay?" *Journal of Product and Brand Management* 21, no. 4 (2012), 275–284. doi:10.1108/1061042121 1246685.

20. Erik Devaney and Erik Devaney, "Stores Are Using Music to Make You Spend More – ThinkGrowth.org." ThinkGrowth.org, January 7, 2016. https://thinkgrowth.org/stores-are-using-music-to-make-you-spend-more-d6c85974b20b.

21. Philip Kotler, "Atmospherics As a Marketing Tool." *Journal of Retailing* 49 (December 1973), 48.

22. Ibid.

23. "History." Adidas. Accessed February 1, 2019. https://www.adidas-group .com/en/group/history/.

24. "Adidas Originals Shoes: Iconic and Classic Sneaker Styles." Adidas. Accessed February 1, 2019. https://www.adidas.com/us/originals-shoes.

25. Robin Mellery-Pratt, "Run-D.M.C.'s 'My Adidas' and the Birth of Hip-Hop Sneaker Culture." *Business of Fashion*, July 18, 2014. https://www .businessoffashion.com/articles/video/run-d-m-c-s-adidas-birth-hip-hop-sneaker-culture.

26. Alisa Hauser. "Adidas Originals Opens Its Biggest Store Ever in Wicker Park." DNAinfo, October 5, 2017. https://www.dnainfo.com/chicago/20171005/ wicker-park/adidas-originals-wicker-park-shoes-1532-n-milwaukee-ave-athletic-shoes/.

27. "Hear the Taste." International Sound Awards. Accessed February 1, 2019. https://www.international-sound-awards.com/hear-the-taste/.

28. Dimple Agarwal, Josh Bersin, Gaurav Lahiri, Jeff Schwartz, and Erica Volini, "Well-being: A Strategy and a Responsibility." *Deloitte Insights*, March 28, 2018. https://www2.deloitte.com/insights/us/en/focus/human-capital-trends/2018/employee-well-being-programs.html.

29. Marianne Garvey, "Meditation Rooms Are the Hottest New Work Perk." *MarketWatch*, October 26, 2018. https://www.marketwatch.com/story/ meditation-rooms-are-the-hottest-new-work-perk-2018-10-26.

30. https://www.theglobeandmail.com/business/small-business/going-global/article-meet-tamara-levitt-the-toronto-woman-who-soothes-millions-on-the-calm/.

31. Connor Casey, "Cities Using Bird Recordings to Reduce Crime." *The Maneater*, February 14, 2012. https://www.themaneater.com/stories/outlook/bird-word-how-chirping-can-cut-down-crime.

32. "Mayor's Muzak Fails To Soothe Some Residents." Transcript. In Weekend Edition Sunday. National Public Radio, June 26, 2011. https://www.npr.org/2011/06/26/137429497/mayors-muzak-fails-to-soothe-some-residents.

33. "Coronoa Electric Beach." Corona. Accessed February 1, 2019. www.coronaelectricbeach.com.

34. "Corona Sunset." Corona. Accessed February 1, 2019. www.coronasunsets.com/.

35. "History of Corona Beer." Mental Itch. January 13, 2015. https://mentalitch.com/history-of-corona-beer/.

36. Lutz Jäncke, "Music, Memory and Emotion" *Journal of Biology* 7, no. 6 (August 8, 2008), 21. doi:10.1186/jbiol82.

37. Joel Beckerman and Tyler Gray, *The Sonic Boom: How Sound Transforms the Way We Think, Feel, and Buy*. Boston: Houghton Mifflin Harcourt, 2015.

38. Ibid.

39. https://www.ama.org/partners/content/Pages/why-customers-attention-scarcest-resources-2017.aspx.

40. Marin Lindstrom, *Buyology: Truth and Lies about Why We Buy*. New York: Doubleday, 2008.

41. "About." Advertising Research Foundation. Accessed February 1, 2019. https://thearf.org/about-arf/.

42. "Few Viewers Are Giving the TV Set Their Undivided Attention." *Emarketer*, November 7, 17. https://www.emarketer.com/Article/Few-Viewers-Giving-TV-Set-Their-Undivided-Attention/1016717.

43. Tom Cheredar, "Shazam Touts TV Success As It Hits 100M Monthly Active Mobile Users." *Venture Beat*, August 20, 2014. https://venturebeat.com/2014/08/20/shazam-touts-tv-success-as-it-hits-100m-monthly-active-mobile-users/.

44. Jack Loechner, "90% of Car Commuters Are Listening to the Radio." *Media Post*, April 25, 2016. https://www.mediapost.com/publications/article/274139/90-of-car-commuters-are-listening-to-the-radio.html.

45. Aaron Baar, "McDonald's New Global Line: 'I'm Lovin' It,'" *Adweek*, June 11, 2003. https://www.adweek.com/brand-marketing/mcdonalds-new-global-line-im-lovin-it-64899/.

46. Alyssa Mertes, "Top 10 Advertising Jingles: CreativeReady/Radio Production Library." *Quality Logo Products*, January 3, 2019. https://www.quality logoproducts.com/promo-university/top-10-advertising-jingles.htm.

47. Marc Hogan, "The Contentious Tale of the McDonald's "'I'm Lovin' It' Jingle." *Pitch Fork*, July 14, 2016. https://pitchfork.com/thepitch/1227-the-contentious-tale-of-the-mcdonalds-im-lovin-it-jingle/

48. "Intel Reports Second-Quarter 2018 Financial Results." Intel Corporation—Investor Relations—Financials & Filings—Annual Reports & Proxy. Accessed January 31, 2019. https://www.intc.com/investor-relations/ investor-education-and-news/investor-news/press-release-details/2018/ Intel-Reports-Second-Quarter-2018-Financial-Results/.

49. "Intel Timeline: A History of Innovation." Intel. Accessed February 1, 2019. https://www.intel.com/content/www/us/en/history/historic-timeline .html.

50. "Sonic Branding (3): Examples of Sonic Branding." *Royalty Free Composer*, January 29, 2013. https://www.royaltyfreecomposer.com/sonic-branding/examples-of-sonic-branding/.

51. Laura Kaufman, "The Man Who Created Intel's Audio 'Signature.'" *Los Angeles Times*, October 20, 1999. http://articles.latimes.com/1999/oct/20/ business/fi-24321.

52. Kathryn Luttner, "Intel CMO Steve Fund on Drones, In-house Agencies, and Evolving a Brand with a Legendary 'Bbong.'" *PR Week*, April 24, 2017. Accessed February 1, 2019. https://www.prweek.com/article/1431326/intel-cmo-steve-fund-drones-in-house-agencies-evolving-brand-legendary-bong#4vJ2wHM9V4iusX7Y.99.

53. Jordan Passman, "Intel, Netflix, Apple and the Power and Influence of Sonic Branding." *Forbes*, November 2, 2016. https://www.forbes.com/ sites/jordanpassman/2016/11/02/intel-netflix-apple-and-the-power-and-influence-of-sonic-branding/#745f04694836.

54. Chris Turner, "In Defence of the Advertising Jingle—(Almost) Gone but Not Forgotten." *The Drum*, June 1, 2015. https://www.thedrum .com/opinion/2015/06/01/defence-advertising-jingle-almost-gone-not-forgotten.

55. Wanda T. Wallace. "Jingles in Advertisements: Can They Improve Recall?" Association for Consumer Research, 1991. Accessed February 1, 2019. www.acrwebsite.org/volumes/7167/volumes/v18/NA-18.

56. Alyssa Mertes, "Top 10 Advertising Jingles of All Time!" Quality Food Products. Accessed February 1, 2019. https://www.qualitylogoproducts .com/promo-university/top-10-advertising-jingles.htm.

57. David Allan, "A Content Analysis of Music Placement in Prime-Time Television Advertising." *Journal of Advertising Research* 48, no. 3 (2008): 404–417. doi:10.2501/s0021849908080434.

58. Julia Marsh, "Cellino & Barnes Still Raking in 'Record Profits' Despite Feud." *New York Post*, October 10, 2018. https://nypost.com/2018/10/10/cellino-barnes-still-raking-in-record-profits-despite-feud/.

59. Gabrielle Fonrouge, Max Jaeger, and Laura Italiano, "Who Will Get the Rights to the Cellino & Barnes Jingle?" *New York Post*, May 11, 2017. https://nypost.com/2017/05/11/who-will-get-the-rights-to-the-cellino-barnes-jingle/.

60. Tiffany Stanley, "What Killed the Jingle?" *The Atlantic*, August 29, 2016. https://www.theatlantic.com/business/archive/2016/08/what-killed-the-jingle/497291/.

61. Kanye West "I See Sounds . . ." Directed by Tom S. YouTube, May 24, 2016. https://www.youtube.com/watch?v=Yu9RBIX5X0k.

62. Veronica Gross, "The Synethesia Project." Boston University. Accessed February 1, 2019. https://www.bu.edu/synesthesia/index.html.

63. Stephen E. Palmer, Karen B. Schloss, Zoe Xu, and Lilia R. Prado-Leon, "Music–Color Associations Are Mediated by Emotion." *Proceedings of the National Academy of Sciences* 110, no. 22 (May 2013), 8836–8841. doi:10.1073/pnas.1212562110.

64. Helen Walters, "The Sound of Color: Neil Harbisson's Talk Visualized." IDEAS TED, July 11, 2013. https://ideas.ted.com/the-sound-of-color-neil-harbissons-talk-visualized/.

65. Patrik Juslin and Petri Laukka, "Communication of Emotions in Vocal Expression and Music Performance: Different Channels, Same Code?" *Psychological Bulletin* 129 (2003), 770–814. doi:10.1037/0033-2909.129.5.770.

66. "The World of Man Made AT&T." Man Made Music. Accessed February 1, 2019. https://www.manmademusic.com/work/att.

67. Katie Richards, "As Voice Continues Its Rise, Marketers Are Turning to Sonic Branding." *Adweek*, January 14, 2018. https://www.adweek.com/brand-marketing/as-voice-continues-its-rise-marketers-are-turning-to-sonic-branding/.

68. Bloomberg, "This Is the Most Name-Dropped Brand in Music." *Fortune*, August 18, 2019. http://fortune.com/2017/08/18/name-brands-pop-music-rap/.

69. Rosana Sanz Segura and Eduardo Manchado Pérez, "Product Sound Design As a Valuable Tool in the Product Development Process."

*Ergonomics in Design* 26, no. 4 (October 2018), 20–24. doi:10.1177/1064804618772997.

70. Lau Langeveld, Rene Van, Reinier Jansen, and Elif Ozc, "Product Sound Design: Intentional and Consequential Sounds." *Advances in Industrial Design Engineering*, 2013. doi:10.5772/55274.

71. "Harley-Davidson Secures Biggest-Ever TM Infringement Win." *World IP Review*, April 17, 2018. https://www.worldipreview.com/news/harley-davidson-secures-biggest-ever-tm-infringement-win-15789.

72. "Harley-Davidson Motorcycle History." Motorcycle-USA.com. February 24, 2008. www.motorcycle-usa.com/2008/02/article/harley-davidson-motorcycle-history/.

73. Steve Oakes and Adrian C. North, "Reviewing Congruity Effects in the Service Environment Musicscape." *International Journal of Service Industry Management* 19, no. 1 (2008), 63–82. doi:10.1108/09564230810855716.

74. Steve Oakes and Adrian C. North, "Using Music to Influence Cognitive and Affective Responses in Queues of Low and High Crowd Density." *Journal of Marketing Management* 24, no. 5–6 (2008), 589–602. doi:10.1362/026725708x326002.

75. Micahel Cappetta and Jo Ling Kent, "Meet the Woman behind Amazon's Alexa." NBC News, August 9, 2018. https://www.nbcnews.com/business/business-news/meet-woman-behind-amazon-s-alexa-n898426.

76. Bridget Arsenault, "Why Barry's Bootcamp Stays Successful." *Forbes*, January 29, 2018. https://www.forbes.com/sites/bridgetarsenault/2018/01/29/how-barrys-bootcamp-continues-to-captivate-an-otherwise-saturated-fitness-market/.

77. Minsun Park, "How to Create the Ultimate Workout Playlist." Barry's Bootcamp, October 1, 2016. https://www.barrysbootcamp.com/how-to-create-the-ultimate-workout-playlist/.

78. "Our Story," Barry's Bootcamp. Accessed February 1, 2019. https://www.barrysbootcamp.com/our-story/.

79. Emma Prenn. "Why Everyone Is Talking about This Workout Studio?" *Self* August 13, 2015. https://www.self.com/story/barrys-bootcamp-workout-expansion.

80. Dieter Bohn, "Amazon Says 100 Million Alexa Devices Have Been Sold—What's Next?" *The Verge*, January 4, 2019. https://www.theverge.com/2019/1/4/18168565/amazon-alexa-devices-how-many-sold-number-100-million-dave-limp.

81. Hannah Jane Parkinson, "Hey, Siri! Meet the Real People behind Apple's Voice-Activated Assistant." *The Guardian*, August 12, 2015. https://www.theguardian.com/technology/2015/aug/12/siri-real-voices-apple-ios-assistant-jon-briggs-susan-bennett-karen-jacobsen.

82. Ibid.

83. "Audio Logo Index 2016." Veritonic. Accessed February 1, 2019. https://blog.veritonic.com/audio-logo-index-2016.

84. Mya Frazier, "This Ad Will Give You a Headache, but It Sells." *Ad Age*, September 24, 2007. https://adage.com/article/news/ad-give-a-headache-sells/120636/.

85. Ibid.

86. "Life Alert Emergency Response." Wikipedia. Last updated on September 16, 2018. Accessed February 1, 2019. https://en.wikipedia.org/wiki/Life_Alert_Emergency_Response.

87. Carl Q. Howard, Aaron J. Maddern, and Elefterios P. Privopoulos, "Acoustic Characteristics for Effective Ambulance Sirens." *Acoustics Australia* 39, no. 2 (August 2011), 43–53.

88. Jason Busch, "Addressing Ambulance Standards." *Emsworld*, July 3, 2015. https://www.emsworld.com/article/12051684/ambulance-design-and-safety-standards.

89. David Brandt and Ingrid Nieuwenhuis, "Understanding Memory in Advertising." Nielsen, February 22, 2017. https://www.nielsen.com/us/en/insights/journal-of-measurement/volume-1-issue-3/understanding-memory-in-advertising.html.

90. Laurence Minsky and Colleen Fahey, with Foreword by Philip Kotler, *Audio Branding: Using Sound to Build Your Brand.* London: Kogan, 2017.

91. Lennox Morrison, "The New Trick to Get You Spending More." BBC, July 7, 2016. http://www.bbc.com/capital/story/20160704-the-music-that-makes-you-spend-the-most.

92. Andy Hines, "National Suicide Prevention Lifeline 1-800-273-8255." In National Suicide Prevention Lifeline. Clios, 2018. Accessed February 1, 2019. https://clios.com/music/winner/social-good/national-suicide-prevention-lifeline/1-800-273-8255-46806.

93. Daniel Jackson, *Sonic Branding: An Essential Guide to the Art and Science of Sonic Branding.* London: Palgrave Macmillan, 2003.

94. Vivienne Decker, "Sweat-Dripping, Beat-Bumping, Candlelit Yoga: Meet the Millennial CEO behind Y7 Studio." *Forbes*, February 29, 2016. https://www.forbes.com/sites/viviennedecker/2016/02/29/sweat-dripping-beat-bumping-candlelit-yoga-meet-the-millennial-ceo-behind-y7-studio/.

95. "Y7 Studio." 2018. Accessed February 1, 2019. https://www.inc.com/profile/y7-studio.

96. Jeff Bercovici, "How the Founder of Y7 Studio Built One of America's Fastest-Growing Fitness Companies for People Who Hate Yoga." *Inc.*, August 15, 2018. https://www.inc.com/magazine/201809/jeff-bercovici/2018-inc-5000-y7-studio-yoga-fitness-trends.html.

# 8

# VISUAL STIMULI

*Branding Objective:
Become a
"Conversational" Brand*

## FLASH-FORWARD

Symbols

Shapes

Colors

Fonts

Signs

Memes

Gifs

Emojis

Images

Videos

## BRAND SPOTLIGHTS

Airbnb

Amazon

DJ Khaled

Kit Kat

Lyft

NASA

NBA

Porsche

S'well Bottles

Sherwin Williams

Signs.com

The Louvre. Beyoncé. Art. A visual collaboration anchored by two powerhouses: an artist known for producing visuals that move culture (from Single Ladies choreography to *Lemonade* on HBO) and the 200-year old museum that is home to reknown pieces from the *Mona Lisa* to the Venus de Milo.[1] Beyoncé and Jay Z's "Apeshit" video shook the art world, attracting aficionados globally with 250 billion online views. Accompanied by a 90-minute, 17-piece museum tour inspired by the works shown in the video, the one-two punch spiked museum attendance by 25% in 2018— the Louvre's best year since 2012.[2,3] As the third element within a strong communication system that includes lexicon and audio, visuals has the power to spur behavior fast and efficiently, while entertaining in the process.

I've traveled to 20 countries and France has always been a favorite. My first trip was in 1989 at age four, which marked the bicentennial celebration of the French Revolution. That year, the Louvre opened its new entrance—the now iconic glass-pyramid-shaped entry designed by I. M. Pei—which the French president almost rejected due to the powerful association of the pyramid symbol to Egypt. Luckily, they changed their mind.

For any global citizen, there is an innate appreciation of strong visual branding made apparent by the basic necessities of finding restrooms, ordering from menus, and navigating transportation. Because we process visual information exponentially faster than text, we go through the world using pattern recognition. According to researchers at MIT, we process images within 13 milliseconds (a millisecond is 1/1000 of a second).[4] How fast is that? Well, the average person blinks every four seconds.[5] Researchers have long proven that before children learn language in the form of words, they can master communication based on understanding basic symbols.[6] So visuals quickly become a universal system comprised of visual elements including symbols, shapes, colors, and images, which can easily be decoded by individuals across age cohorts and geographies. And as digital adds a layer of depth and speed to communication, the opportunity to compress information into fast-growing visual stimuli of gifs, memes, emojis and video will continue to increase in audience appeal, also.

## WORDS ARE FINITE, IMAGES ARE LIMITLESS

According to linguistics professor Stuart Webb at the University of Western Ontario, native English language speakers know about 15,000–20,000 lemmas (i.e., root words found in dictionaries).[7] With only 800 lemmas, he believes an English speaker can understand 75% of the language.[8] There are only 500,000 words coded in Merriam Webster, which means that at best the average English speaker masters less than 10% of the whole language.[9] Each year, fewer than 1,000 new words are added to top dictionaries like Merriam-Webster or Oxford.[10] According to the internet expert and venture capitalist Mary Meeker, whom Forbes calls one of the most important people in business, 35,000 new images are posted to social media every second, amounting to over 3 billion daily.[11] And that's only a fraction of the estimated 1.2 trillion new images captured through digital cameras annually.[12] With an understanding of how fast visuals change as communication elements compared to how slow language (i.e., words) evolve, let's talk about the power of visual stimuli.

# AIRBNB

*Evolving a Brand for a Global Community*

When Brian Chesky and Joe Gebbia founded Airbnb in 2008, home-sharing services were a new product. In 2014, seeking to connect with a new base of global travelers, Airbnb rebranded itself with a pictorial symbol used as a new logo. Airbnb teamed with DesignStudio to create its messaging, strategically opting for a brand and design agency that aims to make a meaningful difference to the most loved brands. The resulting logo was named Bélo and was designed through a compilation of four recognizable symbols: a head, a location icon, a heart and the letter A. "The Bélo is also used as a community symbol that can be expressed differently by each community member and in every listing—it is not bound by language, culture, or location. The end result is a symbol people feel compelled to share—one that accepts we are all different, one to wear with pride," DesignStudio wrote on its website.

The combination of symbols used builds an accessible, easy-to-copy logo that represents the company as a service that brings people together through a sense of belonging. The design is intended to trigger consumers' feelings of connection and comfort, speaking to them on a personal level. And giving the symbol a name adds a level of familiarity to it. The symbol illustrates the company's core mission of belonging, reminding consumers that it's a means for them to feel at home wherever they stay. Bélo has proven to be successful in strengthening brand messaging, as Airbnb has grown from a $25 billion value with 60 million guests to a $38 billion value with 400 million guests.[13,14,15,16]

Most branding consultants, firms, and courses will identify four key brand visuals: mark (i.e., symbol), font, color palette, and shape (e.g., product packaging) (see Figure 8.1). On the next brand rung, they'll add more complex visual applications: imagery and video. As communications evolve, there's another rung to add to the visual branding ladder—glyphs. The surge in glyphs—gifs, memes, emojis—represents modern extensions of ancient hieroglyphics. And the explosion of glyphs, globally, shows no signs of slowing down.

To understand the evolution of visuals in branding, and the role of visuals in culture, we must start at the origins of hieroglyphics—the first "branded" markings. Tracing back over 5,000 years to

FIGURE 8.1

# TRADITIONAL BRAND EXPRESSION ELEMENTS

SYMBOL                                          FONT

**BRAND SIGNATURE**

SHAPE                                           COLOR

*Brand identity traditionally combines four elements into brand signature: symbol, font expressed as lettering, color palette, and shape attributes.*

3,300 BC, Egyptian hieroglyphics contained 24 key symbols akin to present-day letters in the English alphabet.[17] Hieroglyphs codified laws, customs, traditions, and notable stories.[18] According of the British Museum, the entire visual lexicon of hieroglyphics spanned only 7,000 glyphs, reinforcing the adage that a picture, or glyph, is worth 1,000 words.[19]

Consider how glyphs have infiltrated communication through technology such as word processors. Growing from 82 objects when introduced in 1996 to over 140,000 objects in 2018, clip art became the visual library of Microsoft users looking to jazz-up their papers, presentations, and resumes.[20] Rivaled today by the wildly popular site The Noun Project—launched in 2010—has already amassed over one million icons in its online visual dictionary.[21] That means that the under-10-year-old visual dictionary has cataloged an equal number of words as the leading 200-year-old dictionaries (i.e., Merriam-Webster and Oxford). Symbols are core to branding, and critical when you consider that a logo mark is hailed as the prized, protected, trademarked expression of a brand. Not only is the "artwork" (e.g., visual logo) prized, but also the objects that express the brand (e.g., uniforms).

There's more to branding than simply using a common symbol, however. For instance, over 20 companies have the symbol of a smile in their brand logo, including Argos, Danone yogurt, LG, Pepsi, and Weedmaps. Most famously, though, every Prime customer recognizes Amazon's smile when they're handed their grocery delivery, fetch a package from the mailbox, or walk past a distribution point. It's through visibility and consistency that brands start to drive associations between symbols, feelings, and action.

# AMAZON

*Delivering Smiles to Consumers and Businesses*

Currently the most valuable brand internationally, Amazon has secured itself a place in the browser histories of an estimated 300 million shoppers worldwide. As of 2018, its Prime service had 100 million subscribers internationally; twice as many as 2015. Now marketed as a one-stop-shop for everything under the sun, it's hard to remember that Amazon started as a bookstore. When Jeff Bezos founded the retail site in 1994, he selected the name "Amazon" as it included the letters A and Z, and he wanted the title to reflect the wide range of titles that the retailer sold: "everything from A to Z" in the book world.

During the 1990s, Bezos toyed with a few different logos that emphasized the letter A and included the subtitle "Earth's Biggest Bookstore." However, when the new millennium hit and the dot-com era reached its height, Bezos determined that he wanted to expand the marketplace beyond books in a bet that took $5 billion to fulfill. He enlisted the help of creative agency Turner Duckworth to create a logo that painted Amazon as a seller of "everything." The result, a custom font over the signature curved arrow represents a number of factors of the Amazon mission. "We were trying to create something that had an iconic element, that they'd be able to use in the future independent of the logo itself," said David Turner, cofounder of Turner Duckworth.

Enhancing the company's aim, the logo is easy to read and accessible to all shoppers. The curved line resembles a smile, and that is how shoppers feel when using Amazon. It connects the letters A and Z, reminding shoppers that "everything from A to Z" can be found on Amazon. This idea could have been established through any curved line, yet the company selected a curved arrow, ending in a pointer that looks like a dimple. Like the brand itself, the Amazon logo looks to the future. This logo tells us that Amazon is a company that is continuously innovating. It started as an online bookseller in an era before e-commerce, and is now a retail giant and growing exponentially.[22,23,24]

In 1995, the International Olympic Committee (IOC) commissioned research in six countries among 7,000 individuals that showed the startling power of branding—McDonald's was recognizable among 88% of participants while the Christian cross was recognizable by only 54% of participants.[25] The most startling insight is the speed at which a brand like McDonald's used visual stimuli to achieve high recall. McDonald's launched their golden arches during the 1950s; the Christian religion adopted the cross as a symbol almost two millennium prior during the fourth century.[26] While the neurological effects of symbols continue to be studied, we know that they trigger feelings. Adults and children alike are susceptible to symbolism. Ever rode past a McDonald's location and saw the sight of golden arches light up a child's eyes? According to researcher Martin Lindstrom, symbols are nostalgia triggers. Using fMRI technology to track brain activity in over 20,000 consumers in 77 countries, he found that the image of golden arches activates the "reward" zone within children.[27]

Symbols are more than 2D flat art such as clip art or icons; they are also tangible objects. Consider the photo of Kanye West wearing a "Make America Great Again" hat . . . the California-made product sold for $25 during Donald Trump's 2016 presidential campaign, becoming a mainstay at rallies as over 500,000 hats were sold.[28]

Trump's election garnered less than 10% of the Black vote, and the combined image of the wearer (West is a wealthy black man who is immunized from the everyday struggles of minorities) and the MAGA hat (a perceived symbol of white nationalism) conveyed a clashing of values that even "free thinkers" would have trouble accepting. In other words, any verbal argument can get trumped by the feeling laced into the imagery. For most brands, symbols can become profitable licensing opportunities, common among luxury auto brands like Porsche, and a revenue source for the brands that achieve high recall.

# PORSCHE

*Turning Objects of Desire into a Lifestyle Aspiration*

The Porsche logo is deeply embedded with symbolism, now extending into one of the most powerful licenses in the world. When the company was founded by German automobile engineer Ferdinand Porsche in Stuttgart, Germany, in 1931, it had no logo. Its original cars were simply marked with the manufacturer's name. Porsche's automobiles grew in popularity in the second half of the 20th century as it developed racing and sports cars; and in 1952, the company agreed it needed a quality seal. The logo that was ultimately developed by advertising manager Herrmann Lapper and designer Franz Xaver Reimspieß was inspired by the appearance of a coat of arms stemming from symbolism of the Middle Ages.

The iconic black horse in the center of the logo comes from the coat of arms of the city of Stuttgart, which depicted horses in the fourteenth century. Representing power, the symbol of the horse also implies movement and the brand's commitment to tradition. Porsche's logo has changed very minimally in the nearly 70 years since it was first designed. The company writes on its website, "This symbol, steeped in history, signals a continued long life for classic Porsche models." The continued use of a protective coat of arms shows consumers consistency and reliability in Porsche products, as represented in its continued sales growth.[29,30,31,32]

## SAY IT WITH PURPOSE

When Johannes Gutenberg introduced the printing press in the 15th century, the font didn't matter. The most printed work of the day, the Bible, used a mix of fonts. Early typewriters introduced in the later 1880s featured a monospace font. By the 1950s, IBM adopted Courier as their default typewriter font. During that decade, Helvetica was developed in Switzerland.[33] Released in 2007, the 80-minute documentary *Helvetica* pays homage to a font beloved around the world, starting a conversation about the power of fonts in society. In 2018, a team at design firm Icon8 analyzed 1,000 sites that appeared on ProductHunt and found that Helvetica Neue was a favorite among trendy companies.[34] Today, there are over 500,000 fonts, with only a few hundred preinstalled on computer applications, such as Microsoft products, or 245 preinstalled in the Adobe suite.[35]

---

There are five generic font families:
1. Serif (e.g., Times New Roman)
2. Sans-serif (e.g., Helvetica, Arial)
3. Cursive (e.g., Corsiva, Lucida)
4. Fantasy (e.g., Comic Sans, Papyrus)
5. Monospace (e.g., Courier)

---

In 2010, a joint research team at Princeton University and Indiana University sought to determine the connection between font and memory. In two sets of experiments, one with adults aged 18–40 and a second with high school students, both resulted in a fantasy font (i.e., Comic Sans Italicized) beating a wildly popular san-serif font (i.e., Arial). The researchers concluded that disfluency—intentional difficulty in expressing information to force cognition—could be accomplished with font selection and ultimately lead to higher recall.[36] A researcher at RMIT University in Australia, Stephen Banham, has studied fonts for 25 years. In 2018, he created a new font, Sans Forgetica, combining disfluency principles of applying "desirable difficulty" to tasks, and found that the uncommon font helps improve retention of information.[37,38] So, said another way, if you want a message to visually pop and be sticky for an audience, use two or more fonts.

# SIGNS.COM

*Helping Customers Say It with Purpose*

Founded in 2012 in Salt Lake City, Utah, by Nelson James, by 2018 Signs.com was already generating nearly $15 million in annual revenues. The company produces over a million signage pieces annually. The business model is simple: customers can have signage created for their business or events at home on their own devices, submit those and pay for them online, and have their finished product shipped to their home or business. The Signs.com motto is convenience. In 2017, Signs.com was named in Deloitte's North America Technology Fast 500 and Inc.'s 500 Fastest Growing Companies in America, and was one of Utah's Fast 50 in 2018. Placed on Deloitte's list of the 500 Fastest Growing Companies in 2018, for the second year in a row, the company's "three-year revenue growth of 1,112%," ranks them at #458 on the list of prominent businesses.[39,40]

## COLOR

When visiting Europe, I love exploring markets—from Borough Street in London to La Boqueria in Barcelona. As an amateur photographer, the vibrancy of markets is a visual feast for the lens. Spices are my favorite—they are diverse in hue and rich in saturation. The colors become real-life pixels exploding against the backdrop of barrels—visual stimuli that evoke aromas and imaginative thoughts of delightful food. While there are over eight billion colors in a 4k television, 1.6 million colors in Apple iPhone X, and one million colors in the screen of an Amazon Echo Show, according to the Pantone Matching System, there are only 1,800 true colors.[41,42] And as most digital designers may know, there are only 216 universal "web-safe" colors.

The psychological effects of color are deeply known to researchers: color increases brand recognition, aids recall, and drives differentiation. Based on research in 2006, Satyendra Singh of University of Winnipeg notes that "people make up their minds within 90 seconds of their initial interactions with either people or products. About 62–90 % of the assessment is based on colors alone."[43] We are primed by color triggers: color excites, color calms, color conveys danger. Color, then, makes brands matter.

---

Common Color Systems:

**RGB:** Created in 1861 for photography, now used commonly for any screen-based displays (e.g., computer monitors)

**CMYK:** Created in 1906 for printed materials (e.g., magazines, packaging)

**Pantone:** Created in 1956 for paint and manufactured goods (e.g., textiles, plastics)

---

# SHERWIN-WILLIAMS

*Helping Consumers Live a More Colorful Life*

The American company founded by Henry Sherwin and Edward Williams in 1866, didn't have a logo until 27 years after it was born. The eventual logo—a tipped-over paint can pouring red paint over a blue-and-white stylized globe, with the words "Cover the Earth" in white lettering in the red paint—demonstrates to consumers what the company does: manufactures and sells paints and coatings. "Our logo represents our history and our heritage," said Mike Conway, director of corporate communications at Sherwin-Williams. "The Sherwin-Williams logo, which first appeared in 1893, is one of the most recognized in the world. It is not meant to be taken literally, rather it is a representation of our desire to protect and beautify surfaces that are important to people." While consumers might disagree with the logo's message of covering the Earth in paint, they clearly don't let their feelings interfere with their choice to shop from Sherwin-Williams. In 2016, with sales on the rise, Sherwin-Williams acquired competitor Valspar for $9 billion.[44,45]

In the crowded $30 billion women's shoe market in the United States, just ask Christian Louboutin about the significance of their red soles to their bottom line.[46] According to researchers at University of Loyola, Maryland, color can aid brand recognition by over 80%. From catwalks and red carpets to boardrooms and concert stages, Louboutins have been a must-have for stylish consumers since their introduction in 1992. They are now so famous that they've carried a trademark in the United States since 2008.[47] According to Deborah Gerhardt, a professor at the University of North Carolina Law, fewer than 1% of trademarks are for a color, making color one of the most underleveraged branding tools, given the difficulty to monopolize a particular hue in a consumer's mind.[48] For brands in competitive markets like shoes, Louboutin's signature color is known globally, benefiting from being in the pop culture zeitgeist, regularly portrayed on-screen and through oft-cited lyrics, from Cardi B's chart-breaking *Bodak Yellow* (2017) to Ariana Grande's *7 Rings* (2019), in which Ariana notes that "happiness is the price of red bottoms."

Don't be mad, but your favorite color isn't your favorite color. Since the 1970s, researchers have worked to decode color preferences among children and adults.[49,50,51,52] The general consensus: left to our own devices, men are most likely to choose blue and women are most likely to choose a blueish-green hue such as turquoise or teal. Pink? Going, going, gone. With nine out of 10 children having played with a Barbie growing up—making it one of the most popular toys of all time, alongside LEGOs—I'll venture to say that Mattel's marketing worked to convince women that they loved pink.[53] Blue, ironically, happens to be the most crowded color among Fortune 100 company brand identities—Walmart, IBM, HP, Samsung, to name a few. In fact, in any given year, the Fortune 100 companies toggle between blue and red as the most prominent color in logos . . . possibly due to the subliminal signaling of one symbol that all Americans know well—the U.S. flag.

But forget pink and blue for a second, and think purple: FedEx, Yahoo, Taco Bell. In the UK, purple became the subject of a heated legal battle between Cadbury and Nestlé. The 1905-born Cadbury company has used purple since its inception.[54] Fighting a color trademark challenge from Nestlé, the court sided with Cadbury, who argued that after 100 years of constant use, the brand and color are entwined through packaging.[55] Cadbury won, joining Christian Louboutin in the small winner's circle of branded colors.

---

Household brands with trademarks on their signature color include:
- Tiffany Blue
- UPS Pullman Brown

- 3M Post-It Canary Yellow
- T-Mobile Magenta
- Mattel Barbie Pink

---

# LYFT

*Adding Color to the "Black Car" Industry*

Logan Green and John Zimmer didn't necessarily plan on competing with Uber when they founded Lyft in 2012, but that is exactly what has happened. The ridesharing companies have been duking it out like Coke and Pepsi, or McDonald's and Burger King, for real estate on the rapidly expanding rideshare market. Lyft isn't doing too badly in this area. Its market share in the United Stated sits just above 35%. In 2018, the company was valued at more than $15 billion, after raising $600 million in venture capital funding; and in 2019, it became a publicly traded company. If anything, the company has kept pace with the industry, and may soon outflank their competitors.

Lyft always wanted to have the more personal touch. They were the first rideshare company to introduce peer-to-peer hailing, as opposed to the more formal, anonymous-black-car experience of Uber. A recent rebranding also emphasized bright pinks and warm fonts—the opposite of the "black" car. As VP and creative director Jesse McMillin put it, "Everything we've done creatively as a brand is to accentuate that fun, irreverent, human quality, energizing, colorful, any of those types of words might be the way we present a digital experience, an ad out in the world or even in your inbox. Hopefully we're doing that type of stuff there. Then when you get in the car and your driver is a little bit friendlier than the average form of transportation you might be taking that feeling is consistent through those things." Lyft is a human company, and their marketing intends to reflect that. We'll see if that changes with self-driving cars.[56,57,58,59]

Psychologists and color experts Karen Schloss and Stephen Palmer, releasing joint research while studying at University of California–Berkeley, believe that our color preferences are based on the objects we associate with those colors.[60] We associate blue with positive things like sky and water—unlike the associations we have with dark colors. The color that matters most to any tribe, then, becomes a mirror of what objects and artifacts are produced from the culture. And in that mirroring, a brand can use color as a cognitive cue. Looking for a color cue, use Encycolorpedia, an online color bible that cross-matches colors precisely across paint, Web, and print.[61] As you think about communities that interact with your brand, what colors matter most to them based on objects, rituals, or traditions? How do you mirror those colors back across your brand?

**TRY THIS:**

Color
Signature

According to researchers, 95% of Fortune 100 logos feature two colors.[62] Does your brand have two dominant colors, or one primary color and an accent? Is there a singular color you could pursue as a signature brand asset?

## SHAPE

In the United States, 20% of trademarks secured over the past 20 years are related to design (i.e., shape and function).[63] In 2002, Kit Kat started a long legal battle to protect its iconic chocolate bar shape. By the brand's 75th anniversary in 2014, over 650 bars of Kit Kat were being consumed every *second*.[64] During that history, the brand has used the iconic shape as a delivery channel for over 350 different flavors available in over 100 countries.[65] Despite the global chorus of crunches, after a16-year legal battle, their trademark was rejected in the EU in 2018 after the brand omitted four smaller EU member countries from its brand recall evidence.[66] Undoubtedly, the battle of the mind will continue to persuade the courts that their branding through shape warrants protection.

# KIT KAT

*Using Packaging to Deliver 100 Years of Flavor*

One of the world's most beloved candy bars, Kit Kat has seen many variations over its nearly 100-year lifetime—over 350 flavors, to be exact. The one part that hasn't changed? The chocolate-covered wafers' breakable rectangular shape. British company Rowntree's of York first produced the candy in 1935. The long, rectangular pieces—also known as "fingers"—designed to break apart, came about as a portable snack solution, marketed as a treat that could be taken to work in packed lunches. Over the years, the manufacturing has changed hands and grown, yet that shape holds constant. Hershey's has been licensed to produce Kit Kat in the United States since 1970, and Swiss chocolatier Nestlé bought the product from Rowntree's in 1988. With the help of large-scale production, the candy expanded beyond the United Kingdom to the Americas and Asia. The bar is now one of the most produced and eaten snacks worldwide. Nestlé reportedly creates nearly 20 billion Kit Kat bars annually, while Hershey's creates another 90 million. In 2018, Hershey's began construction on a $60 million expansion of its chocolate plant, an addition to be used solely for the production of Kit Kats. "When you make investments like this, you do so because you have confidence," said Todd Tillemans, Hershey's U.S. president. The company expects Kit Kat to be its next $1 billion global brand. Despite the brand's monstrous success, trademark patents for its iconic shape continue to be rejected by courts.[67,68,69,70]

Our need for visuals to guide pattern recognition is most pronounced among consumer packaged goods companies living on store shelves. According to Chicago-based shopper research firm Explorer, who released research in 2016 conducted among 50,000 shoppers, the long-held notion that individuals spend only three to five seconds choosing a product was upheld.[71] In an average-sized grocery store, they noted there are over 1.3 million words on labels, averaging 30 per product, of which 10 are read by consumers. With that attentiveness, any change in packaging design can have disastrous effects as brands try to modernize. In 2009, it took only 46 days before Pepsi pulled redesigned bottles of Tropicana (sporting new orange-shaped squeeze caps) from store shelves, along with its new $35 million ad campaign,[72] citing a 20% decline in sales due to an underestimation of the emotional reaction that consumers would have to changes in the classic product.[73] For brands that consumer buy on autopilot such as fast-moving commodities (e.g., orange juice), even the slightest change in packaging could squeeze a brand's bottom line.

Indiana University professor Ray Burke, a retail and shopper marketing expert, released research that affirmed the role of shape, packaging, and design in stores.[74] Citing research from the school's Customer Interface Laboratory, which he founded, we start to understand that the three to six seconds it takes to watch a gif is about the same amount of time a marketer has to convince someone to buy something in-store based on design principles: eight seconds (for products with a text-only label), six seconds (for products with a visually distinguishable label), and under two seconds (for a product with a unique color and/or shape). Examples of companies that have benefited from design trademarks are Coca-Cola for its iconic curvy bottle and Toblerone with its triangular chocolate bars.[75] Brands need to evolve with advances in communications, as we add new elements in the visual spectrum to keep pace with the shifting attentiveness and emotional triggers of audiences.

# S'WELL BOTTLES

*Using Product Design to Get a Grip on Sustainability*

Sarah Kauss needed a change. The CPA and Harvard Business School alumna wanted to do something more fulfilling with her life, something that would actually impact the world for good. After attending a panel at Harvard on the global water crisis in 2010, she started S'well in her Manhattan apartment. Kauss had a simple goal: make a water bottle that was not only convenient and effective, but also environmentally sustainable and fashionable. Soon after, Harvard began handing out S'well bottles to incoming students during Orientation Weekend. Eventually, Oprah Winfrey's magazine featured the bottle in an issue, and suddenly, Kauss' regional company was on the fast track to becoming a global breakout. Starbucks and Whole Foods came calling. S'well expanded into London and across the European Union. S'well earned $10 million in revenue in 2014; two years later, that figure increased 10 times over.

The bottle is what catches the eye. Its steel design keeps cold liquid colder and warm liquid warmer for longer periods than most plastic bottles. Its sleek, gentle curves contrast with the typically bulky athletic designs for bottles, also. S'well bottles carry over 100 external designs, kept fresh through a personalization business. But, as Kauss notes, she doesn't care whether you buy S'well because it looks cool or because you care about the environment. Either way, she is motivated to do good, and make the planet better, and leave consumers feeling swell in the process.[76,77]

## BECOMING MORE VISUAL SEARCHERS, LEARNERS, AND SHARERS

We are becoming more visual learners, searchers, and shoppers. In 2017, two major companies launched visual search tools—Pinterest and Google—and Pinterest Lens alone has grown to 600 million monthly users in 2018 (up 2.5x from launch).[78] As of 2018, nearly two-thirds of millennials prefer visual search results.[79] The emergence of Google Lens welcomed the 33% of consumers that have conducted a visual search on Google, Pinterest, or Amazon—opening the door for a new type of e-commerce (i.e., shoppable images and videos) as the image recognition market is projected to grow to a $25 billion industry in 2019, thanks to artificial intelligence and machine learning.[80]

Visual search within branded experiences is accelerating, also, allowing customers to shop using visual inspirations. Consider Wayfair, the online furniture store that has experienced double-digit annual growth from 2013 to 2018.[81] Aided by innovations in searching based on photos, companies involved in design and e-commerce, including paint brands like Sherwin-Williams that offer color matching based on a photo, are finding success through meeting the needs of visual searchers and learners. We not only want to take the photos but also make them meaningful inputs to design.

As search algorithms adjust for our visual-driven society, rich media now places higher on front-page results than Web links for Google and Bing, making people with great pieces of content more likely to be discovered than people with text-based websites. And considering the investment differential between one piece of rich media content—image or video—it is significantly more efficient to invest in content marketing than a dedicated and robust home-page or distributed ecosystem of microsites. Considering search trends for 2018, the top searched phrases on Google included two key terms—how to and what is—naturally lend themselves to visual content such as video tutorials, educational infographics, and gifs.

It's no surprise, then, that as marketers become more conversational with audiences in social media, then visual posts are more likely to be liked, favorited, and shared. People want experiences to remain focused on people and human connections, which has resulted in the most "favorited" types of photos on Instagram featuring the

FIGURE 8.2

# VISUAL SPECTRUM

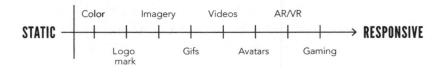

*Visual spectrum ranges from basic visual elements, such as an icon glyph that is static, to interactive elements, such as augmented and virtual reality.*

face of a person. The ever-changing landscape of communication is forcing many brands to start expanding their marketing approach from being a *social* business to a *content-driven* business. The "conversational brand" understands two things: group psychology and glyphs. Group psychology means what motivates communities. And visual glyphs both still (e.g., images) or moving (e.g., video) allow brands to evolve beyond one-way messaging (Figure 8.2).

**TRY THIS:**

Community-Member Point of View

Ditch the stock photography and write a photo brief for a group of micro influencers to capture original photos for your brand. Custom content has higher engagement rates than stock photography. By developing a roster of photographers with social followings, they will already have a sense of what communities like, and thus may increase brand engagement.

## THE JOURNEY TO BRANDS BEING CONTENT

In 2008, Twitter turned two years old and the platform hit six million global users.[82] My job at that time was as a digital strategist, and when a rogue employee of a client decided to turn to the platform to resolve customer issues, our team then worked to ensure some "law and order" in the wild, wild west of social media engagement. The client, Bank of America, then ranked Fortune 25, was already accustomed to being a digital innovator, ranking just behind the *New York Times* in terms of online traffic. Facing financial headwinds from mortgage and wealth management divisions, and an economic recession, the bank wanted to become a "conversational brand" to rebuild trust. A decade later, being a conversational brand is still a priority for businesses, both large and small; however, the parts of that conversation look different. By 2012, I started working on digital PR and branded content for HP, which at the time was ranked Fortune 10. Consumer electronics was one of the most talked about categories online among consumers, and PR was rapidly expanding to include reviews, influencer marketing, and content. The HP brand was the 10th largest branded content producer on YouTube, following Disney and Red Bull, and the notion of "the conversational brand" was starting to crystallize as a mainstream notion that moved from text-based replies to rich media-based audience interactions.

Historically, the most-watched television program in the United States is the Super Bowl, averaging over 100 million viewers.[83] In 2018, the top non-sports show on television was *This Is Us*, attracting over 30 million viewers. With Super Bowl ads fetching $5 million and *This Is Us* charging up to $1 million per commercial, brands have been building their own media channels to connect with consumers at a fraction of the costs, instead investing in content, experiences, and events that create "moments" worth sharing.[84]

No surprise then, that the top brands like Nike have surpassed 100 million followers across their social channels, rivaling the television networks that once were the only channels with efficient mass outreach. With the built-in ability to go direct to consumer, the roles of Fox, ABC, NBC, and CBS in taking brands into 100 million households is becoming less important. Brands that have amassed an army of social media followers larger than media company's liner and digital footprint combined now spans every category, including tech (Google, Samsung, Nintendo, PlayStation), fashion (Chanel, Gucci), and lifestyle (Starbucks, Mac Cosmetics). One unexpected brand that has led the charge in becoming a conversation brand is NASA; originally launched in the 1960s, the space program has over 75 million social followers.

# NASA

*Keeping a Brand in the Pop Culture Orbit*

Most federal agencies would not be featured in an analysis of brand strategies. And yet, the National Aeronautics and Space Administration is the government entity that is undoubtedly the most successful at brand awareness, if one can call it that. The 60-year-old agency is responsible for sending Americans in space to explore the vastly unknown galaxy. It's not just what NASA does that makes people pay attention; their logo is one of the most distinctive and evergreen in American pop culture. Back in 1959, Research Center Reports Division head James Modarelli designed the logo: a blue planet with the letters N-A-S-A across it. Publicly, the logo debuted to many Americans as a patch on the space suits of Neil Armstrong's crew when they landed Apollo 11 on the moon in 1969. NASA's marketing has even expanded into the social sphere. NASA operates accounts on Giphy and Pinterest, ensuring that younger generations will continue to engage with the agency, even if people aren't walking on the moon anymore. NASA gifs have been viewed almost one billion times on Giphy. NASA has maneuvered its way into memory of Americans through box office hits, including *Gravity, The Martian, Hidden Figures,* and Netflix's *IO.* NASA continues to wend its way through the American imagination, and will continue to make us stare up at the sky, and down at our screens, for decades to come.[85,86,87]

Brand reputation is based on what people say about you . . . and brands giving consumers content that fuels positive social conversation are finding success in releasing their own media directly to communities. Communicating using visuals is now a natural part of living in a digital world—thumbs-up (e.g., Facebook Like), hearts (e.g., Instagram), stars (e.g., Amazon), emojis, and gifs—whether leaving reviews, posting on social media, texting, or emailing. As marketers fight for consumer attentiveness, and every second counts, it helps that humans can process visuals in milliseconds, an instant triggering and transferring of feelings and emotions based on visual stimuli. Brands need to reinforce positive feelings by being mindful of what visual systems they're using for customer reviews, feedback, and testimonials.

## WELCOME TO THE NEWEST COMMUNICATION CLUB MEMBERS

So how long does it take a new form of communication like an emoji to cross the chasm into the mainstream? Shorter than you think when we map the rise of emojis and gifs, whose global impact on communication should have every marketer, strategist, and entrepreneur reevaluating their brand guidelines and communication approach. One visual format propelling the conversational brand forward is emojis, invented by Shigetaka Kurita in Japan in 1999.[88] The quickly rising communication format dubbed "visual paralinguistics" by researchers is now used by nearly 98% of mobile phone users to express themselves. In 2015, when the term emoji experienced a 300% increase in popularity, Oxford Dictionaries named it their Word of the Year.[89] To reinforce, it took all of five years for a new format to gain near-perfect market penetration as a dominant visual lexicon. Have your brand guidelines been updated in the past five years?

Other than math, emojis have elevated visual communication to universal levels, helping mitigate ineffable moments. Emojis are updated once a year based on nominations and pop-culture shifts. Although invented in Japan, emojis are centrally regulated by the Unicode Consortium, which is comprised of nearly 200 global members that include major technology companies Apple, Google, Microsoft, and Netflix.[90] Collectively, the consortium regulates over 1,600 official emojis. And still, there have been thousands of unregulated emojis created by brands directly and released through custom mobile keyboards.[91] In the first year that Twitter supported emojis (April 2014 – April 2015), the visual iconography was used 200 million times.[92] By the end of 2015, according to Emogi, a startup that creates emojis for brands to facilitate deeper consumer engagements, nearly 30% of people send emojis several times a day.[93] By 2018, billions of emojis were being used on Twitter by users that ranged from government officials to nonprofits. Ultimately, emojis help convey context, and their staggering growth is forcing brands to expand their brand guidelines and brand personality.

As language and expression evolves, new dictionaries become necessary to catalog meaning. Launched in 2013, Emojipedia catalogs over 2,800 different emoji meaning and nuances, including links to similar emojis across 20 platforms. The creators of World Emoji Day, celebrated annually on July 17 starting in 2014, Emojipedia is one unofficial glyph dictionary for today's lexophile.[94]

Pervasiveness of emojis in visual culture has now infiltrated both product design (e.g., how we give feedback/ratings to companies through survey interfaces with smiley faces) and business models. Several brands have turned to custom emojis (i.e., emoticons) based on their brand personality to connect with audiences. In 2015, as emojis started to gain mainstream global adoption, the World Wildlife Foundation (WWF) launched a campaign to raise awareness for endangered species—enthusiasts could donate to the charity by simply sharing select animal emojis. Launched on World Endangered Species Day, May 17, the use of a new communication tool resulted in nearly 60,000 donation and 200,000 new followers within two months.[95]

Brands are rushing to claim cognitive shelf space of emojis, using the visual communication format to trigger brand recall for products from tacos to pizza. In 2015, soon after their mass adoption, both Taco Bell and Dominos lobbied the Unicode Consortium, as well as operating systems, to add emojis respective to their products. By 2017, Dominos was combining emojis with new platforms like Slack to introduce a new revenue stream of ordering via digital channels. With 90% of consumers using emojis,[96] over 250 brands have created custom keyboards for emojis, including Starbucks and Thompson Bagels.[97] In late 2018, just six months after Thompson Bagels introduced bagel emojis on their own, Apple took note and added the first bagel emoji to iOS devices—a great feat for a brand evolving its role in the visual lexicon of consumers. By 2016, entertainment companies hacked emoji culture: the $700 million Deadpool blockbuster from Twentieth Century Fox featured skull and poop emojis in billboard advertising.[98] The tipping point in the global emoji craze came with the 2017 release of the "Emoji" movie, considered the worst movie of the year by the Razzies. Nonetheless, the movie grossed over $200 million worldwide, signaling our unbreakable bond and infatuation with the new communication format that is giving brands a conversational personality.[99] Yet, rarely still, brand visual identity guidelines actually account for the "can't live without" glyphs of emojis in their communication approach.

**TRY THIS:**

Emoji Vocabulary

What are the top emojis that would represent your brand's personality? What emojis do your customers use most in social media posts?

# DJ KHALED

*Giving Audiences the Keys to Their Success*

The "key" emoji hijacked by DJ Khaled made its debut as a part of the 2008 Apple emoji keyboard. Its founders couldn't imagine it would become one of the most used emojis of all time. The affiliation with DJ Khaled began when the renowned DJ, artist, record producer, and overall social media influencer, used the key emoji as his trademark ascension into the pop culture zeitgeist in late 2015. In addition to his recognition as a brand unto himself in the music business, DJ Khaled is also known for his inspirational social posts, books, and speeches, from which he draws quotes and creates memes to share across social media, specifically Snapchat. Khaled's use of emojis has drawn attention from companies like Mastercard, who used Khaled's phrase and the key emoji in their advertising. Benefiting from quickly making emojis a part of his brand, DJ Khaled started a movement that left audiences feelings positive, motivated, and empowered, all through a visual glyph.[100,101]

## THE NEW MOVING IMAGE

As emojis were infiltrating text messages and social media posts, gifs were awakening for their primetime debut. Benefiting from the rise of video and popularity of emojis, gifs represent a happy medium between image, video, and memes. Google enjoys nearly 90% market penetration, yet even at that scale it is watching newer communication companies like Giphy claim consumer attention. In 2018, Giphy garnered a staggering one tenth of the search volume of Google. And that figure is increasing daily. As a result, gifs mark the second example of how fast communication can shift toward a new format; like emojis, gifs exploded within a five-year period.

According to the founder of Giphy, Alex Chung, who spoke about the surge in usage of the visual format at SXSW in 2018, "gifs are the LEGOs of visual communication ... an entire lexicon of expression and emotion." In a noisy world, the new communication rules of sparking feelings and behavior requires being short and entertaining. In 2018, top brands on Giphy included Cardi B, Hallmark, Absolut Vodka, and the NFL, who all rounded out the top 10 most-sent gifs at nearly a million each. Rounding out the top 20 gifs sent in 2018 were Walt Disney, the NBA, and startup Bubly.[102] Is your brand fluent in the modern communication languages of today—gifs, emojis, and memes? The growth of platforms from Giphy, Imgur, and Bitmoji now requires brands to ask how they are enabling customers to use their brand symbols, assets, and marketing to express ideas in conversations—glyphs for text, group chats, and beyond.

As brand managers create a holistic ecosystem, content initially was the glue between experiences. Data and personalization are now central to experience. We are experiencing yet another shift, from "brand as publisher" to "brand as content." While most brands want to become media publishers (i.e., Red Bull, Mountain Dew, Pepsi, etc.)—creating magazines, television shows, and music labels—consumers are busy hijacking brand moments to create their own memes, gifs, and videos from brand assets. Does your brand make it easy for consumers to make your key visuals a part of their conversations?

| **TRY THIS:** | What symbols and visuals (e.g., images) inspire your desired brand feeling? Which prompt the opposite feeling? |
| Sticky Visuals | |

# NBA

*Putting the "Instant Replay" on Repeat*

The NBA is unique from other professional athletics leagues in its welcoming attitude toward social media. Founded in the late 1940s as a merger between the Basketball Association of America (BAA) and the National Basketball League (NBL), it is much younger than leagues such as the Major League Baseball (MLB) and National Football League (NFL), which have been around since the 1860s and 1920s, respectively. Perhaps it is the NBA's youth that inspired the league to embrace social media tactics as a means of inciting consumer engagement. As social media platforms such as Twitter and Facebook use integrated visual features such as streamlined gif searchability, the NBA uses the visual function as a way to keep younger, tech-savvy consumers interested in the league.

"Gifs enable users to avail themselves of the entire catalog of popular culture to help express themselves," said Jeremy Liew, an early investor of Giphy. "Art, TV, movies, memes, all become part of the alphabet, enabling richer, funnier, more contextual, more personalized communication than ever before." The NBA pushes highlights to Giphy directly following games, enabling and potentially even encouraging social media users to share gifs of the games virally. Gifs allow visual communication, focusing on context as opposed to description, and are therefore quite an accessible marketing technique.

As NBA gifs were shared on social media, the engagement between consumers and the league advanced. Fans could comment and participate in real-time, exchanging clever captions and making observations on small events happening in the stands, huddles, or action of the games. This experiment proved successful for the NBA; in 2018, the NBA was the most tweeted-about sports league, in addition to having the most shared gif moments on Giphy among all sports leagues, proving the power of consumers inviting brands into the conversation when they supply the content types that matter most to their community.[103,104,105,106]

# TRACKING EVOLUTION ONE DICTIONARY AT A TIME

Language is ever-evolving, and its evolution is starting to include more than text-based mental cues. The leapfrogs happening in language are evidenced by the new types of dictionaries and speed of adoption in use among global community members.

Two key trends emerge when we look at the evolution of dictionaries: communities controlling context and a return to glyphs. Communities being able to define language publicly signals the growing influence and strength of tribes in shaping culture and conversation. And all the new dictionaries represent a real-time competition among clusters in culture. Each new dictionary symbolizes a new community emerging, and each new community represents a new connection opportunity for marketers. Second, we are returning to a compressed society of glyphs, participating in an arc of expression that began with markings on cave walls. Now by choice, given the full arsenal of words, audio, and visuals, we are creating and unlocking new meaning around feelings, based on compressing triggers into the zeitgeist of gifs, emojis, and icons (Figure 8.3). Goodbye, words. Hello, glyphs and moving images.

## FIGURE 8.3
## EVOLUTION OF DICTIONARIES

|  | STARTED | CATALOGS | ENTRY COUNT | NEW ENTRIES ANNUALLY |
|---|---|---|---|---|
| **Merriam-Webster** | 1828 | Words | 500K | 1K |
| **Oxford Dictionaries** | 1870 | Words | 1M | 1K |
| **Urban Dictionary** | 1999 | Words | 7M | 100K |
| **Noun Project** | 2010 | Symbols, Icons | 1M | 100K |
| **Emojipedia** | 2013 | Emojis | 2,300 | 100 |
| **Giphy** | 2013 | Gifs, Video | 1M | 100K |

## CONCLUSION

Because the way we consume content is shifting from in-depth to scanning, brands needs to pass a scroll test. In-store, are you identifiable within three seconds? In social and online, does your content visually capture attention among a sea of sameness by compressing information? According to Facebook creative director Andrew Geller, brands are competing to stand out in the 300 feet of content that consumers scroll through on any given day.[107] Taking 3–24 months to get trademarks in the United States, the UK, China, Brazil, France, and Germany, building a brand cannot wait for approval on a logo mark, shape, or color. With over 50% of trademarks initially rejected, "brand" must become more than your mark; and brand leaders and strategists must understand that the long road to building visual recall starts and ends with consistency.[108] And that consistency needs to be positive, and reinforced through positive experiences.

Move over, English, Spanish, and Chinese, which is spoken by one-third of world's population.[109] With over 7,000 tracked languages in the world, we're seeing a return to glyphs as a universal visual language.[110] They're simple, fast, and effective at conveying information and spurring feelings and behavior. Our speed in processing visuals over text, and possibly also over recognizing audio, means visuals are a magic key to unlocking consumer attention. Not only are glyphs like emojis becoming a fast-growing substitute for words, but icons are proliferating in design. A global "flattening" of language into the 2D form abandoned by the Egyptians for what was perceived to be more advanced forms of communication—words—is experiencing a resurgence as the noise around us forces us to find shortcuts to meaningfulness. Based on new social and technological evolutions, the African proverb should shift from "If you want to travel fast, go alone, and if you want to travel far, go together" to "If you want to trend, use a hashtag; but if you want be universal, use a glyph."

## 🔥 FIRE STARTERS

### BECOMING THE "CONVERSATIONAL" BRAND

**VISUAL STIMULI**

☐ *If you had to rewrite your brand mission statement using only five emojis, which would you include?*

☐ *What two or three gifs best describe your brand's internal culture?*

☐ *What colors matter most to your key communities based on their shared culture of objects, rituals, or traditions, and how can your brand mirror those colors back across the brand?*

# Notes

1. Jay-Z and Beyoncé, "Visitor Trails." Louvre. Accessed February 1, 2019. https://www.louvre.fr/en/routes/jay-z-and-beyonce-louvre.
2. Maiysha Kai, "Thanks to Beyoncé and Jay-Z, Visitors Went 'Apeshit' at the Louvre in 2018—But a Fan Cries Foul." *The Root*, January 4, 2019. https://thegrapevine.theroot.com/thanks-to-beyonce-and-jay-z-visitors-went-apeshit-at-t-1831486393.
3. Jake Indiana, "A Breakdown of All the Masterpieces in Beyoncé & Jay-Z's Stunning 'Apeshit,'" *Highsnobiety*, June 18, 2018. https://www.highsnobiety.com/p/beyonce-jay-z-apeshit-video-art/.
4. Anne Trafton, "In the Blink of an Eye MIT Neuroscientists Find the Brain Can Identify Images Seen for as Little as 13 Milliseconds." MIT News, January 16, 2014. http://news.mit.edu/2014/in-the-blink-of-an-eye-0116.
5. Gabriella Munoz, "How Fast Is a Blink of an Eye?" *Sciencing*, May 14, 2018. https://sciencing.com/fast-blink-eye-5199669.html.
6. Claire D. Vallotton and Catherine C. Ayoub, "Symbols Build Communication and Thought: The Role of Gestures and Words in the Development of Engagement Skills and Social-emotional Concepts during Toddlerhood." *Social Development* 19, no. 3 (2009), 601–626. doi:10.1111/j.1467-9507.2009.00549.x.

7. Beth Sagar-Fenton and Lizzy McNeill, "How Many Words Do You Need to Speak a Language?" BBC, June 24, 2018. https://www.bbc.com/news/world-44569277.

8. Ibid.

9. "How Many Words Are There in English?" Merriam-Webster. Accessed February 1, 2019. https://www.merriam-webster.com/help/faq-how-many-english-words.

10. "We Put a Bunch of New Words in the Dictionary." Merriam-Webster. Accessed February 1, 2019. https://www.merriam-webster.com/words-at-play/new-words-in-the-dictionary-september-2018.

11. "Internet Trends Report 2018." KLEINER PERKINS, May 30, 2018. https://www.kleinerperkins.com/perspectives/internet-trends-report-2018/.

12. Caroline Cakebread, "People Will Take 1.2 Trillion Digital Photos This Year—Thanks to Smartphones." *Business Insider*, September 1, 2017. https://www.businessinsider.com/12-trillion-photos-to-be-taken-in-2017-thanks-to-smartphones-chart-2017-8.

13. Catherine Clifford, "Airbnb, Why the New Logo?" *Entrepreneur*, July 17, 2014. https://www.entrepreneur.com/article/235709.

14. Trefis Team, "As a Rare Profitable Unicorn, Airbnb Appears to Be Worth at Least $38 Billion." *Forbes*, March 11, 2018. https://www.forbes.com/sites/greatspeculations/2018/05/11/as-a-rare-profitable-unicorn-airbnb-appears-to-be-worth-at-least-38-billion/#3b0f31a42741.

15. "Fast Facts." Airbnb. Accessed February 1, 2019. https://press.airbnb.com/en-uk/fast-facts/.

16. Lauren Alpe, "The History of Airbnb." *Telegraph*, December 1, 2015. https://www.telegraph.co.uk/technology/technology-video/12021531/the-history-of-airbnb.html.

17. "Ancient Egypt: Symbols of the Pharaoh." British Museum. Accessed February 1, 2019. https://www.britishmuseum.org/PDF/Visit_Egypt_Symbols_KS2.pdf.

18. "An Explanation of Hieroglyphics." History-World. Accessed February 1, 2019. http://history-world.org/hieroglyphics.htm.

19. "Ancient Egypt: Symbols of the Pharaoh." British Museum. Accessed February 1, 2019. https://www.britishmuseum.org/PDF/Visit_Egypt_Symbols_KS2.pdf.

20. "Clip Art." Wikipedia. Last updated on February 1, 2019. Accessed February 1, 2019. https://en.wikipedia.org/wiki/Clip_art.

21. "Noun Project." Made with Creative Commons, September 19, 2017. Accessed February 1, 2019. https://medium.com/made-with-creative-commons/the

-twenty-four-case-studies-in-made-with-cc-were-chosen-from-hundreds-of-nominations-received-from-93f37876733c.

22. "A Smile Is Forever on the Amazon." Story Board, August 12, 2014. http://www.vmastoryboard.com/case-stories/2648/turner_duckworth_amazon_smile_logo/#sthash.RnXOR0o9.FovaTQ9a.dpbs.

23. "The History of Amazon and Their Logo Design." Logo My Way, February 12, 2017. http://blog.logomyway.com/history-amazon-logo-design/.

24. "History of the Amazon Logo." Fine Print Art (blog). Accessed February 1, 2019. https://www.fineprintart.com/art/history-of-the-amazon-logo.

25. "McDonald's 'bigger than Jesus Christ,'" *Marketing Week*, July 21, 1995. https://www.marketingweek.com/1995/07/21/mcdonalds-bigger-than-jesus-christ/.

26. "The Cross." BBC, September 12, 2011. http://www.bbc.co.uk/religion/religions/christianity/symbols/cross_1.shtml.

27. Martin Lindstrom, *Buyology: Truth and Lies about Why We Buy.* New York: Doubleday, 2008.

28. Dean Balsamini, "Trump Campaign Has Sold More Than Half a Million 'MAGA' Hats." *New York Post*, April 29, 2017. https://nypost.com/2017/04/29/trump-campaign-sold-more-than-half-a-million-maga-hats/.

29. "The Original Porsche Crest as a Quality Seal." Porsche. Accessed February 1, 2019. https://www.porsche.com/international/accessoriesandservice/classic/genuineparts/producthighlights/crest/.

30. Loeber Motors, "Find Out How the Porsche Logo Came to Be." Loeber Motors, September 26, 2014. https://www.loebermotors.com/blog/what-does-porsche-logo-stand-for/.

31. "Behind the Badge: Revealing the Historic Porsche Crest's Inspiration." *The News Wheel*, April 28, 2015. https://thenewswheel.com/behind-the-badge-revealing-the-historic-porsche-crests-inspiration/#Emblem-Meaning.

32. "Origins and Making of the Porsche Crest." Logo Design Love, May 30, 2017. https://www.logodesignlove.com/porsche-crest-origins.

33. Nabin Paudyal, "Top 20 Most Popular Fonts of All Time." *Lifehack*, https://www.lifehack.org/428846/top-20-most-popular-fonts-of-all-time.

34. Jesus Diaz, "Designers at Top Companies Don't Use Trendy Fonts. Here's What They Use Instead." *Fast Company*, August 21, 2018. https://www.fastcompany.com/90220770/designers-at-top-companies-dont-use-trendy-fonts-heres-what-they-use-instead.

35. Dave Crossland, "How Many Fonts Are There?" TypeDrawers, December 2015. https://typedrawers.com/discussion/1289/how-many-fonts-are-there.

36. Connor Diemand-Yauman, Daniel M. Oppenheimer, and Erikka B. Vaughan, "Fortune Favors the Effects of Disfluency on Educational Outcomes." *Cognition* 118 (2010), 111–115. doi:10.1016/j.cognition .2010.09.012.

37. Ibid.

38. "Sans Forgetica: New Typeface Designed to Help Students Study." Rmit. edu.au, October 26, 2018. https://www.rmit.edu.au/news/all-news/2018/ oct/sans-forgetica-news-story.

39. Ryan Martin, "Signs.com Named as a Fast 500 Company!" Signs Inc., November 9, 2017. https://www.signs.com/blog/signs-com-fast-500/.

40. "Signs.com: Number 458 on the 2018 Inc. 5000." *Inc.* Accessed February 1, 2019. https://www.inc.com/profile/signscom.

41. "IphoneX." Apple. Accessed February 1, 2019. https://www.apple.com/ iphone-xr/specs/.

42. "Pantone Numbering Explained." Pantone. Accessed February 1, 2019. https://www.pantone.com/color-intelligence/articles/technical/pantone-numbering-explained.

43. Satyendra Singh, "Impact of Color on Marketing." *Emerald Insight* 44, no. 6 (2006): 783–789. doi:10.1108/00251740610673332.

44. Rick Barrack, "You Asked, and Rick Answers: A Revamp Of the Sherwin-Williams Logo." *Fast Company*, August 4, 2011. https://www .fastcompany.com/1663585/you-asked-and-rick-answers-a-revamp-of-the-sherwin-williams-logo.

45. David Griner, "Now It's Sherwin-Williams' Turn for a Much-Needed New Logo, Right?" *Adweek*, September 3, 2015. https://www.adweek.com/creativity/ now-its-sherwin-williams-turn-much-needed-new-logo-right-166701/.

46. Megan Woolhouse, "Men's Shoes Could Soon Outsell Women's." *Boston Globe*, May 4, 2017. https://www.bostonglobe.com/business/2017/05/03/ stepping-their-game-men-shoes-get-makeover/ankLTmsRNOYPuOl-UEd1aTO/story.html.

47. Elizabeth Snead, "Christian Louboutin Continues to Fight for His Red-Soled High Heels Trademark (Poll)." *Hollywood Reporter*, January 31, 2012. https://www.hollywoodreporter.com/news/christian-louboutin-continues-fight-his-red-soled-high-heels-trademark-poll-286183.

48. "Seeing Red: Can a Brand Trademark a Signature Color?" Knowledge@ Wharton, February 21, 2018. http://knowledge.wharton.upenn.edu/ article/louboutin-red-soles/.

49. Abigail Cain, "Why Blue Is the World's Favorite Color." Artsy, August 29, 2017. https://www.artsy.net/article/artsy-editorial-blue-worlds-favorite-color.

50. Sjoerd Wiegersmas and Gerard Van Der Elst, "'Blue Phenomenon': Spontaneity or Preference?" *Perceptual and Motor Skills* 66, no. 1 (February 1988): 308–310. doi:10.2466/pms.1988.66.1.308.

51. Claudia Hammond, "The 'Pink vs Blue' Gender Myth." BBC, November 18, 2014. http://www.bbc.com/future/story/20141117-the-pink-vs-blue-gender-myth.

52. Jessica Alleva, "Blue Is for Boys *and* Girls." *Psychology Today*, September 7, 2018. https://www.psychologytoday.com/us/blog/mind-your-body/201809/blue-is-boys-and-girls.

53. "Does Mattel's Iconic Barbie Doll Need a Makeover?" Accessed February 1, 2019. https://hbr.org/product/does-mattels-iconic-barbie-doll-need-a-makeover/W16090-PDF-ENG.

54. "Name That Color: Cadbury Purple, Tiffany Blue and Other Signature Hues." *Washington Post*, October 4, 2013. https://www.washingtonpost.com/business/economy/name-that-color-cadbury-purple-tiffany-blue-and-other-signature-hues/2013/10/04/6764131e-2d05-11e3-97a3-ff2758228523_gallery.html.

55. "Trademark Dispute on the Colour Purple Cadbury vs Nestlé." Edmonton & Calgary Patents, June 1, 2017. http://trademarkspatentslawyer.com/trademark-dispute-colour-purple-cadbury-vs-nestle/.

56. Kristina Monllos, "Lyft's Poppy, Colorful New Look, Signature Font and Icons Are Meant to Energize the Growing Brand." *Adweek*, May 10, 2018. https://www.adweek.com/brand-marketing/lyfts-poppy-colorful-new-look-signature-font-and-icons-are-meant-to-energize-the-growing-brand/.

57. Simon Mainwaring, "How Lyft Drives Growth through Purpose." *Forbes*, October 16, 2018. https://www.forbes.com/sites/simon-mainwaring/2018/10/16/how-lyft-drives-growth-through-purpose/#11c0cc4c15f1.

58. Greg Bensinger, "Lyft's Valuation Doubles to $15.1 Billion Over One Year in Battle with Uber." *Wall Street Journal*, June 27, 2018. https://www.wsj.com/articles/lyfts-valuation-doubles-to-15-1-billion-over-one-year-in-battle-with-uber-1530115200/.

59. Nandu Anilal, "Lyft's Quiet Success in Ridesharing—The Startup—Medium." *Medium*, May 21, 2018. https://medium.com/swlh/lyfts-quiet-success-in-ridesharing-24f6ca689631.

60. Stephen E. Palmer and Karen B. Schloss, "An Ecological Valence Theory of Human Color Preference." Proceedings of the National Academy of

Sciences 7, no. 19 (May 11, 2010), 8877–8882. https://www.pnas.org/content/107/19/8877.

61. "Hex Colors, Color Picker, Directory, Schemes, Paint Search & Conversions." Encycolorpedia. Accessed February 1, 2019. https://encycolorpedia.com/.

62. Milano K. Valihura, "A Cheat Sheet for Choosing the Best Logo Colors That Will Grab Your Audience's Eye." Foundr, July 24, 2018. https://foundr.com/best-logo-colors/.

63. Business Radio. "Seeing Red: Can a Brand Trademark a Signature Color?" Knowledge@Wharton, February 21, 2018. http://knowledge.wharton.upenn.edu/article/louboutin-red-soles/.

64. Lenore Fedow, "Sake-flavored Kit Kat Released in Japan." CNBC, March 1, 2016. https://www.cnbc.com/2016/02/02/sake-flavored-kitkat-released-in-japan.html.

65. Tingmin Koe, "Kit Kat Japan Hits 350 Flavour Milestone with Matcha Taking Top Sales Spot." FoodNavigator-Asia, December 10, 2018. https://www.foodnavigator-asia.com/Article/2018/12/10/KitKat-Japan-hits-350-flavour-milestone-with-matcha-taking-top-sales-spot.

66. Steve Oakes and Adrian C. North, "Using Music to Influence Cognitive and Affective Responses in Queues of Low and High Crowd Density." Journal of Marketing Management 24, no. 5–6 (2008), 589–602. doi:10.1362/026725708x326002.

67. "Kit Kat." Nestlé. Accessed February 1, 2019. https://www.nestle.com/investors/brand-focus/kitkat.

68. Micheline Maynard, "Kit Kat Lovers, Listen Up: Hershey Is Betting Big That You'll Break Off More." Forbes, March 11, 2018. https://www.forbes.com/sites/michelinemaynard/2018/03/11/kit-kat-lovers-listen-up-hershey-is-betting-big-that-youll-break-off-more/#46a93d007975.

69. James Moore, "Kit Kat Pink Bar: 20 Facts about Choc Favourite as Colourful New Product Launches." Daily Star, April 11, 2018. https://www.dailystar.co.uk/news/weird-news/695340/pink-kitkat-chocolate-bars-20-facts-bestselling-brand-history.

70. Ibid.

71. "Packaging Has Only One or Two Seconds to Engage Your Customer." Explorer Research, May 1, 2018. https://explorerresearch.com/optimize-your-package/.

72. Natalie Zamuda, "Tropicana Line's Sales Plunge 20% Post-Rebranding." Ad Age, April 2, 2009. https://adage.com/article/news/tropicana-line-s-sales-plunge-20-post-rebranding/135735/.

73. Marion Andrivet, "What to Learn from Tropicana's Packaging Redesign Failure?" *Branding Journal*, May 21, 2018. https://www.thebranding journal.com/2015/05/what-to-learn-from-tropicanas-packaging-redesign-failure/.

74. "How Stores Track Your Shopping Behavior." Performed by Ray Burke. YouTube, November 25, 2014. https://www.youtube.com/watch?v=jeQ7 C4JLpug&feature=youtu.be.

75. Scheherazade Daneshkhu, "Why You Can Trademark a Toblerone but Not a KitKat." *Financial Times*, June 28, 2017. https://www.ft.com/content/16351d98-46d9-11e7-8d27-59b4dd6296b8.

76. Chloe Sorvino, "Why S'well Bottle Founder Sarah Kauss Is One of America's Most Successful Self-Made Women." *Forbes*, May 19, 2017. https://www.forbes.com/sites/chloesorvino/2017/05/18/swell-bottle-founder-sarah-kauss-americas-most-successful-self-made-women/#499a532102f9.

77. Carla Rover, "Making Eco-Friendly Eco-Chic—Sarah Kauss, CEO at S'Well Bottle." *Forefont*, January 3, 2013. http://www.forefrontmag .com/2013/01/making-eco-friendly-eco-chic/.

78. Yoram Wurmser, "Visual Search 2018." *Emarketer*, September 26, 2018. https://www.emarketer.com/content/visual-search-2018.

79. Yoram Wurmser, "Executive Summary." *E Marketer*, September 26, 2018. https://www.emarketer.com/content/visual-search-2018.

80. Clark Boyd, "Visual Search Statistics, Trends, Tips, and Uses in Everyday Life." Medium.com, August 6, 2018. https://medium.com/@clarkboyd/visual-search-trends-statistics-tips-and-uses-in-everyday-life-d20084dc4b0a.

81. "Wayfair." Wikipedia. Last updated on January 14, 2019. Accessed February 1, 2019. https://en.wikipedia.org/wiki/Wayfair.

82. Adam Ostrow, "18 Million Twitter Users by End of 2009." *Mashable*, September 24, 2019. https://mashable.com/2009/09/14/twitter-2009-stats/#_99UjoPGfSqx.

83. "TV Viewership of the Super Bowl in the United States from 1990 to 2018 (in millions)." Statista, 2018. Accessed February 1, 2019. https://www .statista.com/statistics/216526/super-bowl-us-tv-viewership/.

84. Garry Levin, "2018 in Review: The Year's Most Popular TV Shows According to Nielsen." *USA Today*, December 17, 2018. https://www .usatoday.com/story/life/tv/2018/12/17/2018-review-nielsen-ranks-years-most-popular-tv-shows/2339279002/.

85. "NASA." Giphy. Accessed February 1, 2019. https://giphy.com/nasa.

86. Steve Garber, "NASA 'Meatball' Logo." National Aeronautics and Space Administration 688 (August 31, 1957). https://history.nasa.gov/meatball.htm.

87. Steven J. Dick, "50 Years of NASA History." NASA. Accessed February 1, 2019. https://www.nasa.gov/50th/50th_magazine/historyLetter.html.

88. Jacapo Priscos, "Shigetaka Kurita: The Man Who Invented Emoji." CNN, May 22, 2018. https://www.cnn.com/style/article/emoji-shigetaka-kurita-standards-manual/index.html.

89. "Word of the Year 2015." Oxford Dictionaries, 2015. Accessed February 1, 2019. https://en.oxforddictionaries.com/word-of-the-year/word-of-the-year-2015.

90. "Levels." Unicode Consortium. Accessed February 1, 2019. http://unicode.org/consortium/levels.html.

91. "Full Emoji List, V11.0." Emoji Charts. https://unicode.org/emoji/charts/full-emoji-list.html.

92. "W K London's 'Endangered Emojis' Turn Tweets Into Donations for WWF." Little Black Book Celebrating Creativity, May 12, 2015. https://lbbonline.com/news/wk-londons-endangered-emojis-turn-tweets-into-donations-for-wwf/.

93. "Insights." Emogi. Accessed February 1, 2019. https://emogi.com/insights.

94. EmojiPedia. Accessed February 1, 2019. https://emojipedia.org/.

95. Natalie Mortimer, "Lessons from WWF's #EndangeredEmoji Campaign." The Drum, July 28, 2015. https://www.thedrum.com/news/2015/07/28/lessons-wwf-s-endangeredemoji-campaign.

96. Asler Aranguiz, "8 Fun and Inspiring Examples of Emoji Marketing Campaigns." Social Seeder, February 22, 2018. https://www.socialseeder.com/blog/8-best-and-worst-emoji-marketing-campaigns/.

97. "Six Ways Brands Successfully Market with Emojis." EmojiOne, June 9, 2017. https://www.emojione.com/blog/six-ways-brands-successfully-market-with-emoji-2.

98. Laura Schembri, "Top 5 Brands with Killer Emoji Campaigns." Redorange Image Consultants, August 28, 2018. https://www.redorange.com.mt/top-5-brands-with-killer-emoji-campaigns/.

99. The Emoji Movie. IMDB, 2017. Accessed February 1, 2019. https://www.imdb.com/title/tt4877122/.

100. Jennifer Walpole. "What the Golden Key Emoji Really Means." The American Genius, February 29, 2016. https://theamericangenius.com/social-media/golden-key-emoji-really-means/.

101. Alex Health, "Here's How DJ Khaled Single-handedly Used Snapchat to Turn the Key Emoji into a Cultural Icon." *Business Insider*, January 13, 2016. https://www.businessinsider.com/dj-khaleds-snapchat-key-emoji-2016-1.

102. Giphy. "GIPHY's Top 25 GIFs of 2018—GIPHY—Medium." Medium, December 3, 2018. https://medium.com/@giphy/giphys-top-25-gifs-of-2018-c07d24b1d29c.

103. Michelle P. "Is That Even Legal? Animated GIFs and Copyright Law." Modicum Agency. Accessed February 1, 2019. https://modicum.agency/blog/animated-gifs-fair-use-copyright-law/.

104. Brandon Wiggins, "Adam Silver Explains Why the NBA Is Far More Liberal with Sharing Highlights on Social Media Than Other Leagues." *Business Insider*, May 4, 2018. https://www.businessinsider.com/adam-silver-nba-ok-highlights-social-media-twitter-gifs-2018-5.

105. Rickj Maese, "NBA Twitter: A Sports Bar That Doesn't Close, Where the Stars Pull Up a Seat Next to You." *Washington Post*, May 31, 2018. https://www.washingtonpost.com/news/sports/wp/2018/05/31/nba-twitter-a-sports-bar-that-doesnt-close-where-the-stars-pull-up-a-seat-next-to-you.

106. Brad Adgate, "Why the 2017–18 Season Was Great for the NBA." *Forbes*, April 25, 2018. https://www.forbes.com/sites/bradadgate/2018/04/25/the-2017-18-season-was-great-for-the-nba/#6b1662f92ecb.

107. Conor Ryan, "How Brands Can Optimize Facebook Ads to Steal Holiday Shoppers from Amazon." *Adweek*, November 17, 2017. https://www.adweek.com/digital/conor-ryan-stitcherads-guest-post-facebook-ads-holiday-shoppers-amazon/.

108. United States Patent and Trademark Office—An Agency of the Department of Commerce. https://www.uspto.gov/dashboards/trademarks/main.dashxml.

109. Joe Myers, "These Are the World's Most Spoken Languages." Weforum, February 22, 2018. https://www.weforum.org/agenda/2018/02/chart-of-the-day-these-are-the-world-s-most-spoken-languages/.

110. "It's Hard to Find Clarity in a Sea of Over 7,000 Languages." Ethnologue. Accessed February 1, 2019. https://www.ethnologue.com/about.

# EXPERIENCE DRIVERS

*Branding Objective:*
*Close the Feedback Loop*

## FLASH-FORWARD

Closed feedback loops

Interaction design

Ecosystems

Diffused experiences

Experience mapping

Cognitive triggers

Systems-thinking

Curation

Community

## BRAND SPOTLIGHTS

Adobe

Alibaba

CVS/MinuteClinic

Dollar Tree

IKEA/TaskRabbit

League of Legends

Lululemon

Margaritaville

Peloton

Samsung

Sephora

Ulta Beauty

Warby Parker

As a digital strategist for Bank of America 10 years ago, our agency was responsible for helping maintain the "experience" within banking centers; well, at least the digital screens. The banking industry was pushed by the economics of technology to reinvent. At the time, customer experience was managed by a handful of people scattered across functional areas. Today, customer experience has a new boss and lieutenants—chief *experience* officers—supported by an army of product managers. Notable companies, including PwC, MasterCard, and Marriott have these new C-suite executives. By 2015, research firm Forrester reported that 6% of S&P 500 Index had a chief experience officer.[1] Their backgrounds usually involve a buzzword bingo of hot-button topics: data, seamlessness, personalization, emerging technology, service, and ubiquity.

According to research conducted by global consulting company McKinsey, managing "experience" requires three key functions: new capabilities, new audiences, and new business opportunities. As chief experience officer roles started to get created to help untangle the web of metrics surrounding the consumer, McKinsey looked at stock performance data from 2010–2014 to find that companies with top customer experiences had an increase in annual growth of three percentage points.[2] Quite a healthy ROI for the newest C-suite member. In spring 2018, technology consultancy Gartner conducted double-blind research among 6,700 consumers in 15 countries. Their research revealed that 80% of consumers felt that *experience* was the important attribute of a brand's product or service.[3] As chatbots, self-service, and cloud solutions increase in use, consumer expectations are signaling that the experience is the brand. However, over 50% of brands do not meet customer expectations, and those customers are actively switching to more innovative companies.

Other experience architects, generally within consumer products, software, and technology are "product managers," who are taking a page from the playbook of brand managers. All departments are converging under the purview of one air traffic control, "customer experience management," or CXM. And between SAP, Adobe, and Oracle, it's a winner-takes-all contest to make data meaningful. In 2017, 6% of Harvard Business School's class became a product manager.[4] What are these new managers managing? Experience. And that ambiguity and control is popular among newly minted executives ready to flex their entrepreneurial and intrapreneurial skills. On LinkedIn alone, in January 2019, there were 45,000 active "brand manager" job postings and 145,000 job postings for "product managers." Both roles focus on the brand ecosystem that falls under experience management—service, product pipeline, operations, marketing, and beyond.

In 2018, the IBM Institute for Business Value partnered with Oxford Economics to conduct research with 2,000 CMO, finding 85% of them cited *experience* as a business threat; *experience* was cited as the number-one threat, ahead of privacy and market changes.[5] And they're feeling the pressure more and more as younger generations crave share-worthy experiences. Studying population dynamics with Nobel laureate Gary Becker taught me one valuable lesson: follow the shifting demographics. In his Nobel Prize speech in 1992, he reminded economist that the "intuitive assumptions about behavior is only the starting point of systematic analysis, for alone they do not yield many interesting implications."[6] A believer in paying attention to trends of shifting demographics, he felt behavior was an outcome of communities. And that audience is made up mostly of millennials. According to the UN World Population, millennials represent over 25% of the world's population, larger than all other generational cohorts.[7] This is an important population dynamic to consider as brands evolve experiences using leapfrog technologies in emerging countries, which are dominated by the FOMO generation.

As defined by a research team composed of professors at Columbia University, University of Rochester, and Bocconi University, whose work first appeared in the *Journal of Marketing* through the American

Marketing Association, "brand experience is conceptualized as sensations, feelings, cognitions, and behavioral responses evoked by brand-related stimuli that are part of a brand's design and identity, packaging, communications, and environments."[8] Simply put, brand experience implies interaction—action-reaction. We generate customer journey maps and plan the purchase pathway. This experience spans a lifetime, and either adds or decreases value for the audience's pursuit to come out ahead.

Experience, then, is the set of behaviors brands engage in with audiences. Those brand behaviors can be human-to-human or they can be digitally led, through technologies like chatbots. An experience manager, then, must sustain a balancing act between quality, customer service, access, and profitability—a feat that can be either difficult or easy, depending on how well your brand reacts to feedback.

# SAMSUNG

*Building an Experiential Ecosystem*

Founded in 1969, Samsung became a leading manufacturer of electronics, globally, from their headquarters in Korea. In 1970, the company produced their first major home appliance, a black-and-white television. After a few years, a blitz began: refrigerators and washing machines in 1974, color televisions in 1978, and microwaves in the 1980s, as their brand became synonymous with household appliances for the whole family. Samsung is a JD Power constant, and as of 2018 remains on their list of electronics companies sustaining excellence over time. Early to the Internet of Things, in 2018, Samsung enjoyed the highest household penetration of Web-connected televisions in North America, in addition to becoming the number-one appliance brand in North America. Their bets on unifying their appliances and wireless devices under a "smart home" ecosystem will further propel them into the years ahead.[9,10]

# CREATE A CROSS-FUNCTIONAL SYSTEM

To revisit systems-thinking, the best experiences are "closed" systems with tight feedback loops. The brand's goal, regardless of who is managing experience, is to learn over time, adapt, and "self-repair." Any well-functioning systems' purpose, as Donella Meadows puts it, is made evident by the behaviors associated with that system. So, if something is created for good, but that thing starts to be used for bad, then the system is broken. From fake followers to fake video counts, marketers are daily confronted with system breakdowns.

In today's noisy world, strong brands grow by building resiliency based on feedback. It's no surprise, then, that some of the fastest-growing brands have some of the most engaged social communities, in which members feel empowered to improve a brand they love by speaking up. In order for us to best serve clients living through changing digital expectations, like Bank of America, we started to close the feedback loop by using online listening platforms to understand macro trends, and combined that with smaller, private forums for actual customers.

Let me give you another example of closing the feedback loop. In 2008, Starbucks was undergoing rapid global expansion, and to maintain empathy for their customer the company launched the MyStarbucksIdea online platform for customers to leave feedback. And in a Reddit-like manner, the best ideas were up-voted by the community. Over the initial five years, Starbucks scaled from implementing 25 consumer recommendations to over 70 annually by end of 2012. Over 180,000 ideas have been submitted in transparency of community voting and Starbucks reaction. By creating a closed feedback loop, Starbucks has harnessed technology to grow its relationship with customers, and grow its bottom line by implementing suggestions that included K-Cup pods, the Starbucks app, and mobile phone payments.[11]

How is your brand listening and reacting, and showing transparency in the process?

The evolution in the banking experience from tellers to ATM to mobile has been a long journey, but banks have adapted, with a consumer that was kicking and screaming in tote. In 2008, when I started working on omnichannel marketing for Bank of America, few consumers thought tellerless banking would have a future. At the time, according to Harris Interactive, only 16% of banking customers preferred a self-serve channel.[12] Ten years later, as of late 2018, according to the American Banking Associate, over 70% of customers prefer self-service through mobile apps, website, phone IVR, and advanced ATMs.[13] The move to tellerless offers the convenience of more access points and has led to a new digital ambassador role that employs 3,500 people.[14] Changing the function of a system requires a coordinated effort between departments, business units, and employees. Experience is central to business growth or failure, and new business models are now being built fully on translating experiences across digital and physical while taking into account the role of both individual and community. So if you "must" disrupt an industry, because your creative brief or board mandate said to, then remember to focus on the feeling audiences will have through that process.

**TRY THIS:**
—
**System Shortfalls**

Ask internally: How do our employees help customers become comfortable in new channels (e.g., switching from teller to ATM)? How do you help customers use our products correctly or with increased ease and pleasure?

# CVS/MINUTECLINIC

*Creating a Full End-to-End Solution for Care*

Once upon a time, pharmacies dispensed the medicines prescribed by physicians, and that was all they did. But that was then, and this is now. For decades, the typical drug store has also been a general convenience store and photo printer, not to mention a purveyor of countless over-the-counter health remedies. Many are open all night. CVS, as one of America's most widely recognized pharmacy brands, exemplifies the current growth strategies in the industry. In 2006, CVS acquired the MinuteClinic chain of walk-in health clinics, which were founded only six years earlier at one location in Minneapolis-St. Paul under the name QuickMedx. Incredibly, MinuteClinic is now considered the largest healthcare provider in the United States, with more than 1,100 outlets across the nation, all of them co-located with CVS Pharmacies or Target stores.[15,16]

## BUSINESS MODELS BUILT ON EXPERIENCE

When you think about the "conversational brand," extend that into personality. Yes: approachable, direct, inviting, motivational. No: closed-minded, rigid, cold, apathetic. Consider the fitness boom being experienced in the United States. More than 61 million Americans visited a health club of some sort in 2017, according to the International Health, Racquet and Sportsclub Association—that's a 6.3% bump from the previous year and a 33% hike from a decade earlier.[17] The trend has been spurred by a rise of break-out startups including Fitbit, SoulCycle, Peloton, Barry's Bootcamp, and Y7 Studios, to name a few. The fitness industry has exploded because companies offer a fully diversified set of solutions built for tribelike mentality.

# PELOTON

*Building "Tribe" Virtually and On-Demand*

Peloton—a name derived from the French word for "platoon," meaning squad or group—took its first steps in 2012. Cofounder John Foley has described Peloton as a technological fitness and media company giving people the opportunity to engage in home exercise classes that are just as efficient as going to the gym. Initially the Peloton company raised $4 million for product development, and produced the first prototype for a new piece of exercise equipment in 2013. They introduced their stationary bike a year later with a hefty $2,000 price tag. Peloton has recently expanded their product into offering digital fitness classes accessible on their equipment through WIFI as part of a digital content studio offering, demonstrating how to make group workouts personal and accessible, while helping their customer feel supported by an instructor and on-demand community.[18,19]

Take a napkin or sheet of paper and sketch the two-by-two matrix shown in Figure 9.1. Use this strategic framework in the development process of products, services, and offerings. There are two key dimensions to experiences in a noisy world: channel and scale. Channel determines whether an experience is physical (i.e., in-person) or digital (i.e., virtual). Scale determines whether the experience is one-to-one (e.g., customer service) or one-to-many (e.g., classes). By considering the intersection of those two dimensions, there are four realities that your company can then operate in. For instance, using the experience matrix for brands

## FIGURE 9.1

# BUSINESS MODEL EXPERIENCE MATRIX

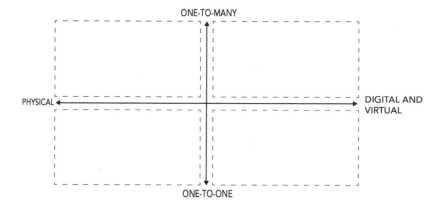

Brands must pressure test their business model diversity against four revenue drivers:
channel, scale, consumer, and community.

# LEAGUE OF LEGENDS

*Creating an Experience-Based Business Model*

League of Legends (*LoL*) has branded itself "a highly competitive, team-based strategy game for those who crave a hard-fought victory." Released in 2009, *LoL* was developed by Riot Games to provide a high-fantasy gaming experience, and to date, that fantasy reality has captured over 100 million daily players. With a business model that spans physical and digital, and one-on-one to one-to-many (i.e., tournaments), the league is growing. By 2012, League of Legends was the most played game on the PC. By 2014, League of Legends had nearly 70 million players monthly in Europe and the United States, with an average of 27 million players per day. As the game increased its digital imprint and expanded its reach to YouTube and other avenues, LoL saw an increase of upwards of 100 million players monthly by 2016. Realizing the potential to up-level the gaming experience through a new combination of channel and scale, Riot Games organized an annual competition. With regional League Championship Series (LCS), in Los Angeles and Berlin, the 2017 annual World Championship had 60 million viewers—compared to that year's NBA Finals that had only 20 million.[20,21,22]

like Peloton and SoulCycle, you can see how their two businesses are designed to cater to different mindsets: Peloton focuses on remote channels (like home) that are one-to-one (single rider), whereas SoulCycle focuses on in-person channels that are one-to-many (group of riders). Yes, they could compete directly. Or, they can own their own parts of a cycling experience matrix. Where do your products, services, and offerings fall within an experience matrix? Where can you push your brand to grow?

## EVOLUTION OF "BRAND"

In 2016, after leaving one of the most buzzed-about venture capital and music management firms, Atom Factory, I rejoined Ogilvy's fast-growing consulting practice. And 10 years after starting my career at Ogilvy following college, the backdrop of marketing had new realities: (1) clients shifted their mindset from digital as a "lab" to digital as a *business imperative*; (2) departments shifted from "digital innovation" to "digital transformation"; (3) digital nearly represented 50% of advertising spend, finally approaching an inflection point once dominated by television, and (4) marketing agencies were facing heat from consultancies (like Accenture, McKinsey, IBM, and Deloitte) that were slowly getting marketing-related work from their Fortune 100 clients who were stuck between pressure to gobble up as much data as possible yet not knowing how to parse meaningfulness

FIGURE 9.2

# BRAND EXPERIENCE EVOLUTION

| 50 YEARS AGO | 10 YEARS AGO | TODAY | 5 YEARS FROM NOW |
|---|---|---|---|
| Static logo | Interactive logo | User-generated | Audio-led |
| Monochromatic | Rich media | Conversational | Video-centric |
| Television-centric | Direct mail–driven | Memorable | Decentralized experiences |
| Print heavy | Television-focused | Digital ecosystem | Ubiquitous brand interaction |
| Door-to-door | Guerilla | Lifestyle-driven | Sensorial and immersive |
| | | | Augmented |

*Brand experience is becoming more sensorial, moving into highly visual, immersive exchanges that redefine value.*

from the web of metrics.[23] The idea of "brand" had passed a tipping point, and startups were pushing 100-year old companies to think and act differently (Figure 9.2), as 150 companies, including Intel, Coca-Cola, and SAP, launched corporate funds to invest in or acquire startups as jumper cables for their growth engines.

The fascination of what made fast-growing companies successful lingered with me after returning to Harlem from Hollywood, where I had helped launch a $100 million media startup for Sean "Diddy" Combs and managed a startup accelerator for Troy Carter. The industry they both were best known for—music—had already undergone a digital transformation, so in many regards they were already ahead of the curve. In returning to Ogilvy, and their consulting practice specifically, there was now a chance to really understand what fast-growing companies were doing through branding to win.

Key questions from clients included: Why do certain companies like Amazon, Apple, and Alibaba keep winning market share? As an established brand, what growth lessons can we learn from digital disruptors? And, how do you design and implement a new "fast-track" lane for growth? Immediately, my experience of working with big brands and startups collided head-on with the future of digital transformations at scale, and we investigated new business models, cross-industry collaborations, and new consumer behaviors. And experience became a recurring theme.

# ALIBABA

*Creating a Work Culture of Being First*

Founded in 1999, Alibaba is now one of the top five internet company in the world—working to defend their global business from e-commerce giants Amazon and eBay. Alibaba offers a unique shopping experience where customers can purchase everything including electronics, home furniture, groceries, apparel, and accessories. Originating in China, they have opened Research and Development (R&D) centers in Singapore, Israel, and the United States. As of 2017, Alibaba had spent $15 billion in R&D, including seven technology labs. Collected data is used to expand their services and find ways to edge out the competition by offering more options for their customers. As of November 2018, they had a total of nearly 700 million mobile users compared to Amazon's 300 million users. In 2018, Amazon announced that it would launch three AmazonGo cashier-less stores in the United States, expanding to a total of 3,000 by 2021. Alibaba has already exceeded this goal, launching their Hema cashier-less stores in 2016, opening 80 of these across China in 2018 alone, with plans to expand worldwide. Expansion plans include restaurants of the future with robots as servers, demonstrating the powerful role of reinventing *experience* in driving business growth.[24,25,26]

In *Great Customer Expectations,* published in 2012, author Matt Watkinson gives his 10 commandments for customer experiences, with the basic premise that "great" experiences are those that exceed expectations, and whether customers articulate their expectations or not, they have them.[27] It's not enough to be great in your category, because customers aren't comparing your brand experience only to your perceived category. Brands today must compete against every single, and any, brand that has a better experience than they do, because great experiences travel and raise the expectation for the next experience anywhere.

During my time in the digital transformation group at Ogilvy Consulting, there were two important projects that the principals empowered me to lead related to my background in omnichannel strategy and startup advisement.

## OMNICHANNEL ATTRIBUTES

In the summer of 2017, I spent a month in London on a project for a large European retailer with 2,500 stores. Our team was asked to advise on a new omnichannel experience strategy. We dug into 100 global retailers from Alibaba to Zara. Several attributes emerged from that research including ubiquity, seamlessness, personalization, value, and being engaging. These areas became experience drivers we used to unlock business transformation pathways.

1. **Ubiquitous and seamless:** Same experience across all channels—products and services. Ability to leave one channel and pick up the experience in another (i.e., continuity of experience). It's about moving beyond labeling simplicity, although that has worked well for international grocer Aldi (owner of Trader Joe's). There should be one consistent feeling that individuals walk away with, whether they use your product end-to-end (e.g., owning a Peloton bike and using their on-demand content) or as one part of their lifestyle (e.g., just watching on-demand content as you ride with another brand's bike).

# ADOBE
*Shifting toward Cloud Services*

Adobe, the software company, has been dubbed one of the most adored and indispensable brands for the creative community. Founded in 1982, their major push was to diversify user base through more accessible and novice-friendly edit and share tools. While conducting consumer research, they found that much of their consumers spent one third of their time on digital software and/or devices, thus increasing their willingness to use digital applications. Pushing into the "cloud" in 2013 with a DIY gale wind, their business model shifted from an in-store CD-rom model to an anywhere, anytime subscription model that has been paying dividends. As of 2018, Adobe's Creative Cloud had a total of 15 million users, up 25% from 2017.[28,29,30,31,32]

2. **Personalization and value:** Actively using data to enhance individual customer experience from promotions to branded content—past purchases, user profile information, location-based data. In 2017, Salesforce commissioned consumer research through Harris Poll to investigate the "connected shopper." The research with 2,000 adults in the United States revealed that millennials and boomers had increasing expectations of real-time inventory management, ability to look up additional product information while in-store, and desire for sales associations to have access to technology that offers personalized product recommendations.[33] The "personal shopper" experience once only afforded to high-end luxury stores was now making its way to the pharmacy aisle and showroom floor, as fast-growing companies were empowering employees by enhancing customer experience with real-time data and branded content, giving new meaning to "brand-in-hand."

# ULTA BEAUTY

*Supporting Value-Based Employee Interactions*

In its battle with Sephora for dominance of the U.S. beauty retail market, Ulta continues to build on the 20% sales growth it realized in 2017, which produced nearly $6 billion in annual sales. Founded in 1990 by Richard E. George, Ulta has over 1,100 stores and more than 21,000 employees, offering an extraordinary array of both prestige and mass-brand beauty products, all at a speed of technology that allows them to personalize the experience to each customer, based on data. The data that Ulta continuously collects is always informing and customizing the brand's interaction with customers via different, connected channels such as email and in-shop interactions.

Another key to Ulta's success is its robust, 28-million-members-strong Beauty Enthusiast loyalty program. Driving over 90% of Ulta sales, these ultimate rewards members receive special beauty tips, early access to new products, trend updates, and invitations to exclusive events. Ulta operates over 1,000 stores and plans to add nearly 10% new stores annually through 2021.[34,35,36,37]

3. **Engaging:** Going where the consumer lives and capturing their attention through familiarity—use of inviting language (from salespeople to call centers to content), inclusion of influencers that represent voices from communities they are members of, and shareworthy content and experiences. Being engaging for a commerce brand might mean retail theater—education, inspiration, and communal learning. Today, retail theater looks like classes at Apple, cooking showcases at Williams Sonoma, lessons at Home Depot, or yoga tips at

Lululemon. Experience, in the context of engaging, means immersing before buying, or learning how to fully unlock the magic of a product or service, after purchase.

# LULULEMON

*Setting the Pace for Growth*

Founded by Chip Wilson in 1998, Lululemon, a yoga-inspired, Canadian-headquartered athletic apparel retailer for women and men, pioneered athleisure wear, one of the hottest new categories in fashion. Now, with more than 400 stores globally, the company continues to grow impressively despite increased competition. As of August 2018, revenue rose 25% over the previous year, fueled by growth in comparable store sales of 10% and online sales of nearly 50%. Success is rooted in the company's devotion to quality and focus on feedback. Hosting yoga classes at its locations and organizing running events provides ample opportunities for learning about customer likes and wants. Lululemon owes much of its marketing success to strong word of mouth recommendations supported by social media. Discussions with product designers occur online through live streaming as well as posts and comments. Feedback has led to new products such as Nulu fabric and a more formal, office-appropriate selection.[38,39,40]

Ultimately, exceptional experiences in omnichannel focus on a "system" view of the brand surrounding the consumer (Figure 9.3), allowing them to choose their own adventure among the channels that work best for them, understanding that just because your brand is not in the channel doesn't mean a competitor won't be. For example, acknowledging that equipment may be a brand hurdle, in 2018 Peloton upped their game against SoulCycle by creating a content platform for trainer-led rides that can be

FIGURE 9.3

## OMNICHANNEL ATTRIBUTES

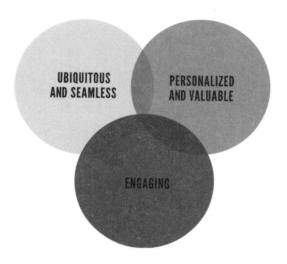

*High-growth companies share common omnichannel attributes: offering ubiquitous and seamless experiences, delivering personalization and valuable guidance, and engaging audiences through retail theater and digital community.*
*Source:* Adapted from Ogilvy Consulting, 2017.

accessed by anyone, anywhere, anytime, cutting down the brand hurdle of buying a new bike or giving up a gym membership, where bikes are available.

## GREAT STRATEGY COMES FROM UNCONVENTIONAL PLACES

Making memorable experiences for consumers starts where and how you get information, and your own understanding of what a great experience is with others in a community. Most senior marketers have been to at least one of the following industry conferences: Ad Age, ANA Masters, Advertising Week. I challenge you to stop going only to the typical industry conferences with panel after panel with rows and rows of seats, where you leave not knowing the people who sat next to you and not knowing any more about culture than when you walked in. If you want to be better at building consumer experiences, then challenge yourself to go outside your comfort zone to newer experiences: Future of Storytelling, BeautyCon, or Fast Company Innovation Festival. Go to places where the *experience* is wired to deliver on four factors:

1. **Engaging format** (i.e., is the format a nontraditional panel that encourages discussion among all attendees?)
2. **Cultural exposure** (i.e., does the experience introduce new forms of culture such as music, art, food, etc.?)
3. **Community intersections** (i.e., are people from different backgrounds present or are the attendees all the same?)
4. **Access to community leaders** (i.e., how easily accessible are the people who can herd tribes toward action?)

Returning from London, there was a new assignment waiting, to evaluate growth moves of digital startups. We looked across a landscape of 200 companies disrupting a broad category of industries, uncovering similarities, best practices, new business models, and ultimately, new growth pathways. Our findings revealed eight "fast tracks" for growth, and those fast tracks all tied into delivering exceptional experiences to audiences (Figure 9.4).

1. **Delivery Dynamics:** Making a greater variety of information, products, and services available under new business models that are direct-to-consumer and on-demand 24/7 (e.g., Netflix, Amazon, Spotify)
2. **Data into Action:** Combining personal and behavioral data with artificial intelligence and IoT to create custom experiences, products, and services tailored to individual consumers (e.g., IBM, Fitbit, Betterment)
3. **Mobility:** Shifting the dynamic of communication, collaboration, and connectivity to increase productivity between people, teams, communities, and companies (e.g., WeWork, Slack)

## FIGURE 9.4
# DISRUPTOR FAST TRACKS

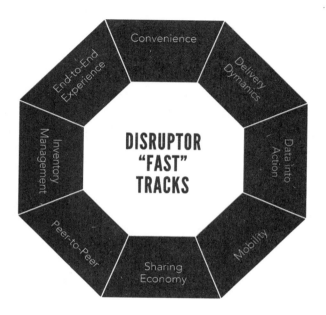

*The eight frequently trafficked growth lanes of disruptive companies: Delivery Dynamics, Data into Action, Mobility, Sharing Economy, P2P, Inventory Management, End-to-end Experience, and Convenience.*
Source: Adapted from Ogilvy Consulting, 2017.

4. **Sharing Economy:** Diffusing ownership of costly goods to communal use for maximum benefit (e.g., Uber, Airbnb)
5. **P2P:** Enabling any consumer to become a direct merchant (e.g., Angie's List, LendingClub, Etsy)
6. **Inventory Management:** Real-time management, routing, and tracking of inventory (e.g., Hotel Tonight, Gilt, JetSetter)
7. **End-to-End Experience:** Managing the full customer life-cycle experience through proprietary combination of company hardware, software, and service (e.g., Tesla, Apple)
8. **Convenience:** Delivering time-saving services and/or products through local, remote and/or digital channels most used by consumers (e.g., CVS/Minute Clinic, Venmo, Plated)

Whether focusing on an omnichannel approach or a disruption approach to experiential strategy, chief experience/marketing/ digital/customer/information/innovation officers are being confronted with a reality: lots of data and more ways for a customer to voice their opinion. Communities are strengthening around cultures and embracing brands, endorsing them for fellow members as a part of the group's communal lifestyle.

To boil this down further, and connect back into feelings and emotions, these companies are doing something under the surface. They're striking a balance in Mehrabian and Russell's PAD model— these brands are empowering consumers by creating a feedback culture rather than focusing solely on connecting the brand into every digital ecosystems (as we did 10 years earlier). According to research conducted among 11,000 consumers in nine major countries[41]—including the United States, China, France, and Australia—there are five key frustrations of customers: (1) waiting in lines, (2) items out of stock, (3) too busy/hectic environment, (4) staff unable to assist, and (4) inconvenient store hours.

# IKEA / TASKRABBIT

*Creating a Full End-to-End Business That Anticipates Customer Needs*

Question: Does anyone really think the World Wide Web needs another Craigslist or Angie's List? There's already a very sizable crowd of online services that offer to connect homeowners or hobbyists with people who can help them with their broken lamps or unfinished tree houses. Well, move over HomeAdvisors. Step aside FindAPro. The world is now meeting Task-Rabbit, courtesy of a new partnership through global retailer IKEA, adding over 50,000 "taskers" to their customer support team. Initially called RunMy-Errand, TaskRabbit is now a prime vehicle for advancing Ikea's strategy in the e-commerce and services arena. By closing a critical feedback loop in the home furnishing industry—putting it together—Ikea is demonstrating the power of "systems-thinking" to ensure customer expectations are exceeded and frustrations remain low in one country after another—in a march to cover all 49 countries where the Ikea brand has a footprint.[42,43,44]

Speaking about "too hectic," what about appearance? In the United States, 80% of shopping for clothes and shoes still happens in physical stores.[45] So at Temple University, Dr. Maureen Morrin has been exploring how customer frustrations with messy aisles and poor lighting affect business. Her recipe for the right sales experience—light, bright, cheery, straight.[46] Why? Because appearance has an effect on mood, and inducing a bad mood in a customer will take exponentially more effort to overcome than maintaining a positive one consistently.

# DOLLAR TREE

*Creating a New Shopping Routine*

Founded in 1953 by J. Douglas Perry, Macon F. Brock, Jr., and H. Ray Compton, Dollar Tree was initially a toy store called K&K. The partners sold K&K to another toy merchant and moved on to discount stores. The original store, *Only One Dollar*, was incorporated in 1986 and went through several name changes before settling into the name we now know.

While Dollar Tree does a significant amount of business online, the majority of revenue is generated in their brick and mortar shops. The empire they built, one dollar at a time, is headquartered in Chesapeake, Virginia. Dollar Tree is a Fortune 150 company with over 14,835 stores throughout the

United States and Canada, having grown from over 2,500 stores in 2002, with 650 of those stores opened in 2018. Dollar Tree buys products in quantities, and most (nearly 40%) are imports and manufacturers' "overruns." This is how they are able to offer discounted prices, and keep the budget- and style-conscious consumer leaving with surprise and delight.[47,48,49,50]

Solving experiential issues is why closed feedback loops are necessary—mechanism to identify elements that should be self-repairing over time, which may not be, or elements that have no function, over time. There are many things to focus on related to experiences that chief experience officers, product managers, and brand managers are working to deliver, from omnichannel to eco-system. But, there are three things that matter most that brands should prioritize delivering (Figure 9.5): rewarding customers, motivating customers, and supporting customers. Through the triad of those three behaviors of a brand, you can build tribes while driving decision-making that makes people feel good.

1. **Reward:** Creating business models with built-in loss aversion favors the consumer by providing incentives for consumption and loyalty (e.g., saving time, paying less in interest). Programs include perks on what matters most to consumers, as determined by them. For instance, Marriott elevates customer stays through access to 8,000 partner perks under the oversight of their chief experience officer.[51]
2. **Motivate:** Helping consumers envision the future while setting public goals that leverage community transparency and trends (e.g., predictive capabilities, modeling, leaderboards, goal-setting). While the number of digital channels to recruit new customers is increasing, the challenge to acquire new customers is not dwindling. Accenture estimates that attracting a new customer can cost 4–10 times as much as retaining a current customer.[52] Motivation means easy access to product and service on-ramps—in the case of Nike it's access to a run club, data, events, connection to friends, and workout routines.

3. **Support:** Building resilient systems capable of anticipating issues and problem-solving at scale to deliver great service. What does good service look like? McKinsey found that customers expect service issues to be resolved in under five minutes.[53] In a 2017 study among 25,000 consumers in 33 countries, Accenture found that nearly two thirds of customers have switched companies due to poor service; consumer expectations were rising the fastest year-over-year in emerging markets.[54]

Brands that successfully manage their experiences through an ecosystem of rewards, motivation, and support benefit from a secret signal to communities: curation. Because in a noisy world of choice, where less is more, the ability to curate for a community is a new rule of brand building. Whether its StichFix or Sephora, curation screams personalization, empathy, and community. Curation is the strength of the DJ competing against a streaming playlist algorithm, a balance of the familiar and the novel. As Diddy once told our executive team during a staff meeting, "the DJ has to be willing to clear the dance floor, not just do what's popular."

## FIGURE 9.5
## CUSTOMER EXPECTATION TRIAD

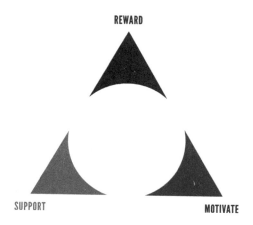

*Brands become valuable to customers when they exceed expectations by demonstrating a triad of brand behaviors that reward, motivate, and support.*

# SEPHORA

*Evolving into an Experience-Based Business Model*

Sephora is a leader in the experience economy, allowing customers to touch and interface with its products in personalized ways. Founded in 1970 by Dominque Mandonnaud, the company helped introduce the "try before you buy" approach to cosmetics, which is now firmly established across the retail beauty market. While many retail outlets currently struggle, Sephora is expanding, with sales up almost double digits year-over-year for the first during 2018, the same year it received recognition from *Fast Company* as a top retail innovator. Today, as the largest beauty retailer in the world, Sephora has over 2,300 retail stores and more than 30,000 employees operating in 33 countries.

Through an omnichannel integration strategy, the company maintains a vibrant and expanding content-connected ecosystem that encourages exploration and discovery among customers. Their growth secrets: making digital a priority and enhancing the physical store experience offline. Other critical factors include applying innovative technologies like facial scanning, making customized data-driven recommendations, building partnerships and acknowledging customers through loyalty, and deepening customer rewards. From beacon technology to beauty influencer videos online, Sephora is in the right place at the right time. In-shop Beauty Hubs provide a lookbook containing thousands of options delivered via iPad stations and interactive mirrors so products can be tried virtually through augmented reality, while beauty classes conducted by beauty professionals keeps shoppers in learning mode. In 2015, to stay ahead of the curve, Sephora developed the Sephora Lab to give the company access to trial technologies such as voice-based shopping.[55,56,57,58]

# THE GOAL OF EXPERIENCE

What, then, is the end goal of an exceptional experience—sales, loyalty, social chatter? No. I challenge you to set a higher goal for experiences: to drive "normative behavior" (i.e., bonding behavior shared between all members of any tribe). Your brand should have a clear behavior-set known and practiced by all your customers; that behavior becomes a measure of brand strength and tribe unity. Want to get married? Buy a diamond ring (DeBeers, 1947). Tired? Take a "coffee break" (Pan-American Coffee Bureau, 1952). Going out for drinks? Bring along a designated driver (AdCouncil, 1983). And in our current social age, if you just bought a gold face mask, then it's time to post on Instagram, to show you're a part of the community. The fastest-growing companies drive and support normative behavior among their customers, behaviors that unite customers into something stronger than a community—a tribe.

In *Nudge*, Richard Thaler and Cass Sunstein discuss the creation of the nationally popular slogan "Don't Mess with Texas," which was voted the most popular state slogan in 2006.[59] And do you know what that campaign is about? Littering. By making recycling "normative behavior," the state had a 70% reduction in litter along roads by 2012. Brands that drive "normative behavior" enter the echelon of pop culture brands: to Google™ it, to Uber™ there, to Xerox™ the flyers, or to Rollerblade™. Normative behavior gradually builds over time into a bandwagon effect (i.e., when individuals are influenced by others, mimicking their behavior and attitudes to conform to a larger group norm). Bandwagon effect is one of the psychological reasons that influencer marketing works—it's the science part of herd mentality.

In order to drive normative behavior, brands need to heavily consider "where" they show up—and whether that place is reflective of a feeling the brand wants to be associated with. I'm not talking about "brand safety" (i.e., avoiding having a toy brand show up alongside violent content), but rather *where*. For instance, toys exude fun, so a toy brand might show up in experiences where people are already having fun, could be having fun, or experiencing the opposite of fun.

Experience managers must shift from building brand-owned eco-systems (e.g., sites, apps) to fostering distributed experiences (e.g., events, immersive engagements, APIs, stores within stores, product collaborations, etc.) that meet the consumer where they are happiest or most frustrated. In the summer of 2018, I had a chance to immerse myself in a study of America's favorite cookie: Oreo. In the past 10 years, the brand has experienced a 300% growth in revenue to become a billion-dollar brand.[60] Looking to evolve the successful "Wonderfilled" campaign to lean more into "playfulness," we developed new experience maps for the brand as an illustrative exercise for how to follow the feeling. By creating experience maps, brands can start to unlock all elements of the

### FIGURE 9.6
## BRAND EXPERIENCE MAP

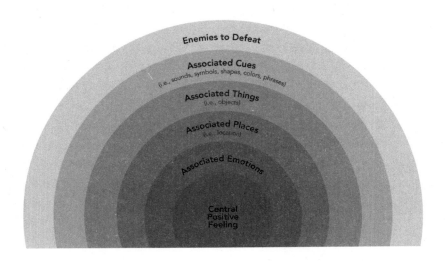

*Brand experience ecosystems should build from stimuli that trigger memories, emotions, and feelings—places, objects, and social cues.*

communication—language, audio, and visuals—to surround consumers in full sensorial experiences (Figure 9.6).

**TRY THIS:**

Experience
Mapping

Focus on meeting communities in their comfort
zone by identifying where key emotional triggers
naturally live in the world. Draw a large bulls-eye
with four rings on a piece of paper (Figure 9.6).

**Center of Target:** Write the intended positive
customer feeling.

**Ring 1:** Write five or more emotions
associated with that feeling.

**Ring 2:** Write the names of places (e.g.,
locations) that may evoke those emotions.

**Rings 3 and 4:** Write the names of things/cues
(i.e., sounds, symbols, shapes, colors, phrases)
associated with the feeling.

**Ring 5:** Write the name of an enemy (i.e.,
opposite feelings) that clashes with the
central feeling.

Your brand's chief goal should be to show up in the places, shapes,
and forms that people most associate with the feeling surrounding
your North Star. For example, "happy" lives in the forms we just
described—lexicon, audio, and visuals—which might manifest
itself in using words like "laughter," playing the sound of an ice
cream truck, or immersing customer in bubbles blowing in the air.
Our goal is to put your brand next to the "feeling zones" that you
want people to associate with you. This is a point that becomes
important when you're an iconic brand like Disney and looking
for growth lanes; it offers a strategic approach to shine a light on
blind spot in areas like licensing, partnerships, and distribution,
which could be meaningful brand experience territories.

# WARBY PARKER

*Reinventing the "At-Home" Appointment*

The overall mission of Warby Parker is to create an alternative to expensive eyewear, a constant since being started in 2010 by Neil Blumenthal, Andrew Hunt, David Gilboa, and Jeffrey Raider. The billion-dollar-valued unicorn has exceeded customer expectations by designing and making their eyeglasses in-house, to ensure quality assurance and deliver affordable prices for eyewear to any and all customers. As of 2014, Warby Parker sold a million pairs of glasses. They offer convenient plans and options for their customers to make purchases—from the initial offer of getting five pairs shipped for free for trial to at-home prescription services to skip the eye doctor visit. Programs like the *Buy a Pair, Give a Pair* have resulted in over four million pairs of glasses being donated to the underprivileged and disadvantaged.[61,62,63]

# MARGARITAVILLE

*Creating the Atmospherics of Eternal Summertime*

"Wasting away in Margaritaville" has been very good for Jimmy Buffett. Not as an actual place, of course, but as the title of the song Buffett wrote in 1977. Margaritaville has become a uniquely branded commercial empire. It has made Buffett one of the wealthiest entertainers in America, with a personal net worth of around $550 million. According to the *New York Times*, "The Jimmy Buffett lifestyle shakes its fist at the Man even while Jimmy Buffett, with his 5,000 employees, is basically now the Man."

His enterprises extend from restaurants to hotels to casinos. And, more recently, he's added Broadway to that list, with the opening of a musical called *Escape to Margaritaville*. This is why some call his overall marketing vehicle the "island escapism brand."

A neighbor and friend of Buffett in Florida, John Cohlan is CEO of Margaritaville Holdings. He had earlier acquired his branding savvy at another holding company, Triarc, where he helped develop businesses like Arby's, Snapple, and RC Cola. Cohlan got his first inkling of what the Margaritaville brand was about when Buffett invited him to the 1998 New Orleans Jazz & Heritage Festival. As he recalls, "I looked out and saw people all dressed up, and I said to myself, 'This is more of a brand than the brands that we [at Triarc] own, because it was a real cultural connection that all these people had as a way of life.'" Cohlan has subsequently grown Buffett's hospitality empire to 10 hotels and resorts, along with several vacation clubs and branded residences.[64,65,66]

## CONCLUSION

According to brand consultant Steve Yastrow, when employees can deliver consistency across interactions to customers then the brand achieves harmony, similar to the way a symphony blends sound into an immersive experience. In his 2010 work *Brand Harmony*, he gives a roadmap to creating a "system" for marketing, communication, and experiences to generate positive brand beliefs in customers.[67] Successful brands empower employees to do the right thing to retain customers.

Achieving the harmony that brands seek requires the ability to have a closed feedback loop with audiences across diffused experiences that centrally feed into how brands improve to meet the expectations of consumers. By keeping community in the forefront, brands can explore, map, and unlock a feelings zone to activate experiences in a manner that rewards, motivates, and supports customers. By managing that trifecta of experience drivers, brands can reinforce normative behavior among customers to ensure the brand maintains relevancy within their lifestyle. The ability to manage the new experience ecosystem that's screen agnostic is dependent on internal corporate culture, also, which is the final mountain to clear in chasing your brand's true north. And internal culture, luckily, is not something that artificial intelligence can create, instill, or distribute for you. This is where good old-fashioned human-to-human effort has to lead.

##  FIRE STARTERS

### CREATING A "SYSTEM" WITH A CLOSED FEEDBACK LOOP

**EXPERIENCE DRIVERS**

- ☐ *What one positive feeling do you want people to have after meeting your leadership team?*

- ☐ *What three words would people who have known you for three years use to describe your personality?*

- ☐ *In what parts of the experience matrix can you add a new product, service, or offering to realize new growth?*

- ☐ *How do you reward employees to report feedback from customers?*

- ☐ *What new territories in the brand experience map can you invest in?*

- ☐ *What normative behavior can you reinforce or create among customers?*

## Notes

1. "More Than 6% of S&P 500 Firms Have a Chief Customer Officer (CCO) Type of Role." Forrester, July 14, 2017. https://go.forrester.com/blogs /14-03-24-more_than_6_of_sp_500_firms_have_a_chief_customer_ officer_cco_type_of_role/.

2. "Customer Experience." McKinsey & Co., June 2, 2017. https://www
.mckinsey.com/~/media/mckinsey/featured insights/customer experience/
cx compendium 2017/customer-experience-compendium-july-2017.ashx.

3. "State of the Connected Customer." Salesforce, 2018. https://www
.salesforce.com/content/dam/web/en_us/www/documents/e-books
/state-of-the-connected-customer-report-second-edition2018.pdf.

4. Lindsay Gellman, "Coveted Job Title for MBAs: Product Manager." *Wall
Street Journal*, March 2, 2016. https://www.wsj.com/articles/coveted-job-
title-for-m-b-a-s-product-manager-1456933303.

5. IBM Institute for Business Value, "The Modern Marketing Mandate: Insights
from the Chief Marketing Officer Study." 2018. Accessed February 01, 2019.
https://public.dhe.ibm.com/common/ssi/ecm/32/en/32014632usen/the-
modern-marketing-mandate_chief-marketing-officer-study_32014632USEN
.pdf.

6. Gary S. Becker, "Nobel Lecture: The Economic Way of Looking at
Behavior." *Journal of Political Economy* 101, no. 3 (June 1993), 385–409.
doi:10.1086/261880.

7. Erik R. Peterson, Ari Sillman, and Courtney Rickert McCaffrey, "Where
Are the Global Millennials?" A.T. Kearney. Accessed February 01,
2019. https://www.atkearney.com/web/global-business-policy-council/
article?/a/where-are-the-global-millennials-.

8. Bernd H. Schmitt, Lia Zarantonello, and J. Brakus, "Brand Experience:
What Is It? How Is It Measured? Does It Affect Loyalty?" *Journal of
Marketing* 73 (2009). doi:10.1509/jmkg.73.3.52.

9. "Appliance Competition Heats Up and Gets Cooking as Six Different
Brands Win J.D. Power Awards." J.D. Power. Accessed February 1, 2019.
https://www.jdpower.com/business/press-releases/2018-kitchen-laun
dry-appliance-satisfaction-study.

10. "History." Samsung. Accessed February 1, 2019. https://www.samsung
.com/us/aboutsamsung/company/history/.

11. "Starbucks Celebrates Five-Year Anniversary of My Starbucks Idea."
*Business Wire*, March 29, 2013. https://www.businesswire.com
/news/home/20130328006372/en/Starbucks-Celebrates-Five-Year-
Anniversary-Starbucks-Idea.

12. "New Harris Interactive Study: Consumers Increasingly Embrace
Mobile Phone Commerce with Banking and Buying On-the-Go."
*Business Wire*, March 12, 2008. https://www.businesswire.com/news
/home/20080312005269/en/New-Harris-Interactive-Study-Consumers-
Increasingly-Embrace.

13. "Survey: Online, Mobile Are Most Popular Banking Channels, Branches Remain Popular." American Bankers Association, October 16, 2018. https://www.aba.com/Press/Pages/101618MCResults.aspx.

14. Jeffry Pilcher, "Bank of America Experiments with Tellerless 'Robo Branches'." The Financial Brand. https://thefinancialbrand.com/64900 /bank-of-america-automated-branches/.

15. "MinuteClinic." Wikipedia. Last updated on November 18, 2018. Accessed January 31, 2019. https://en.wikipedia.org/wiki/MinuteClinic.

16. Kristian Monllos, "CVS Health's Marketing Chief on Turning the Pharmacy Brand Into a Healthcare Player." Adweek, March 28, 2016. https:// www.adweek.com/brand-marketing/cvs-healths-marketing-chief-turning-pharmacy-brand-healthcare-player-170437/.

17. Jeff Bercovici, "How the Founder of Y7 Studio Built One of America's Fastest-Growing Fitness Companies for People Who Hate Yoga." Inc., August 15, 2018. https://www.inc.com/magazine/201809/jeff-bercovici/2018-inc-5000-y7-studio-yoga-fitness-trends.html.

18. Liz Warren, "A Brief History of Peloton: A Look at the Cycling Startup's Explosive Growth." Built in NYC, June 20, 2017. https://www.builtinnyc .com/2017/06/16/history-peloton.

19. Angelica Lavito, "Peloton CEO John Foley Says Fitness Company Is 'Weirdly Profitable.'" CNBC, May 23, 2018. https://www.cnbc.com/2018/05/23/ peloton-ceo-john-foley-says-fitness-company-is-weirdly-profitable .html.

20. Paul Tassi, "Riot Games Reveals 'League of Legends' Has 100 Million Monthly Players." Forbes, September 13, 2016. https://www.forbes.com /sites/insertcoin/2016/09/13/riot-games-reveals-league-of-legends-has-100-million-monthly-players/#522894c85aa8.

21. "What We Do." Riot Games. Accessed February 1, 2019. https://www .riotgames.com/en/what-we-do.

22. David Holloway, "TV Ratings: NBA Finals Is Most Watched Since 1998." Variety, June 13, 2017. https://variety.com/2017/tv/news/tv-ratings-nba-finals-1202464230/.

23. E. J. Schultz, "Creeping on Agencies' Turf, Consultancies Are Shaking Up the Marketing Industry." AdAge, May 1, 2017. https://adage.com/article /news/consultancies-rising/308845/.

24. Craig Smith, "150 Amazing Amazon Statistics and Facts." DMR Business Statistics, December 2018. https://expandedramblings.com/index.php /amazon-statistics/.

25. "Alibaba." Alibaba. Accessed February 3, 2019. https://www.alibaba.com/.

26. Rebecca Fannin, "Alibaba Beats Amazon to New All-Digital Retail Trend." *Forbes*, September 21, 2018. https://www.forbes.com/sites/rebeccafannin/2018/09/21/alibaba-beats-amazon-to-new-all-digital-retail-trend/#75219afa6653.

27. Matthew Watkinson, *The Ten Principles behind Great Customer Experiences*. Harlow: Financial Times, 2013.

28. "2018 Adobe Consumer Content Survey." LinkedIn SlideShare, February 6, 2018. https://www.slideshare.net/adobe/2018-adobe-consumer-content-survey.

29. "Adobe Fast Facts." Adobe. Accessed February 1, 2019. https://www.adobe.com/about-adobe/fast-facts.html.

30. "Adobe Creative Cloud Adoption Grows to 15 Million Paid Members." ProDesign Tools, March 23, 2016. https://prodesigntools.com/creative-cloud-one-million-paid-members.html.

31. Christine Moorman, "Adobe: How to Dominate the Subscription Economy." *Forbes*, August 23, 2018. https://www.forbes.com/sites/christinemoorman/2018/08/23/adobe-how-to-dominate-the-subscription-economy/#438a056152e8.

32. "Adobe Accelerates Shift to the Cloud." Adobe, May 6, 2013. https://www.adobe.com/aboutadobe/pressroom/pressreleases/201305/050613AdobeAcceleratesShifttotheCloud.html.

33. "Salesforce: Retail Campaign." *Salesforce*, September 26, 2017. https://a.sfdcstatic.com/content/dam/www/ocms/assets/pdf/misc/retail-campaign-2017-ebook.pdf.

34. Katie Evans, "Ulta Beauty Buys AI and AR Technology Startups." Digital Commerce 360, November 16, 2018. https://www.digital-commerce360.com/2018/11/16/ulta-beauty-buys-ai-and-ar-technology-startups/.

35. Elliot Maras, "Ulta Beauty Tackles Retail Change by Embracing Change." Retail Customer Experience, May 10, 2018. https://www.retailcustomerexperience.com/articles/ulta-beauty-tackles-retail-change-by-embracing-change/.

36. Hilary Milnes, "How Ulta Beauty Evolved Its Merchandising Strategy to Compete in a Crowded Market." *DigiDay UK*, May 7, 2018. https://digiday.com/marketing/ulta-beauty-evolved-merchandising-strategy-compete-crowded-market/.

37. Pamela N. Danzigar, "Sephora, Ulta and the Battle for the $56B U.S. Beauty Retail Market." *Forbes*, August 6, 2018. https://www.forbes.com/sites/pamdanziger/2018/08/06/sephora-and-ulta-are-on-a-collision-course-then-there-is-amazon-where-is-us-beauty-retail-headed/#476473e055dd.

38. "History." Lululemon. Accessed February 1, 2019. https://info.lululemon.com/about/our-story/history.

39. Adrianne Pasquarelli, "Lululemon Stretches Digital Marketing Wings, Sees Success." *AdAge*, March 29, 2018. https://adage.com/article/cmo-strategy/lululemon-stretches-digital-marketing-wings-sees-success/312909/.

40. Dejan Gajsek, "Lululemon Athletica—How One Company Succeeded in One of the Most Ruthless Industries." *Medium*, July 8, 2018. https://medium.com/@dgajsek/lululemon-athletica-how-one-company-succeeded-in-one-of-the-most-ruthless-industries-bd3f2bf685aa.

41. "The State of Brick and Mortar 2017." Mood Media, 2017. https://us.moodmedia.com/assets/2017-state-of-brick-and-mortar.pdf.

42. "Task Rabbit." Task Rabbit. Accessed February 1, 2019. https://www.taskrabbit.com/.

43. Andrea Kramer, and Mary Stevens, "Some of the Strangest Jobs People Have Paid Others to Do on TaskRabbit." CNBC, January 17, 2017. https://www.cnbc.com/2017/01/17/strangest-jobs-people-have-paid-others-to-do-on-taskrabbit.html.

44. Aaron Pressman, "Why TaskRabbit's Gig Economy Model Is Thriving under Ikea's Ownership," *Fortune*, July 17, 2018. http://fortune.com/2018/07/17/taskrabbit-ikea-brown-philpot-undercover/.

45. Diana Pearl, "Apparel Stores Can Survive the 'Retailpocalypse.' Here's How Some of Them Are Innovating." *Adweek*, September 3, 2018. https://www.adweek.com/brand-marketing/with-80-of-apparel-purchases-made-in-stores-the-retailpocalyspe-may-not-be-quite-here-yet/.

46. Ryann Reynolds McIlnay, Maureen Morrin, and Jens Nordfalt, "How Product–Environment Brightness Contrast and Product Disarray Impact Consumer Choice in Retail Environments." *Journal of Retailing 93*, no. 3 (September 2017), 266–282. doi:10.1016/j.jretai.2017.03.003.

47. Paul R. La Monica, "Activist Wants Dollar Tree to Sell Stuff for More Than $1." *CNN Business*, January 7, 2019. https://edition.cnn.com/2019/01/07/investing/dollar-tree-family-dollar-starboard/index.html.

48. "Dollar Tree Stores, Inc." Funding Universe. Accessed February 1, 2019. http://www.fundinguniverse.com/company-histories/dollar-tree-stores-inc-history/.

49. Hayley Peterson, "Dollar Tree Is One of the Only Chains That Amazon Can't Beat—and It Runs the Most Appalling Store We've Ever Seen." *Business Insider*, May 5, 2018. https://www.businessinsider.com/how-dollar-tree-is-so-successful-2018-5.

50. 99 Cents Only Stores, "99 Cents Only Stores Reports Strong Fourth Quarter and Full Year Fiscal 2017 Results." *PR Newswire*, April 20, 2017. https://www.prnewswire.com/news-releases/99-cents-only-stores-reports-strong-fourth-quarter-and-full-year-fiscal-2017-results-300442495.html.

51. Tanya Dua, "Dollar Shave Club, Warby Parker, and Casper Are Transforming Customer Experience, and It's Forcing Big Brands Like Mastercard and Marriott to Fight Back." *Business Insider*, January 14, 2019. https://www.businessinsider.com/legacy-brands-are-responding-to-the-dtc-threat-by-appointing-chief-customer-experience-officers-2019-1.

52. Dave Klimek and Kunal Mehta, "From Lip Service to Customer Service." Accenture Strategy. Accessed February 1, 2019. https://www.accenture.com/t00010101T000000Z__w__/au-en/_acnmedia/Accenture/Conversion-Assets/DotCom/Documents/Global/PDF/Strategy_8/Accenture-Strategy-Workforce-Lip-Service.pdf.

53. "Customer Experience." McKinsey & Co., June 2017. https://www.mckinsey.com/~/media/mckinsey/featured%20insights/customer%20experience/cx%20compendium%202017/customer-experience-compendium-july-2017.ashx.

54. "Exceed Expectations with Extraordinary Experiences." Accenture. Accessed February 1, 2019. https://www.accenture.com/t20171220T024439Z__w__/dk-en/_acnmedia/PDF-68/Accenture-Global-Anthem-POV.pdf.

55. Pamela N. Danzigar, "Sephora, Ulta and the Battle for the $56B U.S. Beauty Retail Market." *Forbes*, August 6, 2018. https://www.forbes.com/sites/pamdanziger/2018/08/06/sephora-and-ulta-are-on-a-collision-course-then-there-is-amazon-where-is-us-beauty-retail-headed/#476473e055dd.

56. Alex Samuely, "Sephora's Commitment to Digital Beauty Leadership Includes Beacons, Augmented Reality." Retail Dive. Accessed February 1, 2019. https://www.retaildive.com/ex/mobilecommercedaily/sephora-commits-to-digital-beauty-retail-via-beacons-augmented-reality-app.

57. Benoit Clement Bollee, "What Retailers Can Learn from Sephora's Winning Strategy." *Storefront*, February 2018. https://www.thestorefront.com/mag/what-retailers-can-learn-from-sephoras-winning-strategy/.

58. "How Sephora Built a Beauty Empire to Survive the Retail Apocalypse." *CB Insights*. Accessed February 1, 2019. https://www.cbinsights.com/research/report/sephora-teardown/.

59. Richard H. Thaler and Cass R. Sunstein, *Nudge: Improving Decisions about Health, Wealth and Happiness*. New York: Penguin, 2009.

60. Kraft Foods Inc., "OREO Enters 100th Year Crossing the $2 Billion Mark; Plans to Reach $1 Billion in Developing Markets in 2012." *PR Newswire*, May 4, 2012. https://www.prnewswire.com/news-releases/oreo-enters-100th-year-crossing-the-2-billion-mark-plans-to-reach-1-billion-in-developing-markets-in-2012-150144495.html.

61. "Warby Parker." Warby Parker. Accessed February 1, 2019. https://www.warbyparker.com/app.

62. Mark Spera, "How Did Warby Parker Grow to a $1.2 Billion Ecommerce Company in 5 Years?" *Growth Marketing Pro*, September 11, 2018. https://www.growthmarketingpro.com/warby-parker-grow-1-2-billion-ecommerce-company-5-years/.

63. Erin Mayer, "Warby Parker Has Sold (and Donated) One Million Pairs of Glasses . . ." *Bustle*, June 27, 2014. https://www.bustle.com/articles/29630-warby-parker-has-sold-and-donated-one-million-pairs-of-glasses-5-celebs-who-are-big.

64. Emily Price, "Jimmy Buffett Is More Business Than Booze These Days." *Fortune*, February 8, 2018. http://fortune.com/2018/02/08/jimmy-buffett-margaritaville-business/.

65. Taffy Brodesser Akner, "Jimmy Buffett Does Not Live the Jimmy Buffett Lifestyle." *New York Times*, February 8, 2018. https://www.nytimes.com/2018/02/08/arts/jimmy-buffett-does-not-live-the-jimmy-buffett-lifestyle.html.

66. Jena Tesse Fox, "How a Strong Brand Proposition, CEO Keep Margaritaville from Wasting Away." *Hotel Management*, July 13, 2018. https://www.hotelmanagement.net/own/how-margaritaville-ceo-john-cohlan-built-a-brand.

67. Steve Yastrow, *Brand Harmony: Achieving Dynamic Results by Orchestrating Your Customer's Total Experience*. New York: SelectBooks, 2003.

# CULTURAL CONNEC- TIONS

## *Branding Objective: Align Thoughts and Actions*

| FLASH-FORWARD | BRAND SPOTLIGHTS | |
|---|---|---|
| Conscious consumerism | Ben & Jerry's | 🍦 |
| Values | Disney | 🏰 |
| Purpose | Marriott | 🏨 |
| Policies | Mod Pizza | 🍕 |
| Protocols | Patagonia | 🥾 |
| Point of view | Ritz-Carlton | 🚪 |
| Positioning | Snickers | 🍫 |
| Corporate narrative | The Story | 🏛 |
| Storytelling | TOMS | 👟 |
| Shared enemy | WeWork | 👫 |
| | Zara | 👗 |

The birth of *conscious consumerism* (i.e., originally signaled under economic theories of "conspicuous consumption") began far before Wall Street bucked at "brand purpose" or Simon Sinek challenged leaders to dig deeper into their "why." In 1892, the University of Chicago opened. Aside from recruiting students, they needed to hire faculty for every part of the school. Little did they know that economics would become their world-class beacon. One of the initial 200 faculty members teaching the first incoming class of 600 students, Norwegian-American Thorstein Veblen joined the newly formed economics department in 1892 to eventually pen his observations on culture in *The Theory of the Leisure Class*.[1] Courted by James Laughlin, a well-respected economist who chaired the department and later founded the Federal Reserve Bank, Veblen also notably collaborated with John Dewey, who later founded the New School in New York, which includes the present-day Parsons School of Design.[2]

Before offering his perspective on consumption, Veblen formally studied and worked for notable economists including John Bates Clark, who has a prestigious medal given in his honor by the American Economic Association (AEA) to one promising economist under age 40 (often as a precursor to winning the Nobel Prize in Economics). Possibly, John Bates Clark saw a spark in Veblen. Characterized as a smart yet frequent voice of dissent, Veblen left us with an important consumer nugget: seeds for conscious business (i.e., sustainability, CSR, and purpose). In his 1899 work *The Theory of the Leisure Class,* Veblen notes that "conspicuous consumption of valuable goods is a means of reputability to the gentleman of leisure."[3] Translation: people with disposable income will want to display that income through their purchase behavior. While his early thoughts on conspicuous consumption choices applied to more affluent individuals, companies have now come to see the necessity of weaving the principle into everyday products to allow all consumers to use everyday purchase behavior as a badge that they support sustainability, socioeconomic, and environmental issues. And companies such as

Bath & Body Works, TOMS shoes, and Whole Foods, to name a few, have now built their business around values of conscious consumerism, laying a blueprint for how fast-growing companies must anchor themselves in values and purpose carried out by their practices, policies, and brand behaviors.

# TOMS

*Showcasing Global Accountability*

TOMS Shoes—known for its "Shoes for Tomorrow" charity—began in Texas. Its founder, Blake Mycoskie, took only six years to grow the company to a value of $300 million, while retaining 100% ownership. By 2012, he did something almost unheard-of for a successful CEO of a multimillion-dollar corporation: Mycoskie took a break. Mycoskie later said the reason for this sabbatical was that he felt "lost because TOMS had become more focused on process than on purpose." When he returned, he felt a renewed sense of purpose, wanting to bring TOMS back to its origins when the company, which designs and sells Argentine-style shoes, eyewear, coffee, apparel, and handbags, was more of a movement than a business. As of 2018, TOMS had given away over a million pairs of shoes to those in need in over 40 countries across the world and vowed to continue this type of philanthropy as part of their business mission.[4,5]

Pitting global brands like Pepsi and Nike against consumers to determine if the brands care enough or have done enough for the social issues and causes featured in their marketing with Kendall Jenner and Colin Kaepernick, consumers want brand behaviors to align with corporate rhetoric and marketing narratives (see Culture-Ethics test later in this chapter). Consumers are forcing brands to consider how they're making them better off, rather than creating a fading pop-culture moment through a mix of controversial imagery and empathyless PR ambition for impressions. The pre-turn-of-the-century notion of conscious consumerism has taken well over 100 years to permeate capitalism through triple-bottom-line reporting but seems resolute on staying top-of-mind for leaders through purpose, CSR, sustainability, and responsible supply-chain practices.

# BEN & JERRY'S

*Fighting for Social Justice One Scoop at a Time*

Is there a more iconic brand of ice cream these days than Ben & Jerry's? Ben Cohen and Jerry Greenfield opened their first parlor in Burlington, Vermont, in 1978, and even though Dutch conglomerate Unilever gobbled them up in 2000, that hasn't meant the brand has become stale. On the contrary, Ben & Jerry's maintains an active sense of social justice, something its founders cared about deeply. CEO Jostein Solheim has continued this mission ever since he took over the brand in 2010. After a controversy in the 1990s over the use of artificial ingredients (all products were advertised as containing only natural ingredients), Ben & Jerry's currently employs fair-trade workers, uses only cage-free eggs, and works with sustainable dairy farms. Profits are donated to racial justice, voting rights, and campaign finance reform organizations, among many other issues. The company even incorporates the product itself into this mission. The Empower Mint flavor was released in North Carolina as a protest against the state's suppression of voting rights among its African American residents; proceeds went to local chapters of the NAACP to help black voters register to vote. Ben & Jerry's may not hold the largest market share among ice cream brands, but it is undoubtedly the most visible, and the one most attached to a brand identity that engages with its customers in a substantive, sustainable way.[6,7,8,9]

Launched in 1991, Edelman's Trust Barometer tracks "trust" levels of citizens toward media, businesses, NGOs, and governments.[10] With the aftereffects of the financial crisis bailouts, outsourcing of jobs, and automation, consumer trust for "big business" continues to fall, at least in the United States. While trust of businesses has been trending down, over 73% of global participants from 20 countries agreed that a company can simultaneously improve both profits and socioeconomic conditions, with 76% of participants agreeing that the change must come from the CEO's leadership.[11] According to Forbes's annual ranking of the Most Reputable Companies, calculated based on nearly 250,000 participants from 15 countries, the top brands are: Rolex, Lego, Google, Canon, and Disney.[12] Companies are most successful, arguably, when they have clear and consistent values that are well known among their tribe of enthusiasts, yet are inclusive and welcoming to anyone new to the brand. All brands with a clear North Star and shared positive feeling ingrained in the brand ethos are on the right track to navigate a noisy world where consumers can, do, and will continue to raise their voices in protest, or vote through their spending behaviors.

Managing over $6 trillion in assets, BlackRock CEO Larry Fink joined the company in 1988 and has since grown it to be bigger than Warren Buffett's Berkshire Hathaway, Thomas Jefferson's BNY Mellon, and JP Morgan Chase's banking empire. In leading over 10,000 global employees, he writes a letter to shareholders each January to provide guidance on the year ahead. In his 2018 letter, Fink recognized, "To prosper over time, every company must not only deliver financial performance, but also show how it makes a positive contribution to society."[13] This is a reminder echoed almost annually on major shareholder guidance as a result of conscious consumerism crossing over from Veblen's elite "leisure class" into the middle class. And into the near future, a tug of war between Wall Street and Main Street will demand more from companies as digital shifts the macro culture toward rewarding greater transparency.

# PATAGONIA

*Supporting Employees Who Care about the Environment*

Sometimes, it pays to invest in your passions. Rock climber Yvon Chouinard planted the seeds of what would blossom into Patagonia when he started selling climbing gear in 1957, at the tender age of 19 years old. More than a decade later, Chouinard expanded into apparel, and formally founded the company in 1973. Chouinard's personal investment in environmental activism demanded that the brand be associated with the cause. When so many companies adopt a brand purpose to merely talk the talk, Patagonia stays busy walking the walk. Today, the Ventura, California–based company builds its commitment to the environment into its corporate culture. As the organization puts it, they seek to "build the best product, cause no unnecessary harm, use business to inspire and implement solutions to the environmental crisis." One percent of annual net revenues have been donated to environmental nonprofit groups in every year since 2002. Giving each employee ample time to volunteer and immerse in the great outdoors, the brand's dedication to protecting public lands led to the formation of Conservación Patagonia, which helped establish a national park in Chile.[14,15,16]

The same as with economics, navigating culture requires an understanding of what people really want—and how those nuances differ between communities. Over the past decade, the transparency offered through (social) media has had many benefits that few marketers fully anticipated. For instance, social media allowed consumers to go from being faceless demographics in media buys to being viewed as real people in dynamic communities that have views and voices. It took employees from being optimized as productivity inputs (i.e., human capital) for profit to being supported as people who cannot escape the reality of socioeconomic issues of disparity and injustice. And it took companies from being able to sit on the sidelines to having to justify silence and inaction.

In many regards, our oversharing of information has led to an accelerated understanding of communities—an always-on, unfiltered look at humanity through their beliefs, behaviors, and norms—through one selfie at a time. It's in this intersection that the rigor of trend analysis and pattern recognition starts to reveal how shifts in consumption are indicative of much deeper shifts in culture. And not just external consumer culture, but rather corporate culture inside brands. In this chapter, we will talk about how to bring together two inescapable communities for any brand striving for growth—consumers and employees. We get reinforcement that culture is an amalgamation of artifacts and customs from communities. We will come to understand that a community is just a collective consciousness hived together. Aptly last, in finding your brand's North Star, it's necessary to develop a customer-centric company culture in an attempt to build a fast-growing company through a holistic branding system. How and where do you start? The first step is to humbly acknowledge that no company is too big to fail, and that every company must figure out how to wire their internal culture to meet expectations of operating responsibly.

## THE MYTH OF "SAFETY IN SIZE"

Following the global financial crisis of 2007–2008, there started to be glimpses of a public understanding that "too big to fail" policies, practices, and perspectives were no longer working.

There was a public awakening to the crack in the veneer that companies can operate indefinitely on old value systems. Consulting firm Capgemini reviewed Fortune 500 companies listed from 2000 to 2015, and found that 50% of them weren't too big to fail, having gone extinct, bankrupt, or merged with other companies.[17] Gone are the days of status quo, in which one or two family-owned companies control an industry or market leaders are protected. Business today requires agility, boldness, and leapfrog innovations. Consider General Electric, having appeared on the Fortune 500 list a record 24 times since the list launched in 1955, lost 50% of its stock value in 2018.[18] In that same year, retail giants, and once Fortune 500 mainstays, Sears and JC Penney struggled to stave off young, hungry, tech-centric digital retail startups from StichFix to Rent the Runway. In fact, only 12% of companies appearing on the 1955 Fortune 500 list re-appeared in the 2017 ranking.[19]

In an age of convergence, collaboration, and confluence, no brands should feel comfortable. That unease should compel you to keep reading to find how fast-growing companies are breaking records, outsmarting leader brands, and riding a positive consumer feeling to records sales and revenue, whether it's StichFix (one of the fastest brands to get a $1 billion valuation), Spotify (one of the fastest brands to gain over 100 million users), or SoulCycle (one of the only brands to average double-digit growth for a consecutive five-plus-year period). According to Martin's CEO Kristen Cavallo, "When you impact culture, you impact sales."[20] Having reinvented their own internal culture while influencing pop culture, The Martin Agency has created over 100 Geico ads over the past 20 years.[21] Based on brand recall, Geico is a brand firmly in the pop culture zeitgeist of 90% of Americans.[22] Martin understands that paying attention to the convergence of community and culture leads to brand building in a noisy world.

# MARRIOTT

*Treating Guests with Mindfulness*

Little could J. Willard Marriott have imagined that his Washington, DC, root beer stand, opened in 1927, would turn into a hospitality megalith with revenues of nearly $23 billion by 2018. Marriott was already one of the biggest hotel chains in the world before 2015, but its acquisition of Starwood Hotels and Resorts brought such brands as St. Regis, W Hotels, and Sheraton into the fold, helping to rapidly increase its market share to become the largest hotel operator.

In 2018, the company decided to emphasize a new brand purpose, one that tapped into the essential element of hospitality—empathy. They launched the "Golden Rule" campaign for their four core brands (Fairfield, Court-yard, Four Points, and Spring Hill), signaling a new internal culture. The corporate effort across four brands that delivered one third of Marriott's revenue represented an effort to strip away the stress and fear of a cold, clinical hospitality experience that so many customers dread. Marriott got personal. The universal values of caring and compassion could have been at risk of disappearing in such a structured, corporate environment; Marriott broke through that, and their growth continues apace.[23,24]

## COMMUNICATION'S ROLE IN CULTURE

Communication is arguably one of the most important parts of "culture." Every culture has a unique relationship with elements of communication—lexicon, audio, and visuals—and it is that unique relationship with communication that makes customer experience and internal culture powerful branding tools. Culture, whether internal to employees or external for consumers, comes from communities. And we immerse in those expressions of community through music, literature, art, traditions, religion, fashion, and so on, all the way down to values.

In late 2018, I attended an event that happens annually for a hand-selected group of 300 senior marketers, technology leaders, and influencers. During one session, Super Bowl champ turned CEO, Martellus Bennett, took the stage to tell about his journey from the field to the boardroom, noting an observation that "knowledge evaporates between the streets and the top floor."[25] His words ring true among all rungs of upper management struggling to understand what motivates communities, offering a valuable lesson that

# WEWORK

*Fostering Community-Building through Immersion*

Started in 2010, WeWork seeks to promote the spirit of community in the most positive way. With locations in 100 cities, WeWork's estimated value is nearly $50 billion, nipping at the market caps of T-Mobile and Walgreens. The company doesn't just manage real estate, it also helps businesses, small and large, foster a sense of community through a shared culture of access and diversity. To build a strong internal culture, WeWork hosts an annual camping trip where longtime employees and new employees have the chance to bond with and learn from community members. In 2018, they hosted over 8,000 attendees, hailing from communities all over the world, representing the vast reach of their co-working spaces. As part of their enterprise, WeWork partners with corporations like Microsoft, Facebook, Adidas, and CitiFinancial, to help unlock their own intrapreneurial aspirations by co-locating alongside startups.[26,27,28] you can't look at a printed report or screen with a persona and feel you "know" anything about an audience. His underlying message: immersion and empowerment of more voices. As evidenced by Undercover Boss, it's sometimes those at the top who need to take time with employees and consumers as a reminder of whether their brand is resonating on the frequency of communities.

Through immersion alongside people—not just immersion in data alone—you start to understand that culture is ever-changing (Figure 10.1). Culture has fluidity, shifting over time depending based on which community dominates politics, economics, art, and commerce. Culture is an iceberg—both ever-present and invisible to the naked eye. And culture is a shared experience—inclusive of behavior, beliefs, and values. Culture comes from communities, and communities grant permission to brands to participate in their culture. Brands can have a domino effect within culture, but only if communities and tribes react.

## FIGURE 10.1
# CHARACTERISTICS OF CULTURE

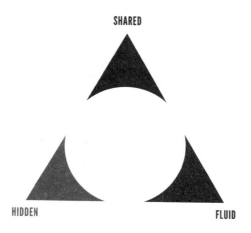

*Culture functions as a shared yet fluid flow between people and communities, operating with often invisible social norms and behaviors.*

# GETTING OUT OF YOUR SEAT, AND INTO THE FIELD

So how do you learn about "culture" and how can companies encourage employees to immerse at scale? The marketing and communications industry have taught us that "creatives"—designers, art directors, copywriters, and so on—are the only ones who can generate great ideas. That those individuals are "trained" to solve problems in time-boxed situations, and that those individuals must provide their seal of approval before an idea is ready to go-to-market. This notion is flawed. While there is a design process that they facilitate and several paths to unlock creativity that they traverse, everyone within an organization needs to be a creative problem solver with the confidence to talk about, create ideas for, and engage to inspire action among communities. When only a small team or community manager can determine what moves a community's culture, then the entire organization will suffer from inauthenticity.

However, getting individuals to be creative problem solvers is easier said than done. Organizational structure often limits the ability of employees to immerse within culture. For example, employees are often given little time to generate ideas, and within that limited time must weigh a number of factors: past actions (for company, client, and industry); audience insights; objectives/intended outcomes; and realities of execution (budget, timing, staff). To fully immerse in culture, you must untether employees from their desks and let them play in the zoo of life. We must stop expecting employees to Google their way into strategy; people need to immerse in order to become effective problem solvers.

Over the past decade, global companies from Google to 3M have begun to explore how to best inspire creative problem solving while not putting extreme pressure on their employees to perform. During that time, several models have emerged:

- Give employees free time (3M, Google)
- Provide creative/play spaces (IDEO, Zappos, Red Bull, agency digital and innovation "labs")
- Create unconventional working environments (Pixar desks are like cottages; Timberland offices features a rock wall; Cisco has sleeping pods for employees to take naps)
- Facilitate innovation/case competitions (Deloitte)
- Create resident experts to predict the future (futurists at AOL, Microsoft, Edelman, Altimeter)

As a vice president at global communication agency Porter Novelli, I created and led an initiative called "!magination @ Work" that was modeled after successful cultural immersion programs. Our mission was simple: give employees a structured way to explore the world and bring those insights back into the company to drive deeper engagement with communities . . . to loosen our over-reliance on data and fine-tune our ability to interpret the plentiful signals around us in music, art, fashion, and beyond. In its simplest form, the program included 15 participants from planning, creative, and account management in roles ranging from producers to vice presidents. Participants could do one of three things: (1) go on a two-hour exploration (e.g., new restaurant or store), (2) conduct a half-day exploration (e.g., museum, theatre), or (3) complete site visits to innovative companies like Quirky. The goal was to introduce new ways of thinking about how to develop communication and engagement based on culture; and the one commitment was to bring the insights back to the organization to diffuse the learnings.

Challenge to all brand leaders: stop hiding behind computer screens, data sets, and corporate firewalls; rather, go experience what your audience experiences. Leave the comfy VIP section of your events to walk the floor, go stand in line to buy a product in your retail channels, or call your service line for support. Only in doing so will you learn how to fix customer frustrations and, more important, anticipate their expectations before they negatively articulate them publicly, on the record, to other tribe members. Only through immersion will you and your executive leadership keep moving your brand forward with improvements in consumer sentiment, attitude, and preferences. Choose a day of the week, and commit to the immersion.

# ZARA

*Creating a Cosmopolitan Brand That Moves*
*at the Speed of Local Style*

The Spanish fashion retailer Zara, founded in 1975 by Amancio Ortega and Rosalía Mera, is one of the more globally known brands among sister companies including Massimo Dutti, Pull&Bear, Bershka, Stradivarius, Oysho, and Uterqüe. Zara is the most popular store in the holding group with nearly 20 clothing collections introduced to consumers annually. In 2018, Zara was number 46 on the Forbes List of Most Valuable Brands with annual revenues of nearly $20 billion. What sets Zara apart from the competition is the company's tight closed feedback loop between sales and production: they can produce a product within a week's time compared to the six months it takes most stores in the fashion industry, and if a product isn't selling, it's pulled off the shelf within a week to make room for another potential mover. This pace allows for the company to produce nearly 12,000 new designs each year, all at the speed that the culture among their buyer community shifts. According to founder Ortega, "Innovation and commitment toward our customers defines our corporate culture," and that is why they are constantly improving their inventory.[29,30,31]

Senior executives, strategists, entrepreneurs, and investors all have the same question—how do you influence culture? To answer their question, I lead groups through an interactive workshop on how to hack and hijack culture and cover some of the principles from my *Battle of the Mind* course at Columbia University. Over a series of exercises, we drill down into how to evolve from cold "target audience" thinking into a fluid "community" tribalism, explore the origins and artifacts of communities, and discuss the nuances of ethically engaging communities. During one early exercise, the group is challenged to write a list of the many "communities" to which they belong. And then we talk about what's a community and the observations from the exercise. Regardless of the group, participants have several revelations that change how they view culture, and the role of the brand in supporting communities.

After completing the exercise, a few things become clear to participants. First, each community has a unique culture, and that culture adds a layer to each person's identity. Second, we belong to dozens of communities, and the values of those different communities clash. And third, in those clashes we see that every community has a villain and a hero, because every community has something to protect. It's no surprise, then, that fast-growing brands are good at identifying, naming, and rallying a tribe against an enemy—a strategy that can effectively bond a community together.

## WHO'S THE VILLAIN IN YOUR BRAND STORY?

When starting my career in marketing at global advertising agency Ogilvy in New York, the allure of working for a big brand was intoxicating. Their creative motto was to "Make Brands Matter," and they knew how to spark behavioral change. Launched in 1957, over the decades, Dove started losing ground among women as the standard of "beauty" shifted under the influence of pop culture to include rampant misrepresentations in advertising of beauty, body type, and self-image.[32] The biggest victims—young girls who were barraged with airbrushed, color-corrected, and augmented visuals. Ogilvy's planning team uncovered that women were losing self-confidence in the race toward unachievable beauty standards. Through the iconic Real Beauty work launched in 2004, Dove named an enemy: stereotypes propagated to young girls and women through imagery that ultimately lowers self-esteem. It was one of the first case studies that was taught to me as a young planner and strategist, and a memorable lesson in how people rally against villains. Ten years after the campaign launched to spark a new, positive brand feeling through coordinated marketing, operations, partnerships, and licensing efforts, Dove accomplished products sales growth of nearly 80%.[33] The beauty brand was playing its role in conscious consumerism, and building it into the fast-moving consumer packaged goods category.

# SNICKERS

*Naming a Shared Enemy*

By 2010, Snickers was in a rut. The 80-year-old brand was finding that their ability to retain customers was next to impossible, and for that matter, their messaging was trying to attract too narrow a demographic. Snickers was part of the Mars legacy, the same outfit that gave the world the Milky Way, Three Musketeers, and M&Ms treats. Snickers was one of the family-owned company's oldest brands, but it needed a major shakeup in order to become a household name again. BBDO global head of strategy James Miller put it more bluntly: Snickers needed fame.

In stepped the "You're Not You When You're Hungry" campaign, launched during Super Bowl XLIV in 2010. One should not recognize satisfaction when they buy a candy; if you're satisfied already, what's the point in grabbing a candy bar off the shelf? Instead, the campaign targeted the fundamental feeling of hunger, and the immediate resolution of such a feeling that a candy bar can give you. Hunger was an enemy, and a Snickers bar was the sword with which to vanquish it. It worked. Within two years, global sales of Snickers increased nearly 16% after the campaign launched while market share of Snickers grew in 56 of the 58 markets where the first spot aired. According to Euromonitor International, by 2012, Snickers had overtaken Mars labelmate M&Ms as the biggest international confection brand, a leadership spot it has since enjoyed. [34,35,36]

Shared enemy branding works for three key reasons. First, we try to minimize negativity (and those that cause it). That negativity minimization is bedrock to Daniel Kahneman's behavioral principle of loss aversion. And "enemies" fall in that category of things to minimize in our noisy lives. Second, hating an enemy creates normative behavior toward the villain, which we learned in the previous chapter is imperative for using *experience* to differentiate and foster community. For instance, the enemy of cigarettes (and nicotine) has been slowly getting vanquished by communities through legislations—package labeling, anti-smoking laws indoors, and laws regulating distance of smoking areas near building entrances. Third, we gravitate toward mystery. According to communication and culture researcher Jens Kjeldgaard-Christiansen, based at Aarhus University in Amsterdam, villains elicit disgust, which drives more empathy for the victim, which could be the community itself. [37] It's through the three hooks of minimizing negativity, creating normative behavior, and leaning into mystery that make enemy positioning effective in producing fast-growing brands.

---

Common shared enemies might include:
- Social issues (e.g., laws)
- Physiological states (e.g., hunger)
- Mental states (e.g., boredom)

- Health conditions
- Stereotypes (e.g., industry and consumer)
- Rivals

---

## FINDING YOUR NORTH STAR

Simon Sinek has inspired millions of people to *Start with Why*, the title of his best-selling book, when determining purpose.[38] When defining your brand's *why*, I'd implore you to name a positive feeling you want to impress upon others. Make that feeling a compass to navigate toward your brand's North Star of what you do and how you do. In a time when collaboration is making companies reconsider once competitive threats, following the feeling creates partnerships that can unlock new value propositions. Exercises such as experience mapping (from Chapter 9) help define where those new collaboration opportunities can organically exist. As leaders, challenge your teams to shift internal culture from using "policies, practices, and protocols" that penalize employees, to an internal culture that grants permission and empowers employees to take positive action to further the brand values in dealing with co-workers, partners, and consumers.

Our heritage . . . what heritage?

Let's face it, most founders don't start a company from the benevolence of their heart. Their *why* is sometimes being good at something technical and thus being able to turn a profit from that expertise. Our insta-fame isn't the result of longing for the limelight, as in the movie *20 Feet Away*. Most companies have to engineer doing good into their DNA now, and that's fine. There are strategic ways to define a company's true north and ensure that practices quickly realign.

According to Harvard Business School professor Michael Porter, known for creating Porter's Five Forces, ultimately, "companies are widely perceived to be prospering at the expense of the broader community."[39] He urges businesses to move beyond CSR and into shared value,[40] defining shared value as "creating economic value in a way that also creates value for society by addressing its needs and challenges."[41] Companies great at influencing culture share traits: finding tension, standing up to an enemy, changing the narrative, challenging the status quo, changing trajectory of society through policy, and making a difference in people's lives.

How do you know if your efforts in improving internal culture to affect external community cultures are working?

- New people joining the brand community (i.e., bandwagon effect)
- More voices are amplified that represent leaders within communities
- Behavior shifts among communities toward "normative behaviors" that involve the brand (i.e., shared conduct, habits)
- Sense of belonging and hive effect that brings community closer together (e.g., new technology)
- Communities start to reflect inclusion and accessibility to all (e.g., no socioeconomic barriers to belonging)
- Community willingness to defend and protect the brand, more so than simply recommending or promoting the brand

## BUILDING A NARRATIVE

In essence, strong companies have strong points of view and are able to articulate that point of view in a way that consumers can easily repeat to others. While others may call that point of view your brand story, narrative, why, purpose, or raison d'être, whatever it is called, it should be singular-minded. And that point of view should

## FIGURE 10.2

# BUILDING POINT OF VIEW

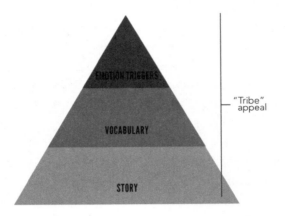

*Point of view has three core elements: a story (e.g., a breakthrough moment), a focused field of language (e.g., branded vocabulary), and communication triggers (e.g., lexicon, audio, visuals) that appeal to tribe.*

inform how you navigate the noisy world around us. Through point of view, we start to see interconnections between parts of the LAVEC branding system (Figure 10.2): lexicon that triggers emotions, branded vocabulary that makes the point of view attributable back to the company, and rich stories supported by strong audio and visuals and experiences that immerse audiences in values. This takes us a step further than retail theater toward tribal appeal.

## AN AGE WHERE POV MATTERS

In 2010, content marketing was quickly becoming the currency of social media. Craving a deep-dive into storytelling, I joined Radical Media, the production company that filmed the pilot of *Mad Men*. We were just launching the fifth season of *Iconoclast*, a critically acclaimed branded content property created for Grey Goose, featuring paired activity-based interviews between Charlize Theron and Jane Goodall, Hugh Jackman and Jean-Georges Vongerichten, and David Blaine and Chuck Close. The experience taught me about the power of owning your point of view, even if your brand is you, as an individual, and the power of converging perspectives with someone seemingly dissimilar. The result of bringing together the point of view pairings: stories that both captivated through relatable characters and challenged the status quo, stories that gave a new perspective, and stories that brought communities together around a common mission of empathy.

Storytelling is a powerful medium. Disney, for instance, masterfully imparts lessons and value through stories. Through these powerhouse studios, we see that a good story is a Trojan horse—people will listen and often be disarmed. As brands—products, services, and people—we must have compelling stories built on a point of view of the world around us. To be silent in a noisy world is slow brand death.

# THE STORY

*Making Retail Theater a Curated Experience*

"So, what's the story?" That must be the question that inspired Rachel Shechtman when she named the little fashion shop she opened in 2011 in the west Chelsea neighborhood at the corner of 10th Avenue and 19th Street in Manhattan. The story about the Story is one of original and inventive branding. With a mere 1,600 square feet of selling space, and far from the regal midtown glitz of Fifth, Madison, and Park Avenues, the shop called Story has become a remarkable magnet for high-powered fashion executives as well as small-business owners. On a typical Saturday the Story—visible from the highly frequented High Line and steps away from Chelsea Market occupied by Google—draws in 2,000 visitors.

Describing their business model, Shechtman notes, "We change every three to eight weeks like a gallery, and we sell things like a store." Her strategy is to stock an eclectic range of fashions and wares from interesting but little-known suppliers, to give those brands exposure to major retailers and influencers on a national stage. With 20 years' experience as a fashion consultant, Shechtman had the branding know-how to bring industry power players into Story's orbit, including Target, J. Crew, Drexler, and Lands' End, as well as people like Martha Stewart and Whoopi Goldberg. Call it branding with a cast of characters. In 2018, only seven years after Story's founding, Shechtman sold the enterprise to Macy's. Story's operations continue, with Rachel's daughter taking over the shop, while Rachel moved on to become Macy's new brand experience officer, reporting directly to Macy's president. [42] [43]

So how do you make your story sticky? According to research conducted by University of Pennsylvania Wharton professor Jonah Berger, people are more likely to share information that makes them look good. In *Contagious*, he argues that people mostly want to look smart, cool, and in-the-know. "People don't think in terms of information. They think in terms of narratives. But while people focus on the story itself, information comes along for the ride."[44] Partnering with Hearst Magazines to launch a magazine for hosts and guests, Airbnb ventured into publishing to use narrative and storytelling to inspire travelers[45]—a "branded" point of view that now represents a new business model, with titles also being launched for fast-growing company Bumble.

In 2007, Fox premiered *Are You Smarter Than a Fifth Grader?* The overnight sensation attracted over 10 million viewers regularly, and spawned into a trivia empire including video games, toys, and license deals. The show succeeded in America largely because, well, the average person actually is just about as smart as a fifth grader. And, in fact, speech analysis shows how most U.S. presidents acknowledge that reality by speaking at a middle-school level. When that "make me look good" information is wrapped in emotional triggers and useful, then stories has a high chance of becoming viral. No story, though, has a chance of becoming well-known, unless it's framed at the right communication level for targeted communities.

In 1975, wanting to ensure consistency in one form of story-telling—manuals—the U.S. Navy commissioned researchers to develop the Flesch-Kincaid scale to measure reading grade level. The scale is commonly used as a communication pressure test within politics, legislation, and official government documents, to ensure ease of comprehension. Several free online tools include readability tests that can help you craft a brand story that reso-nates with your audience. U.S. presidents in the past 20 years have spoken on a fifth- to eighth-grade level, while earlier presidents such as Abraham Lincoln communicated on an eleventh-grade level. What level are your key communities? What level are your ads and marketing? On what level are your policies written? Flesch-Kincaid provides a military-grade precision to honing your brand story to appeal to your key communities and is an underleveraged tool in culture building.

**TRY THIS:**

Passing the Grade

Use an online version of the Flesch-Kincaid reading test on your brand communication—social media posts, executive keynotes, company handbook, and beyond. What level are they? Based on social media posts, using the Flesch-Kincaid scale, what level are your target audiences? Are your communications and communities on the same page?

In 2016, tech editor Adrienne Lafrance investigated the science behind storytelling. In her piece in *The Atlantic*, she detailed how researchers at the University of Vermont and the University of

Adelaide analyzed over 1,500 books, scoring language along the way as either happy or negative.[46] Surprisingly, AI could use sentiment to predict when a story arc was forming and about to change. Based on their analysis, there are only six types of emotional arcs. What kind of story arc is your brand in right now? What's the next chapter you need to tell?

1. Rags to Riches (rise)
2. Riches to Rags (fall)
3. Man in a Hole (fall then rise)
4. Icarus (rise then fall)
5. Cinderella (rise then fall then rise)
6. Oedipus (fall then rise then fall)

## OWNING YOUR NARRATIVE

So what matters most, then, related to a brand story or founder's story? Psychologist and Harvard professor Amy Cuddy ventures an answer: trust and respect.[47] In *Presence*, she argues that trust comes through character and respect through competence. "Trust is the conduit for influence; it's the medium through which ideas travel."[48] When crafting your narrative and living in the world, be sure that it leaves the audience with a strong feeling of both trust and respect.

What unites Barbz, the Navy, or the Beyhive? What unites SoulCycle enthusiasts, Barry Bootcamp fanatics, and Equinox loyalists? What unites fans of the Cubs, Warriors, and Cowboys? Normative behavior. And when your community starts to demonstrate normative behaviors they create themselves or ones your brand creates with the invitation for them to join, then you will have a brand signal for healthiness. Normative behavior—not your logo or mark—is your brand signature and reminder that a compelling story, once it becomes a truly powerful narrative with a strong point of view, will motivate and move people to action.

As we teach graduate students, awareness is not an objective. Only with behavior can a brand measure its full magnitude.

**TRY THIS:**

Executive POV

Need a narrative in a pinch? Trying to figure out how to tell a story that motivates interviewers? Sticky and compelling leadership messaging comes from the following avenues:

1. Personal story of being outside a comfort zone, being a change agent, or being a humble servant
2. The fours Cs (controversy, conflict, contradictions, catchphrases)
3. Insider information/access
4. Answers to questions people ask you most often

So how literal should a story be? Well, we tend to think in terms of metaphors that help us relate to the world around us. Harvard Business School professor Gerald Zaltman specializes on the intersection of emotions and decision-making. In his 2008 book *Marketing Metaphoria*, Zaltman relies on 12,000 interviews with consumers in 30 countries, he argues "deep metaphors play powerfully yet silent in the unconscious minds of consumers, are relatively few, and are universal."[49] Through his collective body of academic research, he concludes that 95% of our "thought, emotion, and learning" happen without our awareness.[50] To translate those feelings into meaning, he concludes there are seven cord metaphors that marketers can build strategy:

- Balance (e.g., food and beverage)
- Transformation (e.g., health)
- Journey (e.g., apparel and travel)
- Container (e.g., auto)

- Connection (e.g., wireless and media)
- Resource (e.g., technology and software)
- Control (e.g., home security)

**TRY THIS:**
—
**"POV FRAMING"**

How could you reframe an issue, cause, or community using branded vocabulary? Are there new metaphors you could introduce into your narrative to achieve greater saliency?

## UNDERCOVER BOSS

Launched in 2010 on CBS, the show *Undercover Boss* takes viewers on a journey to see the inner workings of a company from the perspective of select employees. Participating companies have included: NASCAR, MGM Grand, Subway. As managers, your role is to ensure that brand values are clear in external customer experiences and internal culture. Consumers and employees pledge their loyalty to companies with clear values, which requires brands to have more transparency than ever. A surge of rankings—sustainability cores, human rights ratings, best places to work, and so on—means there are a dozen "systems" for rating companies based on their values. As of 2017, 85% of companies on the S&P 500 tracked and reported their sustainability efforts; up 300% from 2011 when only 20% of companies reported their efforts.[51] In 2017, politics forced the hand of many companies

# RITZ-CARLTON

*Empowering All Employees to Be Problem Solvers*

The most famous name in luxury accommodation has its roots in the original Hôtel Ritz, opened in Paris back in 1898, and its London sibling, the Carlton, opened a year later. The modern iteration began in 1911, when hotelier Albert Keller bought the franchise rights to both brands and opened the Ritz-Carlton in New York. The modern Ritz-Carlton Hotel Company launched in 1983, followed by a takeover by Marriott in 1998. They are Marriott's premier luxury hotel brand, with 130 locations operating worldwide.

It is no surprise that the core of Ritz-Carlton's brand purpose is service, but unlike the "Golden Rule" effort that Marriott launched for four of its portfolio brands, Ritz-Carlton struck gold in a different way. The brand employs what it calls the *Gold Standards*, codes of conduct to which all of its staff must hold themselves. Most intriguing is "The 6th Diamond" category, the area in which the hotel hopes to distinguish itself even beyond the highest standard of evaluation. One of the credos of the 6th Diamond is mystique. There must be a certain alluring air of mystery about the hotel in order for it to feel exclusive and special. In fact, each staffer is permitted to spend up to $2,000 to make every guest's stay as rewarding as possible. The brand may face stiff competition in cities like New York and London, but it dominates smaller cities. Overall, Ritz-Carlton's 5% market share among luxury hotel brands leads all comers.[52,53]

in showing their values—both a healthcare and technology council for the president dissolved after corporate partners pulled out, citing corporate values, including Merck (whose stock rose 35% in 2018). Values can no longer be internal only—employees must wear them on their sleeve.

When values resonate with audience values, the brand becomes a "parachute of happiness." Consider Disney, the most magical place on Earth, which through nearly every touchpoint ignites the brand around ONE central feeling that is universal. So much so, that even when Disney sponsors a night on ABC's *Dancing with the Stars*—despite the typical rules—no contestants are eliminated. What does your brand do that makes it a "parachute of happiness"?

---

Based on work from social psychologist Shalom Schwarz, who has conducted research among 60,000 participants in 80 countries, there are 10 universal values.[54]

His widely accepted values system includes sparks for brands to use narrative, points of view, and internal culture as growth springboards:

1. **Power:** Demonstrating control, dominance, and strength
2. **Achievement:** Projecting success and excellence
3. **Hedonism:** Satisfying pleasure
4. **Stimulation:** Chasing novelty
5. **Self-direction:** Being a free thinker
6. **Universalism:** Championing rights and equality for all
7. **Benevolence:** Caring for community
8. **Tradition:** Respecting heritage and custom
9. **Conformity:** Upholding norms
10. **Security:** Ensuring safety and stabilization

# DISNEY

*Tapping into Universal Values*

What do you feel when you hear the word "Disney"? You probably feel happy, or at least recognize that Disney is a company in the happiness business. It has been that way for over 90 years, when a young Walt Disney first started making cartoons. The release of *Steamboat Willie* in 1928—the world's first audio-synced cartoon, which introduced audiences to Mickey Mouse—catapulted Walt to fame. He built a major movie studio that expanded into feature films, live action films, television, theme parks, merchandise, sports, theatre, cruises, and so much more. With Fox by its side, Disney is set to continue delivering entertainment to families worldwide in mixed formats, including augmented reality. But first and foremost, it wants its name to make you feel happy.

Because of that history, that brand purpose must hold true in all aspects of Disney's ever-expanding empire. Their goal is to create a "parachute of happiness" that permeates across platforms. Happiness is a universal feeling, and Disney hopes to protect its place as a universally appealing brand. *Dancing with the Stars*—broadcast on ABC, a Disney network—holds a "Disney Night" every season, wherein no contestants are eliminated. Instead, they are encouraged to "make their dreams come true on the dance floor." The next phase of the Disney story is going to be written somewhere between the digital space of now—gaming and streaming—and infinity—*Star Wars*.[55,56]

So how does a company, nonprofit, or startup ensure that their brand exudes strong values? When brands embark on cultural explorations internally and externally, they do so with ethics in mind. Below are two widely accepted approaches to being a responsible corporate agent, from covering the depth of total operations to tactical executions.

FIGURE 10.3
# TRIPLE BOTTOM LINE

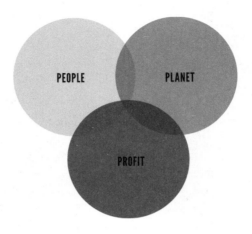

*Source*: Adapted from John Elkington, "25 Years Ago I Coined the Phrase 'Triple Bottom Line'. Here's Why It's Time to Rethink It." *Harvard Business Review*, June 25, 2018.

Triple-bottom-line measurement and reporting focuses on business models, operations, supply chain, and human resources. Coined in 1994 by writer John Elkington,[57] the concept evolved from the 1970s "social enterprise" model introduced by UK consultant Freer Spreckley, who pushed companies to balance financial performance, environmental protection, and social conditions of workers.[58] The method has three core parts: profit, planet, and people (Figure 10.3). Used by Novo Nordisk, a $100 billion pharma company continually ranked as one of the best places to work, triple bottom line has become so central to their operations that it is in their corporate bylaws. Since 2004, they have publicly reported performance, and, after three years of a flat stock price from 2001 to 2003, they experienced growth to the tune of 10x by 2019.[59] Triple bottom line has become common as companies move toward CSR and sustainability reporting, ultimately to activate conscious consumption.

In 2017, the backlash was so swift against Pepsi and Kendall Jenner for appropriating imagery, specifically Black Lives Matter protests,

## FIGURE 10.4

# TARES TEST

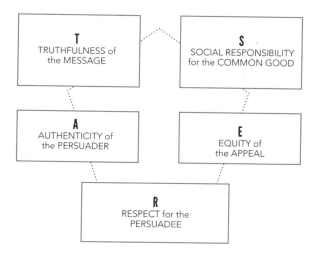

| | |
|---|---|
| **T**<br>TRUTHFULNESS of<br>the MESSAGE | **S**<br>SOCIAL RESPONSIBILITY<br>for the COMMON GOOD |
| **A**<br>AUTHENTICITY of<br>the PERSUADER | **E**<br>EQUITY of<br>the APPEAL |

**R**
RESPECT for the
PERSUADEE

*The limits of persuasion should be tested based on five factors: Truthfulness, Authenticity, Respectfulness, Equity, and Socially Responsibility.*
Source: Adapted from Sherry Baker and David L. Martinson, "The TARES Test: Five Principles for Ethical Persuasion." *Journal of Mass Media Ethics* 16 (2001), 148–175.

that the ad didn't even air for a full 24 hours before being pulled.[60] This was a cultural appropriation fumble that *Wired* editor Angela Watercutter noted "united the internet." While most social chatter focused on the gut reaction to the commercial, in my classroom we were debating the epic ethics failure using the TARES test. As a back-of-the-napkin system, the TARES test is a five-minute pressure test necessary in an age of "brand safety" and swift social backlash.

The TARES test is applicable to programs, campaigns, tactics, messaging, introduced in 2001 by Sherry Baker and David Martinson through the *Journal of Mass Media Ethics*.[61] Common among service companies, nonprofits, NGOs, and healthcare, the model gives five core considerations for persuading others (Figure 10.4):

1. **Truthful:** Can audiences make an informed decision? Do they have access to the right information?
2. **Authentic:** Are intentions good?

3. **Respectful:** Are the interest and culture (e.g., beliefs and social norms) of other parties being considered?
4. **Equitable:** Is there fair value for all parties that does not take advantage of vulnerabilities?
5. **Socially Responsible:** How do people benefit?

In 2017, Boston Consulting Group devised a new approach called Total Societal Impact that covers environmental, social, and governance (ESG) effects. Known for the BCG growth-share matrix taught for decades as a business school staple alongside Porter's Five P's, the firm creates waves within corporate strategy. Their research gives large, matrixed companies a framework and reality check: compared to 40 years ago, a company in 2017 had six times the chance of being delisted from stock exchanges due to the instability among businesses.[62]

As a combination of methods, I developed a "culture-ethics" pressure test for clients: be earnest, empower, and express empathy (Figure 10.5).

## FIGURE 10.5
# CULTURE-ETHICS TEST

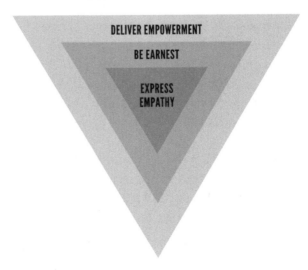

DELIVER EMPOWERMENT

BE EARNEST

EXPRESS
EMPATHY

*Culture is a byproduct of communities, and brands active within culture-based marketing have a responsibility to be earnest, express empathy, and deliver empowerment.*

Being earnest requires finding and defining a time commitment needed to move a community forward. Ask your team, agency, and partners two critical questions: How do you demonstrate you're committed to them? What time commitment matters to the community? Nike's 2018 "Believe" ad featuring the voice of Colin Kaepernick, the center of the kneeling controversy in the NFL, was instantly hailed by many as one of the greatest ads of all time along Apple's 1984 ad. But, in actuality, what did the ad change? Who did it help? What commitment did Nike make to the social issues that Kaepernick risked his career for? Once the ad cleared and the creative praise and awards stopped rolling in, were any of the reasons Colin took a knee improved by Nike's message or money? Earnestness means staring at a creative idea and saying, we can make this campaign, initiative, ad, or message stronger by aligning it to community expectations of sincerity.

Delivering empowerment involves creating meaningful change for the community. Two critical questions to answer are: What are the everyday barriers and struggles for this community? What would this community consider the "good life?" As a tip, engage employee resource groups internally; they're often underleveraged in giving the opinion of the communities they represent. Aside from planning cultural celebration, speaker series, or art exhibits, employee resources groups need to be leveraged to inform actual branding and business decisions. Moreover, find voices of leaders in communities to amplify and invite into the conversation early. Early means when the idea is in creative development, not just treating influencers as media buys. Arguably, they are influencers because they know communities better than you; brand humility to let them influence creative direction will lead to much stronger creative work and greater community reception. Since communities are driven by herd mentality, when you don't empower people from the community to lead creative ideas, you only limit the impact of your brand.

Showing empathy requires developing community-specific solutions. Key questions to ask include: How does this community see the world? Who are the voices that the community trusts? To answer these questions, executives need to immerse in the "culture" of their consumers—food, music, art, fashion, and beyond. If you're not comfortable immersing yourself in a community, then your sense of empathy toward them will be misaligned because no report can make you empathize with someone in the same way as leaving the office to coexist in their reality. There's no substitute for immersion—not focus groups, not man-on-the-street interviews, or any other "fly-by" tactic that checks the box of seeing a consumer in the wild. The speed to get insights must not trump one's assumptions that they can market to anyone they have persona for. Through immersion, passing ethical test such as TARES becomes more achievable while ways to promote societal impact become more apparent.

# MOD PIZZA

*Turning Diversity into a Winning Recipe*

Scott and Ally Svenson just wanted to feed their sons. In 2008, Scott had moved his family back from London, where he had been running Starbucks Europe, back home to Bellevue, Washington. In the transition, he noticed that all the fast-food options around were below his standards. He and his wife partnered with pizza entrepreneur James Markham to develop a fun, delicious fast-food pizza chain that put the customer's needs first. Nearly 10 years later, MOD has 300 locations, raking in over $200 million in 2016—a two-third sales jump from the previous year.

MOD has become more than just a place to grab a quick pie. Their employee and HR strategies are encompassed by their "Come as you are" philosophy. Most fast-food restaurants put their employees in an anonymous corporate uniform and expect them to follow a script. MOD emphasizes diversity and personality, allowing the staff to be themselves. MOD cares about the individual over the "corporate drone," and that has meant direct community activism. Those with intellectual disabilities are frequently hired, and then supported to thrive. MOD partnered with Pioneer Human Services to provide job opportunities for those recently released from prison or drug rehabilitation. For the Svensons, the rapid growth of the business is one pathway to give back to communities where they operate shops. And in the process of following strict values, MOD has become the fastest-growing restaurant chain in America.[63,64,65]

## AIMING FOR SUCCESS IN ACTION AND COMMITMENT

In a noisy world of fake followers, news, and video views, how do you achieve a modicum of *brand safety*? In entering the speedway of culture, companies need to keep four considerations aligned with their value. First, use allies for change: as a best practice, companies dealing with sensitive topics in culture should consult and empower independent experts, organizations, or nonprofits with already established credibility that can halo onto the brand. Second, consider using the healthcare model of partnering with advocacy-type groups to drive acceptance of new methods, solutions, and thinking. Third, leverage the best of the brand: with companies adopting more CSR and socially responsible business practices, it is expected that companies will use the "best" of their resources (e.g., reducing waste in supply chain, donating excess from supply chain). Efforts should be rooted in what the consumer-employee community values; engage them in determining what to support. And fourth, prioritize positive outcomes: it is expected that brands (and their content) that touch on sensitive subjects (e.g., suicide, domestic violence) will also provide solutions—in context—that make viewers, users, or communities better off.

Try pressure testing ideas, innovations, with these questions:

- Does it change/reframe the **narrative**?
- Does it change the **trajectory** of an industry or community?
- Could it create **share-worthy moments** within media?
- Could consumers take this campaign to the **next level** (i.e., memes, gifs, user-generated content)?
- Does it reinforce what we **stand for** and **stand against**?
- Will it be **remembered** in history? Why?
- Does it make a community **"better off"**?

## FINDING YOUR BRAND'S NORTH STAR

Confucius' view on the world summarizes how marketers should approach brand development inside a company: "I hear and I forget. I see and I remember. I do and I understand." Our modern interpretation of how we learn—seeing, hearing, and doing—stems from Edgar Dale, a former Ohio State University professor and audiovisual expert. His research over five decades resulted in a precursor for present-day pedagogy, which informs how we teach children and adults. Similar to Confucius, Dale's directionally descriptive "Cone of Experience" prioritized first-hand experience over being exposed to the elements of lexicon, audio, and visuals.[66] In essence, it's the doing that matters, not what you say as a brand. And as earlier discussed in their book, communication as a system is largely about actions and delivery rather than words themselves.

In a community-driven economy controlled by tribes, a community manager should no longer be the only person on your team who fully understands what your community wants. It is equally all parts of the organization's responsibility to instill a central positive feeling at every touchpoint. Essentially, in brand speak, all of the elements of communication—lexicon, audio, and visuals—build into a brand ecosystem that gets taught to consumers, customers, and clients through their experiences (Figure 10.6). Those three elements are the master keys to building a brand that triggers positive action. The role of the company, through its internal culture then, is to ensure an environment of collaboration and immersion in the brand DNA, so every member understands *why* they do what they do, so every brand touchpoint triggers a consistently positive feeling in a noisy world.

## FIGURE 10.6
# LAVEC MODEL

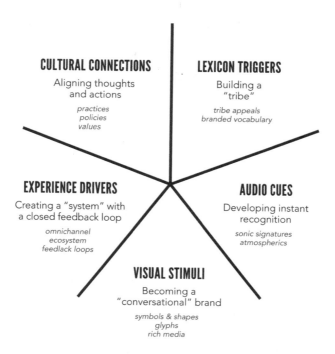

*Every brand has a unique North Star based on its five defining attributes: Lexicon Triggers, Audio Cues, Visual Stimuli, Experience Drivers, and Cultural Connections.*

## ALIGNING THOUGHTS AND ACTIONS (I.E., POLICIES, PRACTICES, AND PROTOCOLS THAT BOTH REINFORCE AND EMPOWER)

**CULTURAL CONNECTIONS**

☐ *What are the three most important facts for someone to know about your brand's history?*

☐ *What is your brand a "defender of" or what/who is the enemy of your brand (e.g., Teach for America stands as a defender of equal access to quality education while Snickers makes an enemy out of hunger)?*

☐ *In under 100 words, what was the brand's breakthrough moment?*

☐ *In one sentence, how would you describe your ideal company "culture"?*

☐ *What do you consider "high performance" for your company, and do employees know that?*

☐ *Do you have a written Code of Conduct for employees, vendors, or partners?*

☐ *What is the most important benchmark of success for your brand related to improving the lives of consumers?*

☐ *What single issue in the world does the brand care most about (that affects customers/clients)?*

## Notes

1. Chicago Fire Newspaper Collection 1871–1909. Accessed February 1, 2019. https://www.lib.uchicago.edu/projects/centcat/fac/facch09_01.html.
2. "Thorstein Veblen." The Library of Economics and Liberty. Accessed February 1, 2019. https://www.econlib.org/library/Enc/bios/Veblen.html.
3. Thorstein Veblen, *The Theory of the Leisure Class*. New York: Penguin, 1994.

4. Blake Mycoskie, "The Founder of TOMS on Reimagining the Company's Mission." *Harvard Business Review*, January/February 2016. https://hbr.org/2016/01/the-founder-of-toms-on-reimagining-the-companys-mission.

5. "Together We Stand." TOMS. Accessed February 1, 2019. https://www.toms.com/.

6. "Market Share of the Leading Ice Cream Vendors in the United States in 2017, Based on Sales." Statista. Accessed February 1, 2019. https://www.statista.com/statistics/255054/market-share-of-the-leading-ice-cream-vendors-in-the-united-states/.

7. Jessica Leber, "Empower Mint, a New Ben & Jerry's Flavor, Protests the Dough in Politics." *Fast Company*, May 17, 2016. https://www.fastcompany.com/3059864/empower-mint-a-new-ben-jerrys-flavor-protests-the-dough-in-politics.

8. Aaron Hurst, "Why Ben And Jerry's CEO Pushes His Company To Merge Ice Cream And Social Justice." *Fast Company*, January 27, 2017. https://www.fastcompany.com/3067597/why-ben-and-jerrys-ceo-pushes-his-company-to-merge-ice-cream-and-social-j.

9. Claudia Dreifus, "Passing the Scoop; Ben & Jerry." *New York Times Magazine*, December 18, 1994. https://www.nytimes.com/1994/12/18/magazine/passing-the-scoop-ben-jerry.html.

10. "2019 Edelman Trust Barometer." Edelman, January 20, 2019. https://www.edelman.com/trust-barometer.

11. "2019 Edelman Trust Barometer Executive Summary." Edelman. Accessed February 1, 2019. https://www.edelman.com/sites/g/files/aatuss191/files/2019-01/2019_Edelman_Trust_Barometer_Executive_Summary.pdf.

12. Vicky Veloni, "The World's Most Reputable Companies 2018." *Forbes*, March 15, 2018. https://www.forbes.com/sites/vickyvalet/2018/03/15/the-worlds-most-reputable-companies-2018/.

13. Richard Feloni, "BlackRock CEO Larry Fink Says within the Next 5 Years All Investors Will Measure a Company's Impact on Society, Government, and the Environment to Determine Its Worth." *Business Insider*, November 1, 2018. https://amp.businessinsider.com/blackrock-larry-fink-investors-esg-metrics-2018-11.

14. "Annual Benefit Corporation Report." Patagonia Works. https://www.patagonia.com/static/on/demandware.static/-/Library-Sites-PatagoniaShared/default/dw824fac0f/PDF-US/2017-BCORP-pages_022218.pdf.

15. "Conservación Patagonica." Patagonica. Accessed February 1, 2019. https://www.patagonia.com/conservacion-patagonica.html.

16. Rose Marcario, "Our Urgent Gift to the Planet." Linkedin, November 28, 2018. https://www.linkedin.com/pulse/our-urgent-gift-planet-rose-marcario/.

17. "When Digital Disruption Strikes: How Can Incumbents Respond?" Capgemini, LinkedIn SlideShare. February 20, 2015. https://www.slideshare.net/capgemini/digital-disruption-44929928.

18. "Investor." GE. Accessed January 30, 2019. https://www.ge.com/investor-relations/overview.

19. Mark J. Perry, "Fortune 500 Firms 1955 v. 2017: Only 60 Remain, Thanks to the Creative Destruction That Fuels Economic Prosperity." *History Studies International Journal of History* 10, no. 7 (October 20, 2017). doi:10.9737/hist.2018.658.

20. "Martin Agency." Martin Agency. Accessed January 30, 2019. https://martinagency.com/about.

21. "US' Most Creative Partnerships: Geico & The Martin Agency." Martin Agency, June 22, 2016. https://martinagency.com/news/us-most-creative-partnerships-geico-the-martin-agency.

22. Ibid.

23. "Marriott International, Inc." SEC. Accessed February 1, 2019. https://www.sec.gov/Archives/edgar/data/1048286/000162828018001756/mar-q42017x10k.htm#sA53300A7ACF959D38150A44B9951CBE5.

24. "Goldenrule Marriott." Marriott. Accessed February 1, 2019. http://goldenrule.marriott.com/.

25. Kai D. Wright, "Overheard at Stream. . . ." Medium, December 3, 2016. https://medium.com/@WPPStream/overheard-at-stream-75d35022fe8e.

26. Mark Sullivan, "At WeWork Summer Camp, 8,000 People Come Together With a Purpose." Wework Blog, August 21, 2018. https://www.wework.com/blog/posts/wework-summer-camp-2018.

27. "Wework." Wework Blog. Accessed February 1, 2019. https://www.wework.com/enterprise.

28. Charisse Jones, "WeWork Puts Its Stamp on More than Office Space, but Profits Remain Hard to Come by." *USA Today*, September 17, 2018. https://www.usatoday.com/story/money/2018/09/17/wework-spreads-its-wings-some-say-may-forgetting-its-roots/755608002/.

29. "Zara." *Forbes*, May 23, 2018. https://www.forbes.com/companies/zara/#2c662b477487.

30. "Quotes Amancio Ortega." Quoteswise. Accessed February 1, 2019. http://www.quoteswise.com/amancio-ortega-gaona-quotes.html.

31. "The Secret of Zara's Success: A Culture of Customer Co-creation." Martin Roll, May 2018. https://martinroll.com/resources/articles/strategy/the-secret-of-zaras-success-a-culture-of-customer-co-creation/.

32. "Discover the Difference." Unilever. Accessed February 1, 2019. https://www.unileverusa.com/brands/personal-care/dove.html

33. Jack Neff, "Ten Years In, Dove's 'Real Beauty' Seems to Be Aging Well." *AdAge*, January 22, 2014. https://adage.com/article/news/ten-years-dove-s-real-beauty-aging/291216/

34. "Case Study: How Fame Made Snickers' 'You're Not You When You're Hungry' Campaign a Success." Campaign US, October 26, 2016. https://www.campaignlive.com/article/case-study-fame-made-snickers-youre-not-when-youre-hungry-campaign-success/1413554.

35. Lydia Gordon, "Snickers to Pass M&M's as Top International Confectionery Brand." Euromonitor International (blog), September 21, 2012. https://blog.euromonitor.com/snickers-to-pass-mms-as-top-international-confectionery-brand/.

36. E. J. Schultz, "Snickers Surging to Top of Global Candy Race." *AdAge*, September 20, 2012. https://adage.com/article/news/snickers-surging-top-global-candy-race/237349/.

37. Jens Kjeldgaard-Christiansen, "Evil Origins: A Darwinian Genealogy of the Popcultural Villain." Research Gate, January 2015. doi:10.1037/ebs0000057.

38. Simon Sinek, *Start with Why: How Great Leaders Inspire Everyone to Take Action*. New York: Portfolio, 2009.

39. Michael E. Porter and Mark R. Kramer, "Creating Shared Value." *Harvard Business Review*, January/February 2011. https://hbr.org/2011/01/the-big-idea-creating-shared-value.

40. "Creating Shared Value Explained." Harvard Business School, Institute for Strategy & Competitiveness. Accessed February 1, 2019. https://www.isc.hbs.edu/creating-shared-value/csv-explained/Pages/default.aspx.

41. Porter and Kramer, "Creating Shared Value."

42. Pamela N. Danziger, "Will Story's Rachel Shechtman Be Able to Revolutionize Macy's? Bluemercury Offers a Clue." *Forbes*, May 3, 2018. https://www.forbes.com/sites/pamdanziger/2018/05/03/how-will-rachel-shechtman-and-story-fare-under-macys-hint-look-at-bluemercury/#535ccf3636de.

43. Rosemary Feitelberg, "The Continuing Story of West Chelsea's Story Boutique." *WWD*, December 5, 2015. https://wwd.com/business-news/retail/story-west-chelsea-boutique-10288909/.

44. Jonah Berger, *Contagious: Why Things Catch On*. New York: Simon & Schuster, 2013.

45. Carleigh Stiehm, "Hearst Magazines' New Airbnbmag Encourages Readers to Be at Home in the World." Hearst, May 22, 2017. www.hearst .com/newsroom/hearst-magazines-new-airbnbmag-encourages-read ers-to-be-at-home-in-the-world.

46. Adrienne Lafrance, "The Six Main Arcs in Storytelling, as Identified by an A.I." *The Atlantic*, July 12, 2016. https://www.theatlantic.com/ technology/archive/2016/07/the-six-main-arcs-in-storytelling-identified- by-a-computer/490733/

47. Amy Cuddy, *Presence: Bringing Your Boldest Self to Your Biggest Challenges*. New York: Back Bay Books, 2018.

48. Elyse Romano, "A Harvard Psychologist Says People Judge You on 2 Things When They Meet You." *D'marge*, May 15, 2016. https://www .dmarge.com/2016/05/amy-cuddy-how-people-judge-you.html.

49. "Deep Metaphors." Olson Zaltman. Accessed February 1, 2019. http:// olsonzaltman.com/deepmetaphors.

50. Ibid.

51. Mark R. Kramer, "The Right Way for Companies to Publicize Their Social Responsibility Efforts." *Harvard Business Review*, April 2, 2018. https:// hbr.org/2018/04/the-right-way-for-companies-to-publicize-their-social- responsibility-efforts.

52. "The Ritz Carlton." The Ritz Carlton. Accessed February 1, 2019. http:// www.ritzcarlton.com/en/about/gold-standards.

53. Yin Chu, "A Review of Studies on Luxury Hotels over the Past Two Decades." Master's Thesis, Iowa State University, 2014. Accessed February 1, 2019. https://lib.dr.iastate.edu/cgi/viewcontent.cgi?article=4920&context =etd.

54. Shalom H. Schwartz, Jan Meuleman Cieciuch, Michele Vecchione, Eldad Davidov, Ronald Fischer, Constanze Beierlein, Alice A Ramos, Markku Verkasalo, Jan-Erik Lönnqvist, Kursad Demirutku, Ozlem Dirilen-Gumus, and Mark Konty, "Refining the Theory of Basic Individual Values." *Journal of Personality and Social Psychology* 103, no. 4 (2012): 663–688.

55. "About The Walt Disney Company." The Walt Disney Company. Accessed February 1, 2019. https://www.thewaltdisneycompany.com/about/.

56. "Walt Disney." Wikipedia. Last updated on February 3, 2019. https:// en.wikipedia.org/wiki/Walt_Disney.

57. John Elkington, "25 Years Ago I Coined the Phrase 'Triple Bottom Line.' Here's Why It's Time to Rethink It." *Harvard Business Review*, June 25, 2018. https://hbr.org/2018/06/25-years-ago-i-coined-the-phrase-triple-bottom-line-heres-why-im-giving-up-on-it

58. "Social Enterprise." Wikipedia. Last updated on January 19, 2019. Accessed February 01. 2019. https://en.wikipedia.org/wiki/Social_enterprisev.

59. "Performance on Our Triple Bottom Line." Novo Nordisk. Accessed February 1, 2019. https://www.novonordisk.com/sustainable-business/performance-on-tbl.html.

60. Constance Grady, "Pepsi Has Pulled Its Controversial Ad Suggesting You Can Solve Police Brutality with Soda." *Vox*, April 5, 2017. https://www.vox.com/culture/2017/4/5/15186216/pepsi-ad-kendall-jenner-black-lives-matter-controversy.

61. Sherry Baker and David L. Martinson., "The TARES Test: Five Principles for Ethical Persuasion." *Journal of Mass Media Ethics, 16* (2001), 148–175. doi:10.1080/08900523.2001.9679610.

62. Douglas Beal, Robert Eccles, Gerry Hansell, Rich Lesser, Shalini Unni Krishnan, Wendy Woods, and David Young, "Total Societal Impact: A New Lens For Strategy." Boston Consulting Group, October 25, 2017. https://www.bcg.com/en-us/publications/2017/total-societal-impact-new-lens-strategy.aspx.

63. "Mod Pizza Announces 2017 Full-Year Results." Mod Pizza. March 13, 2018. Accessed February 1, 2019. https://modpizza.com/press/mod-pizza-announces-2017-full-year-results/.

64. "MODs Rule." MOD. 2015. Accessed February 1, 2019. https://vimeo.com/90686640.

65. Soloman Micah, "MOD Pizza, America's Fastest-Growing Restaurant, Supports People In Recovery or Just out of Jail." *Forbes*, February 5, 2018. Accessed February 1, 2019. https://www.forbes.com/sites/micahsolomon/2018/02/05/how-mod-pizza-americas-fastest-growing-restaurant-puts-people-first-including-felons-ex-addicts/#3487f6726dda

66. Edgar Dale, *Audio-Visual Methods in Teaching*. New York: Holt, Rinehart & Winston, 1969.

# 11

# FOLLOWING
# THE FEELING

*What's the Role of
Technology in Following
the Feeling?*

With the speed to technology and facial recognition growing faster, the time to cross the technology chasm is shortening. Should we fight machine learning advances like emotion identification and facial recognition that could make customer experience feedback more real-time and seamless, or embrace the new methods? In a 2018 Medium post, Netherlands-based innovation manager Daan de Geus paints the picture of the "smart museum" of the future.[1] Imagine the Louvre installing facial recognition software that enabled them to track attentiveness of visitors by work (e.g., Mona Lisa versus Venus de Milo), pleasantness of various exhibits or museum attractions, or simply gather higher quality visitor data by age and gender based on dwell times. Would consumers be open to anonymous biometric feedback exchanges through technology that ultimately makes the brand experience more enjoyable?

Like most new technologies, the adoption of software that measures emotions and feelings will increase as use cases build for how problems are being solved, frustrations are being addressed, and speed to customer experience improvements are cataloged. And in terms of those use cases, over the past 10 years, we've finally moved from gestural expression for fun (e.g., in gaming) to facial expression as a lifeline (e.g., in hospitals).

Use cases for emotion-tracking and facial recognition software have increased to now range from helping consumers with disabilities to helping organizations deter crime. At the Consumer Electronics Show (CES) 2019, held annually in Las Vegas, NV for 200,000 technology buyers, vendors, and influencers, Intel unveiled a wheelchair powered by facial expressions, putting their technology in primetime to interpret our 43 facial muscles.[2] The technology can scan the user's face to operate devices, such as a wheelchair, or scan a patient's face in a hospital bed to determine their pain level when the patient cannot verbally communicate.[3] That technology, though, first appeared publicly in 2016, and is just starting to gain attraction and interest as the world becomes noisier.

And the crime deterrence part? For 20th Century Fox's 2002 *Minority Report,* there was no expense spared in the $100 million budget to imagine "next generation" technology from the year 2054.[4] The idea of using surveillance of the future in order to prevent crime was appealing to consumers, making the futuristic movie a box office hit. So much so, that in 2004 the same movie studio released a follow-up $100 million film set in 2035, *I, Robot*.[5] While they got the tech being used to fight crime part right, the timelines for both movies were vastly miscalculated. Because in 2018, the facial recognition plotlines from the films were already realities, controversially, when police in Florida and Washington purchased the technology from Amazon.[6] So when then, will we think that the benefits outweigh the criticism?

As consumers became tethered to the Web, marketers benefited from all the data being tracked based on digital behavior. The innovation of personalization was not because of a marketer, but rather the byproduct of tracking clicks, causing a wake of data in the watershed. Introduced in order to optimize screen-based experiences, facial recognition and eye tracking are close cousins. The popularity of one will lead to the popularity of the other. They are inseparably linked to real-time measurement of noncognitive states that consumers would not be able to accurately communicate in a focus group, survey, or usability test. They are, in essence, improving customer experience. And isn't that improvement the goal of both brand and consumers—to make experience better?

In 2012, WPP-owned Kantar TNS launched a new emotion-based offering called ConversionModel to help brands secure more favorable decisions with consumers using facial recognition and emotion detection for testing brand creatives such as advertisements. As of 2018, Kantar TNS called half of the Fortune 500 companies a client. Their competitors, Ipsos and GfK, both have offerings that use emotion-tracking software to test commercials and creative works in a controlled environment. But the real leap will occur when out-of-home experiences take hold of the technology.

Companies with major efforts related to facial recognition and emotion detection include: Intel RealSense (2014); Google Vision developer toolkit (2015); IBM Watson Visual Recognition (2015); Microsoft Face Detection (2016); and Amazon Rekognition (2016). According the American Civil Liberties Union (ACLU), facial recognition usage is more prevalent in our growing "surveillance society" than consumers realize, and, if you look to the far east, already a common occurrence. As of 2018, the ACLU tracked facial recognition pilot programs for retailers Walmart, Target, and Saks Fifth Avenue, in addition to sports giant Madison Square Gardens. Speaking to *New York Magazine*, Donna Lieberman, executive director of the New York Civil Liberties Union, noted the key issues: data collection methods, transparency, storage and consumer access.[7] Fighting with companies looking to use technology to protect their bottom line, the National Retail Foundation (NRF) represents 18,000 members.[8] The association estimated that in 2017, theft cost the industry 1.3% in sales, or $40 billion.[9] Facial recognition helps prevent theft.

One place consumers will soon encounter facial recognition at scale is aviation. Aside from CLEAR, which uses biometric data, airlines are more than interested: they're investing. In 2018, Atlanta-Hartsfield Airport was the busiest airport in the world, a record it has held since 1988.[10] With over 3,500 flights daily to 50 countries, Delta calls the airport home. Each year, over 100 million customers pass through the global crossroads. By testing biometric facial scanners, the airplane promises that the new technology will reduce waiting lines while increasing airport security.

In 2018, researchers in Spain also made a leap forward in emotional mapping outside of labs and inside real environments. Based in Valencia, the Emotion Research Lab houses behavioral scientists, technologists, engineers, and computer scientists. The startup has developed proprietary technology that goes beyond the common six primary emotions (e.g., happiness, joy), to identify over 100 secondary emotions (e.g., amazement, excitement), all within milliseconds. Their pilots outside the lab have been able to accurately capture a trail of data in real-time, using noninvasive GoPro cameras, including: "attentive time," age, gender, people count, primary emotions, and secondary emotions. All of the activity, interest, and investment point to one thing: This technology is imminent, so when will it be used to improve brand building through customer experience management?

## ACHIEVING BRAND LIFT-OFF

The difference between two fast-growing startups may not be the product or service, but rather the brand feeling: Uber versus Lyft, SoulCycle versus Peloton, GrubHub versus Deliveroo, Southwest versus Delta, Kit Kat versus Snickers. Companies are now forced to go head-to-head in a way that not only creates a relationship between the brand and the consumer but extends that relationship to touch the third-rail of community.

With thousands of emotions, each with an ineffable expression, triggering a positive feeling requires consistency across an organization. If "seeing is believing," then "feeling is being." And for those brands that transcend others to create happiness or to provide escapism to their consumers, emotions become a universal cognitive trigger in brand building. Standing the test of time from childhood, emotional triggers generate a gravitational pull toward a brand ecosystem that creates normative behavior, and that drives company growth (Figure 11.1).

In an increasingly noisy world of content, data, platforms, and technology, all producing more data signals for brand health, the single most important "expression" of your brand, whether a person, company, or nonprofit, is simple . . . *it's how you make others feel.*

## FIGURE 11.1
# BRAND LIFT-OFF

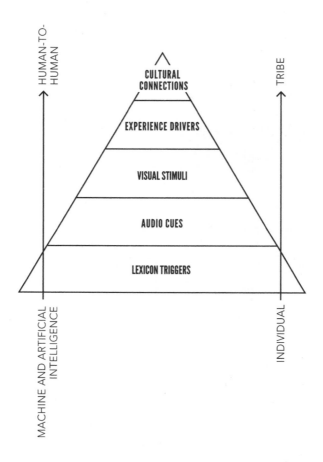

*In an evolving communication system, the function of humans will be emotional transfer while machine learning and artificial intelligence will offer more personalized experiences through micro branding.*

## Notes

1.  Daan De Geus, "Here's What a Smart Museum Could Look Like." A Medium Corporation, October 11, 2018. https://medium.com/iotforall /heres-what-a-smart-museum-could-look-like-5a872e8567f9.

2.  Alex Cranz, "This Wheelchair Is Controlled With Smiles and Kissy Faces." GIZMODO, January 9, 2019. https://gizmodo.com/this-wheelchair-is-controlled-with-smiles-and-kissy-fac-1831581930.

3.  "Wheelie—Facial Expression Controlled Wheelchair with Intel® Real-Sense Intel Software." Produced by Stephanie Essin. YouTube, August 23, 2016. https://www.youtube.com/watch?v=YhD9OjOX36A.

4.  *Minority Report.* IMDB, 2002. https://www.imdb.com/title/tt0181689/.

5.  *I, Robot.* IMDB, 2004. https://www.imdb.com/title/tt0343818/.

6.  Nick Wingfield, "Amazon Pushes Facial Recognition to Police. Critics See Surveillance Risk." *New York Times*, May 22, 2018. https://www.nytimes.com/2018/05/22/technology/amazon-facial-recognition.html.

7.  Nick Tabor, "Smile! The Secretive Business of Facial-Recognition Software in Retail Stores." *Intelligencer*, October 20, 2018. http://nymag.com/intelligencer/2018/10/retailers-are-using-facial-recognition-technology-too.html.

8.  "NRF Retailer Membership." National Retail Federation. Accessed February 1, 2019. https://nrf.com/about-us/nrf-membership/nrf-retailer-membership.

9.  "2018 National Retail Security Survey." National Retail Federation, 2018. https://cdn.nrf.com/sites/default/files/2018-10/NRF-NRSS-Industry-Research-Survey-2018.pdf.

10. "Hartsfield-Jackson Atlanta International Airport." Federal Aviation Administration, September 10, 2018. https://www.faa.gov/nextgen/snapshots/airport/?locationId=54.

# INDEX